Immigrants, Schooling and Social Mobility

Also by Hans Vermeulen

THE POLITICS OF ETHNIC CONSCIOUSNESS (*co-editor with Cora Govers*)

Also by Joel Perlmann

ETHNIC DIFFERENCES: Schooling and Social Structure among the Irish, Italians, Jews and Blacks in an American City, 1880–1935

Immigrants, Schooling and Social Mobility

Does Culture Make a Difference?

Edited by

Hans Vermeulen
Professor and
Co-Director of Research
Institute for Migration and Ethnic Studies
University of Amsterdam
The Netherlands

and

Joel Perlmann
Senior Scholar and Research Professor
Jerome Levy Economics Institute
Bard College
USA

First published in Great Britain 2000 by
MACMILLAN PRESS LTD
Houndmills, Basingstoke, Hampshire RG21 6XS and London
Companies and representatives throughout the world

A catalogue record for this book is available from the British Library.

ISBN 0–333–79342–0 hardcover
ISBN 0–333–79343–9 paperback

First published in the United States of America 2000 by
ST. MARTIN'S PRESS, LLC,
Scholarly and Reference Division,
175 Fifth Avenue, New York, N.Y. 10010

ISBN 0–312–23488–0

Library of Congress Cataloging-in-Publication Data
Immigrants, schooling, and social mobility : does culture make a difference? /
edited by Hans Vermeulen and Joel Perlmann.
p.   cm.
Papers originated from the conference "Does culture make a difference?" held in
Amsterdam in Nov. 1996.
Includes bibliographical references and index.
ISBN 0–312–23488–0 (cloth)
1. Immigrants—Education—Social aspects—Congresses. 2. Educational
anthropology—Congresses. 3. Social mobility—Congresses. I. Vermeulen, Hans.
II. Perlmann, Joel.

LC3705 .I52 2000
306.43—dc21

00–026943

This book is printed on paper suitable for recycling and made from fully managed and sustained
forest sources.

10   9   8   7   6   5   4   3   2   1
09   08   07   06   05   04   03   02   01   00

Printed and bound in Great Britain by
Antony Rowe Ltd, Chippenham, Wiltshire

Contents

Acknowledgements

Except for the two introductions and the essays by Gibson and Sansone, all contributions originated at the conference 'Does Culture Make a Difference?', held in Amsterdam in November 1996. 'Does Culture Make a Difference?' was also the title (in Dutch) of the dissertation of Flip Lindo, another contributor to this volume and co-organizer of the conference. The text by Vermeulen and Venema is an extension of an example given by Vermeulen in an introductory lecture at that conference. The conference formed the conclusion of a research programme entitled 'The Interrelation between the Socioeconomic and Cultural Position of Immigrants in Dutch Society'. This was financed by the Netherlands Organization for Scientific Research (NWO) and the Universiteit van Amsterdam. The issues addressed in this volume were among the central themes of the conference. Our special thanks go to Michael Dallas for the English-language editing of the texts by the non-Anglophone authors; to Tijno Venema for assisting with several production tasks for this volume, including preparing the index; and to Astrid Meyer for her careful standardization of the contributions.

Notes on the Contributors

Maurice Crul studied political science at the Universiteit van Amsterdam and ethnic studies at the Vrije Universiteit Amsterdam. He currently works at the Institute for Migration and Ethnic Studies of the Universiteit van Amsterdam and the Interuniversity Centre for Social Science Theory and Methodology of the University of Groningen. His PhD thesis on school careers of second-generation Turkish and Moroccan youth has been published in Dutch (De Sleutel tot Succes: Over Hulp, Keuzes en Kansen in de Schoollooppanen van Turkse en Marokkaanse Jongeren van de Tweede Generatie (2000)). Together with Flip Lindo and Ching Lin Pang, he is editor of *Culture, Structure and Beyond* (1999). His present research interests are intergenerational downward mobility and comparative European research on the second generation.

Margaret A. Gibson is an educational anthropologist at the University of California, Santa Cruz. Her research has focused on the variability in immigrant and minority students' school achievements. In her fieldwork she has given particular attention to ways in which ethnicity, gender and social class interact to shape students' school-adaptation patterns. In addition to ongoing fieldwork in several multiethnic high schools in California, Gibson has conducted field research in the US Virgin Islands, India and Papua New Guinea. Major publications include *Accommodation without Assimilation: Sikh Immigrants in an American High School* (1988), *Minority Status and Schooling: A Comparative Study of Immigrant and Involuntary Minorities* (co-edited with John Ogbu, 1991) and *Ethnicity and School Performance: Complicating the Immigrant/Involuntary Minority Typology* (1997). Gibson also serves as associate editor of the journal *Race, Ethnicity and Education*.

Flip Lindo is an anthropologist and senior researcher at the Institute for Migration and Ethnic Studies of the Universiteit van Amsterdam. He has published on a variety of topics including ethnic mobilization, migrant organizations, migrant policy and differences in social mobility patterns between migrant groups. Recent publications include a monograph in Dutch on differences in school attainment among migrant adolescents in the Netherlands (*Maakt cultuur verschil?*, 1996) and a book, also in Dutch, on a conflict between an Amsterdam city district council and a community of Turkish orthodox Muslims over the establishment of a mosque (*Heilige Wijsheid in Amsterdam*, 1999). With Maurice Crul and Ching Lin Pang, he is editor of another book on a subject similar to the present one (*Culture, Structure and Beyond* 1999). His current research interests include the relationship between local ecology, youth culture and risk behaviour among children and adolescents from migrant families.

Mies van Niekerk is an anthropologist and researcher at the Institute for Migration and Ethnic Studies of the Universiteit van Amsterdam. She has done research among immigrants in the Netherlands and has published on ethnic identity, ethnic youth, interethnic relations, immigrant elderly and urban poverty. In 1993 she published *Kansarmoede: Reacties van allochtonen op achterstand*. Her more recent publications are on Surinamese immigrants in the Netherlands. Her doctoral thesis is on ethnic differences in social mobility among Surinamese immigrants and their offspring (in publication). Current research interests include immigrant entrepreneurship and informal economic activities.

Joel Perlmann is senior scholar at the Jerome Levy Economics Institute of Bard College, and Levy Institute Research Professor at the College. He is the author of *Ethnic Differences: Schooling and Social Structure among the Irish, Italians, Jews, and Blacks in an American City, 1880–1935* (1988), and of a forthcoming study (with Robert Margo) entitled *Women's Work?: School-teaching in America, 1650–1920*, as well as of numerous papers.

Livio Sansone is vice-director of the Centro de Estudos Afro-Asiáticos in Rio de Janeiro and lecturer in Anthropology at the Universidade Estadual in the same city. He has carried out fieldwork on race relations and black culture in London, Amsterdam, Paramaribo, Bahia and Rio de Janeiro. His main areas of interest are the relationship between youth culture, globalization and ethnicity, and race relations in Latin America. Publications include 'The Making of Black Culture', *Critique of Anthropology* 14, 1994 and 'Funk in Bahia and Rio: Local Versions of a Global Phenomenon', *Focaal*, Special Issue on Globalization/Localization, 30–1, 1997.

Stephen Steinberg is a professor in the Department of Urban Studies at Queens College, New York, and in the PhD Program in Sociology of the City University of New York. His most recent book, *Turning Back: The Retreat from Racial Justice in American Thought and Policy* (1995), received the Oliver Cromwell Cox Award for Distinguished Anti-Racist Scholarship. He is also author of *The Ethnic Myth: Race, Ethnicity, and Class in America* (1989). In addition to his academic publications, he has published articles in *The Nation*, *New Politics*, *Reconstruction*, and the *UNESCO Courier*.

Tijno Venema is research assistant at the Institute for Migration and Ethnic Studies of the Universiteit van Amsterdam. In 1992 he published *Famiri nanga kulturu: Creoolse sociale verhoudingen en Winti in Amsterdam*, a fieldwork-based study of the social life and the Afro-American Winti-cult among the Surinamese Creoles of Amsterdam.

Hans Vermeulen is an anthropologist and co-director of research of the Institute for Migration and Ethnic Studies, Universiteit van Amsterdam. He has published extensively on migration and ethnicity and is currently working on multiculturalism. His most recent publications are *The Politics of Ethnic Consciousness* (co-edited with Cora Govers, 1997) and *Immigrant Integration: The Dutch Case* (co-edited with Rinus Penninx, forthcoming), the original edition of which was published in Dutch in 1994.

Pnina Werbner is Reader in Social Anthropology at Keele University and Research Administrator of the International Centre for Contemporary Cultural Research (ICCCR) at the Universities of Manchester and Keele. Her most recent publications are *Embodying Charisma: Locality, Modernity and Emotion in Sufi Cults* (with Helene Basu, 1998); *Debating Cultural Hybridity* and *The Politics of Multiculturalism in the New Europe*, both co-edited with Tariq Modood (1997); and *Women, Citizenship and Difference*, co-edited with Nira Yuval-Davis (1999). Her monograph is *The Migration Process: Capital, Gifts and Offerings among British Pakistanis* (1990). Her forthcoming book, *Diaspora, Islam and Millennium* is on the political imaginaries of British Pakistanis. Her current research on multiculturalism and on transnational Sufi cults was conducted in Britain and Pakistan.

1

Introduction: The Role of Culture in Explanations of Social Mobility

Hans Vermeulen

During recent decades, the notion of culture has become more popular and more controversial at the same time. A booming new discipline, cultural studies, has put 'culture' at the centre of its attention. Economists and economic sociologists proclaim the 'value of culture' and argue that the time has come to 'bring culture back in' (Holton 1992: 179–214). Scholars of politics and international relations insist that 'culture matters' (Ellis and Thompson 1997) and warn that the cultural factor has been neglected. Notions of cultural diversity and productive culture have taken centre stage in management, and giving training to others in intercultural communication and cultural diversity has become a goldmine for enterprising individuals. So 'culture' has gained currency not only within the walls of academia, but also (or even more so) outside them. Culture is on everyone's lips, as the anthropologist Sahlins phrased it some years ago.

The popularization of the culture concept has been accompanied by growing unease among social scientists about the way it tends to be applied, both inside and outside academia. As Keesing (1994: 304) has pointed out, we are confronted by a deep irony. Just as the concept of culture has come to pervade popular thought, some of us are starting to question its very utility. This has led some scholars to propose replacing it by variants like 'the cultural' (Keesing 1994: 309) or 'cultural sets' (Wolf 1982: 387). Others simply avoid the concept altogether, and some have even begun to 'write against culture' (Abu-Lughod 1991). Yet it seems that no one yet has seriously proposed relegating the concept of culture to the dustbin, or even to a place between quotation marks, something now quite common in the case of 'race'.

Perhaps nowhere is the issue of culture so controversial as in the study of the differential social mobility of immigrant groups, those which are perceived to be so different from mainstream society that we consider them 'ethnic' or 'racial'. Critics argue that talking about the cultures of immigrant groups usually means drawing attention to the specific character of ethnic groups – thus stirring up ethnic prejudice rather than combating it.

If a 'failure' to achieve upward social mobility is ascribed mainly to the culture of an ethnic or 'racial' group, that is condemned as 'blaming the victim'. Attributing *rapid* upward mobility to a group's culture, as has been done in many past studies on the Jews in the USA and many current ones on certain Asian groups in immigration countries, is accepted more readily. It is often propagated by the groups themselves, or at least by some of their members and organizations. But here, too, objections have been raised, if only because of the implicit comparison with other, less 'successful' groups.

The question of whether culture makes a difference is therefore, as Steinberg argues in his contribution to this volume, not a morally neutral or politically innocent question. However, to understand the moral and political pitfalls of the question is not to answer the question itself. To avoid the term 'culture' may reduce the risks of walking into the trap of the culturalistic fallacy, but it might also make us less aware that a trap exists, one which is not linked exclusively to the word itself. It could well be that by shunning the concept of culture we run the greater risk of obscuring some very important issues, however controversial and sensitive these may be. So the question remains: does culture make a difference? As a first step in an attempt to find answers, let us look in more detail at some of the dangers that lurk when we employ the notion of culture.

The culturalistic fallacy

Ways of speaking and writing about culture can often be designated as 'culturalistic'. As far back as 1953, Bidney was already warning about the 'culturalistic fallacy'. I will use the phrase *the culturalistic fallacy* to refer to those ways of speaking and writing about culture which depict cultures as sharply bounded, homogeneous and relatively unchanging entities, transmitted on from generation to generation. Culturalistic discourse presents a culture as existing more or less independently of everyday reality, as something following its own laws of development. It reifies culture, portraying it as a 'thing' or approaching it as an 'organism' or a 'collective individual' (Handler 1988).

In the course of the past few decades, 'culture' has become a common word in everyday discourse. It has also come to be used more and more as a political instrument in claiming rights. Having a culture of your own may entitle you to special treatment. Though the culturalistic fallacy is now perhaps most common in everyday discourse, it would be mistaken to assume things got out of hand when the concept of culture was stolen from the anthropologist's tool kit by people who did not know how to use it. Bidney was not criticizing the public, but his colleagues. And indeed, in anthropology and the other social sciences, the culturalistic fallacy is as old as the use of the word culture itself. As Wolf has reminded us, the anthropological notion of culture is a product of the age of nationalism:

> We need to remember that the culture concept came to the fore in a specific historical context, during a period when some European nations were contending for dominance while others were striving for separate identities and independence.
>
> (1982: 387)[1]

Wolf's assertion highlights why, and since when, the tendency has existed to see cultures as homogeneous, sharply bounded entities. At the same time, it makes more understandable when and where this notion of culture came under more frequent and systematic attack – after the heyday of nationalism in the Western world, in an era of increasing globalization. As Hannerz has written:

> Our historical understanding of culture, with its roots in nineteenth-century European thought, has mostly made us see the world as a cultural mosaic, of separate pieces with hard, well-defined edges. The emphasis is on the distinctiveness, integrity and purity of cultures. (...) In our times, however, the interrelatedness of cultures forces itself upon our awareness. Notions of 'a society' or 'a culture' are more problematic than we find it convenient to admit.
>
> (1989: 201)

Culture is often defined as a social heritage, something handed down from generation to generation. To the degree that collective notions or values can be viewed as adaptations to changing social circumstances, rather than as part of a social heritage, they tend not to be included in the notion of culture.[2] This leaves little room for discontinuity, change and creativity (Bidney 1953: 27).

The social heritage conception of culture thus goes hand in glove with the idea that continuity is natural and discontinuity is unnatural – that continuity needs no explanation, only change does (Wolf 1982: 387). The emphasis on the transmission of culture and on its continuity suggests furthermore that culture is practically impervious to external influences, so that the 'laws' of cultural development become virtually independent of political and economic changes. Culture – ethos, values, ideology, world view or whatever a specific author refers to when using the notion of culture – comes to be viewed as one of the driving forces of history.

Culturalistic explanations are often adduced to 'explain' behaviour for which no other explanation is available.[3] They tend to be circular and do nothing more than declare the behaviour in question to be specific to a certain group.[4] Despite their emptiness, culturalistic explanations are often presented with an (often implicit) claim that they are the final answer, one that raises no further questions. People, especially *other* people such as ethnic minorities,[5] behave in particular ways because that is just the way they are. Unlike 'our' behaviour, which seems a natural, logical response to each situation, 'their' behaviour seems determined by 'culture'. That makes 'our' behaviour appear rational, based on reason, while 'theirs' is irrational, deriving from tradition. In this way, 'their' behaviour becomes exoticized, incomprehensible. Obviously it is untenable to partition rationality off from culture in this way.[6] Adequate cultural analysis will show plainly that behaviour in a given situation is comprehensible and 'rational' in the light of the cultural assumptions involved. That applies to 'their' behaviour as well as to 'ours'.

All this is not to say it is useless to elucidate certain behaviours, ideas or values by relating them to the whole body of cultural notions held by a group. But that alone is not sufficient. It is necessary to question the *why* of these cultural notions – to trace, as far as possible, when and how such notions originated and how they have been maintained. That entails a focus on context and on political and economic processes.

Culture and progress

Probably there have always been people who explained the pathways of social mobility taken by specific ethnic or religious groups, or the economic development of nation states, by an almost exclusive reference to culture – values, traditions or the like. Although such culturalistic explanations are rejected by many experts in the field, they still enjoy some currency in the academic world and, by virtue of their simplicity, they are also attractive to a larger audience.

A fairly recent example is Harrison's book *Who Prospers? How Cultural Values Shape Economic and Political Success* (1992). Harrison believes that values and attitudes – which to him form the essence of culture – explain the differential economic success of minority groups and nation states alike. Central among the values leading to economic success in Harrison's view are hard work, frugality, trust and an orientation towards the future that encourages planning and saving and engenders a positive attitude towards education. Trust was later to receive special attention in the work of Fukuyama (1995).[7]

Harrison is concerned about 'the erosion of American culture' and 'the present-oriented aspects of the post-industrial value system' (1992: 247), which he contrasts with 'the Confucian values of work, education, and merit, and the Taoist value of frugality' characteristic of Asians from countries like Taiwan, Korea and Japan (1992: 149).[8] The erosion of traditional American values threatens the economic progress of the United States and the continuation of its leadership role in the world. In Harrison's eyes

America needs reforms in the fields of religion, education, management and childrearing. This all comes down to an appeal for a 'cultural renaissance', a moral regeneration, a new commitment 'to the future, to education, to achievement and to excellence' (1992: 247).

Harrison refers to many earlier works that emphasized the cultural factor – albeit in varying degrees – such as Max Weber's classical study *The Protestant Ethic and the Spirit of Capitalism* (1976), Banfield's *Amoral Familism* (1958), McClelland's *The Achieving Society* (1961), Foster's *Peasant Society and the Image of the Limited Good* (1965) and Lewis's work on the 'culture of poverty' (for example Lewis 1966). Weber tried to answer the question of why capitalism developed in Western Europe and not elsewhere. He believed capitalism required a specific outlook, the continuous accumulation of wealth for its own sake. Such an outlook, he argued, was characteristic of some Protestant denominations and he focused specifically on one of them – Calvinism. In Calvinism God called on the faithful to work for His glory. Work thus became a positive value. This doctrine of calling, together with a belief in predestination, put a premium on hard work. Hard work and occupational success were a sign of grace. Calvinism also had a strong ascetic aspect, stressing frugality and thrift. A final element in Weber's characterization of the Protestant ethic was the belief in the possibility of rational control over all aspects of life, contrasting with the more magical, sacramental Roman Catholic system of beliefs. Ever since Weber, explanations of socioeconomic success in terms of culture have emphasized values like hard work, frugality, saving and trust. In her contribution to this volume, Werbner argues that especially under postmodern conditions the 'aesthetic appreciation of the hedonistic pursuit of luxury' may be more important than frugality, rationality and thrift.[9]

Although Weber did give attention to other factors than the Protestant ethic, the main thrust of his argument was to show that ideas can become effective forces in history, and this was a criticism of economic determinism. Weber's research was part of a more general discussion of the relationship between religion and socioeconomic development. Well-known is his debate with Sombart (1911) about the contribution of the Jews to the development of modern capitalism. Sombart had argued that the Jews had made significant contributions; Weber believed they had not, since their ethics had remained strongly traditionalistic and lacked an attitude of economic rationality. Weber's thesis on the Protestant ethic is still highly controversial. Though it has been criticized on many points, and though the criticism constitutes a 'formidable indictment' of his views (Giddens 1976: 12), many still find the thesis appealing.[10] In explaining 'Asian success' in Asia itself or among Asian immigrants elsewhere, some have argued that Confucianism is a source of an ethos similar to the Protestant ethic as portrayed by Weber. Ironically, this is rather contrary to Weber's own view of Confucianism as a symbol of oriental bureaucratic stagnation.

Weber was one of the sources of inspiration for McClelland's *The Achieving Society* (1961). McClelland's work can be interpreted as an attempt to translate Weber's thesis into a more general theory of psychological motivation, by arguing that the psychological notion of motivation is strongly related to the sociological notion of value. McClelland's thesis is that the need for achievement plays a central role in economic growth. This need for achievement is a product of childrearing practices influenced by 'background factors' like religious traditions. Foster's image of the limited good, Banfield's amoral familism and Lewis's notion of the culture of poverty were all developed to explain the *lack* of development and prosperity in some groups. Foster used the phrase 'the image of the limited good' to denote a cognitive orientation whereby all desirable goods exist in very limited quantities. This orientation, supposedly characteristic of peasants, implies that they distrust one another and believe that improvement of their condition is only possible at the expense of others and by having luck rather than by working hard. Banfield saw the ethos of 'amoral familism' – according to which people pursue only the limited interests of the nuclear family while distrusting all others – as the chief cause of the underdevelopment of southern Italy. Lewis's 'culture of poverty' deals mainly with the urban poor.

Although these theories differ in the amount of attention they devote to the structural causes of a given culture, ethos or cognitive orientation, they all imply that the cultural factor is an important determinant of economic success or failure. They also share another characteristic: they all became highly controversial almost immediately after publication and sparked heated debates between their advocates and opponents. One can disagree with much of Steinberg's essay and still appreciate his point that the basic issues involved keep coming back. This is perhaps most evident in the literature on the urban poor and topics directly related to it. The basic idea of the culture-of-poverty thesis is that living under conditions of poverty may, the longer it continues, bring about a cultural adaptation to those conditions. This may serve survival as long as those conditions continue, but it makes it harder to take advantage of new opportunities if and when they arise.

Sansone addresses these issues in this volume, looking also at the role the internationalization of black culture and the changing international economy play in the process. The harsh criticisms of the culture-of-poverty thesis (see for example Leacock 1971 and Valentine 1968) have led to an avoidance of that concept, but they have also spawned a multitude of new notions like 'anti-school culture', 'oppositional culture', 'adversarial culture' and 'underclass culture', which centre around the same basic issues (see Steinberg's contribution). This can be seen either as proof that the evil cannot be eradicated and that combating it is like fighting a many-headed dragon, or as evidence that real issues are involved that cannot be addressed by simply ignoring contaminated concepts.

Patterns of differential social mobility in immigrant ethnic groups

The study of social mobility has been one of the classical themes of sociology since De Tocqueville, Marx, Weber and Sorokin.[11] Since the 1960s the field has become ever more specialized and technical, and dominated almost entirely by the survey method. At least since the early 1970s, it has also been criticized for attaching greater value to statistical virtuosity than to substantive issues. Social mobility research has come under attack on other grounds too. Partly because of its over reliance on surveys, it has been criticized for its individualistic bias. It has tended to treat the randomly chosen individuals in the survey research as isolates, giving scant attention to their social embeddedness within specific contexts. Related to this, its excessive focus on occupations, and thus on the individuals expected to have those occupations, has resulted in an almost exclusive focus on men. Researchers have tried to accommodate such criticisms in various ways. Qualitative approaches have been adopted to supplement quantitative ones (for example Bertaux and Thompson 1997a), and quantitative techniques are being developed to measure contextual effects and avoid the exclusive focus on occupations and the resulting male bias.

The contributors to this volume make use of both quantitative and qualitative methodologies, and they focus on education as well as the labour market. Most put a strong emphasis on comparison. Several compare groups that are similar in at least some respects and have migrated to the same country at about the same time under similar conditions. There are also other types of comparisons. One article deals with the 'same' group in different countries and many contributions make within-group comparisons. The emphasis is not only on differences between immigrant groups, but also on similarities between them and on differences between immigrant groups and the majority population. Crul's analysis of second-generation Moroccan and Turkish school careers, for example, stresses their cultural and other similarities as immigrant groups in the Netherlands.

Differential social mobility of immigrant groups is often studied as part of ethnic studies or the study of migration, with *integration* or *incorporation* used as central concepts, rather than social mobility. Our choice of the term *social mobility* here is not meant as a rejection of those other concepts. The notion of social mobility – itself not without certain ideological pitfalls, as I have just indicated – does have the advantage of being more specific than 'integration' or 'incorporation', which refer to all aspects of the process of becoming part of the receiving society. 'Social mobility' also sets immigrant groups less apart from the rest of the population than concepts used predominantly for immigrant populations.

A common procedure in the quantitative study of differential ethnic mobility processes is to try first to determine whether differences between ethnic groups can be explained by their present class position, usually measured by some variant of the socioeconomic status (SES) score, or structural location. The last notion is usually conceived as broader than class position, also including, for example, aspects of social structure (for example family structure). The usual candidates for explaining the possible residual variance are *culture* (that is, the cultural notions and values of the groups included in the research), *exclusion* by the dominant society (racism) and *contextual effects* such as the class composition and class relations of the ethnic communities. The primary opposition in both quantitative and qualitative research is usually conceived as that between *culture* and *structure or class*.

Two books appeared in the United States in 1981 which are very similar in certain respects: *Ethnic America* by Thomas Sowell and *The Ethnic Myth* by Stephen Steinberg. Both review the histories of a wide array of ethnic groups in that country over an extended period of time, and both ask how we can account for the fact that some groups have attained a better socioeconomic position than others. The answers they give, however, are diametrically different. Sowell (1981: 282) explains the economic histories of immigrant ethnic groups in the United States primarily in terms of the 'human capital' they have at their disposal. Human capital refers to 'the whole constellation of values, attitudes, skills, and contacts that many call a culture.'[12] So Sowell seeks the main causes in the *cultures* of the groups in question, while Steinberg vehemently opposes such an explanation. For him it is *class*, not culture, which is the strongest determining factor. The differences between the two authors relate to the different ways they use the word culture. Both conclude that the possession of certain skills has influenced the position immigrants were able to achieve, but while for Sowell this shows the importance of culture, for Steinberg it confirms the centrality of class. By no means, though, is the disagreement between these two writers reducible to a mere difference in definition. The following passage makes this clear, while also conveying the essence of Sowell's viewpoint:

> Specific skills are a prerequisite in many kinds of work. But history shows new skills being rather readily acquired in a few years, as compared to the generations – or centuries – required for *attitude* changes. Groups today plagued by absenteeism, tardiness, and need for constant supervision at work or in school are typically descendants of people with the same habits a century or more ago.
>
> (1981: 284)

In this passage, at least, Sowell evinces a culturalistic outlook, taking culture as a relatively timeless given, an ahistorical category.

Steinberg's attitude towards the notion of culture is ambivalent. In some of his more programmatic statements he seems to assign some measure of significance and explanatory value to culture. At such moments he particularly stresses that culture does not exist in a vacuum and is not unchangeable, and he points to the interaction between cultural and material factors (see for example 1989: xiii–xiv, 87). In other places, however, and notably in his concrete analyses, Steinberg is mainly out to convince the reader that culture is a myth. He does this by zeroing in on the static and ahistorical notions of culture he encounters in the writings of his adversaries. But having rejected such notions of culture, he fails to replace them with the more dynamic one he advances elsewhere. Instead, at least in his analysis of specific cases, he tends to reject the notion of culture altogether, dismissing it as a myth. He is right to challenge his opponents views, and most of his criticism is insightful and to the point, but his alternative is not entirely convincing.

The antithesis between culture and class (or structure) also pops up regularly in the European literature. Here I will only mention a debate that took place about a decade before the publication of Sowell's and Steinberg's works. This discussion did not centre on social mobility, but – with postwar immigration still a relatively recent phenomenon – on the adaptation of the first-generation immigrants. Marxist approaches were strongly represented among the early studies of immigrants, as in the work of Castles and Kosack (1973) and Nikolinakos (1973 and 1975). The behaviour of first-generation immigrants was understood almost exclusively in terms of their class position. This class analysis was later strongly criticized by Shanin as being ahistorical. He warned that 'a Marxist, or any other class analysis can dismiss history only at its analytical peril' (1978: 281). Shanin argued as follows. Labour migrants can only be understood by looking at their origins. You cannot come to understand immigrants' behaviour by viewing them exclusively in their present class position. You have to include in your analysis their class position from before their migration: labour migrants tend to behave more like the peasants they *were* than the workers they *are*. Though Shanin did not use the word 'culture', his analysis can be taken as an appeal to consider culture. For culture, in the sense of collective consciousness, is the medium through which the past makes itself felt in the present. Conceived in this way, culture is a historical concept by definition. Yet Shanin's article was not a call for the study of *ethnic* culture, but of *class* culture. In his view, peasant culture played an important – and generally positive – part in the process by which immigrants adapt to the conditions in their new country.

In at least some of the more recent approaches, the debate on structure versus culture, and especially any reference to culture, seem to be avoided. How should we interpret this? Is it simply a translation of the same issues into a different vocabulary, or is it an attempt to avoid a 'loaded' issue? Or, is it an indication that an ancient and sterile opposition has finally been overcome? If the latter is the case, could it not be that something is being lost in the process? Some of these questions are addressed by Joel Perlmann in the next introductory text.

The contributions to this volume

Following our two introductory essays, we present two contributions which, from different perspectives, are very critical of any attempt to explain differential social mobility in terms of culture – even if the cultural factor is only considered to be part of a broader explanation. Since his book *The Ethnic Myth,* Steinberg has been known for his fierce criticism and virtual rejection of explanations in terms of culture, which in his view become almost inevitably culturalistic. His contribution can best be regarded as an update of that book with a discussion of some of the relevant literature of the past decade.

Notwithstanding his criticism, Steinberg still accepts the terms of the 'culture–versus–structure' debate. Werbner rejects these. One of her principal arguments is that no universal 'culture-free' measure of success exists. She rejects the measurement of success in purely economistic terms such as income and occupation. All other contributors seem to agree with Roosens (1989: 157 and 1998: 59) that globalization has resulted in at least some degree of transcultural consensus of values and desires in this area, that is most contemporaries regard economic betterment as an end for themselves. Van Niekerk explicitly argues this. One could even contend that without this relative consensus it would not be possible to speak about inequality on an international as well as an intrasocietal basis.

The contributions by Steinberg and Werbner are followed by six case studies. I will focus here specifically on two issues regarding these case studies: what they add to our understanding of the social mobility of immigrant groups and what light they shed on the question of whether and how culture might play a role in this process. In doing this, I do not claim to adequately represent the richness of insights that the contributions provide. I can only highlight some of the issues.

In the case of the European immigrants who entered the United States before the 1920s, it is now possible to study social mobility processes over several generations. Such research generally indicates that all these prewar immigrant ethnic groups, though following different paths and moving at an unequal pace, have all ultimately reached roughly similar socioeconomic positions at the aggregate level, positions well above those from which they started (see for example Lieberson 1992 and 1996, Waters and Lieberson 1992). One of the prime questions as we study *new* immigration is whether the course of social mobility will be similar for the newcomers. Some believe it will be, but others predict more pessimistic outcomes, at least for some groups.[13] Most observers would probably agree that it is still too early to know and that much depends on the future capacity of the labour market to provide jobs (for example Lieberson 1996: 203). Postwar immigration to Western Europe shows a number of similarities to the new immigration in the United States, whereas no comparable large-scale immigration took place to Europe early in the 20th century. This debate is highly relevant, then, for understanding the European situation.

This volume contains two case studies on the old immigrant groups in the United States. These studies benefit from a long-range perspective. The authors of the remaining articles deal with postwar immigration, and, as far as the second generation is concerned, they confine themselves mainly to educational achievement, since this generation is still young and has barely entered the labour market.

This book asks whether culture makes *a* difference, not *the* difference. The question assumes that the role of culture can at most be a modest one in a complex of interacting factors. So in the detailed analyses of the case studies which follow, many aspects other than the cultures of the immigrant groups are also considered, such as racism or opportunity structures at the time of immigration. I will not go into these other factors, except for one issue which is related to the cultural factor and difficult to separate from it, namely aspects of social structure characteristic for a given ethnic group and part of what Waldinger, Aldrich and Ward (1990: 22) have called 'group characteristics'. Several essays focus attention on the role of the family or of family members in social mobility processes.[14]

It is most central in Crul's analysis of educational achievement among second-generation Moroccans and Turks in the Netherlands. Crul investigates why at least some of the children of lower-class immigrants from peasant backgrounds succeed very well in school. It emerges that older brothers and sisters – and sometimes more distant relatives or coethnics – play a crucial part in the process. Lindo points to the pivotal role played by mothers. He argues that the greater educational achievements of Iberian in comparison with Turkish children can be partly explained by the greater participation of Portuguese immigrant mothers in social life outside the family, including the labour market. Van Niekerk relates differences in family structure and cohesion to differential strategies of upward social mobility. Early marriage and the larger, more cohesive and hierarchical Surinamese Hindustani families are associated with a strategy of accumulation of economic resources, while the smaller, more 'democratic' and more individualistic families of the Surinamese Creoles follow a strategy of accumulating educational qualifications.

The nature of ethnic communities and the networks with coethnics also receives a great deal of attention in this collection. Vermeulen and Venema show that the majority of lower-class Italian immigrants in the United States, who originated from southern Italy, profited little from the presence of more well-to-do Italians. Most of the latter were from northern Italy, had their own separate communities and looked down on the southerners. But even among southern Italians themselves, class barriers were formidable. Within Greek communities this was very different. Successful Greek immigrants might come from the same social backgrounds as the poorer immigrants, some of whom were likely to be their kin. The result was not only that poorer immigrants could expect help from those better off, but also that upward mobility seemed within reach for many. In this totality, it seems that the collective experience of the Greek trading diaspora – with its emphasis on 'useful contacts', co-operation, organization, education, and last but not least, business and niche-building – played a vital role.

A related and interesting aspect is the role of social cohesion – of families, ethnic communities or various intermediate-level entities. Comparing Mexican and Punjabi immigrants in Valleyside – a contrast that resembles somewhat the one described by van Niekerk for the Surinamese Creoles and Hindustani – Gibson argues that the more closely knit communities of the Punjabis, with their strong ethnic and religious identities, promote educational success. The Mexican case forms a contrast on all these points. This seems to be in line with Crul's argument that the cohesiveness of Turkish families and communities promotes school achievement. Unlike Gibson, who concentrates on the role of cohesiveness in building secure identities that can shield immigrants from racial hostilities, Crul focuses on actual help in school careers. Both studies contrast with Lindo's findings on the relative educational success of Iberian compared to Turkish children. In the Turkish community, cohesive networks based on region of origin are able to enforce conformity in a way that traditional patterns of behaviour – which interfere with educational achievement – can be maintained. In the Iberian communities, ethnic networks are not unimportant, but relations within the family and ethnic communities afford more freedom to the younger generation.

If we assume that Thompson's statement that a loosening of family ties may often be an essential prelude to social mobility (Thompson 1997: 53) can be extended to other primary group relations, Thompson's findings resemble those of Lindo. How can these differences be explained? First of all, it seems clear that cohesiveness does not have uniform effects. The influence it brings to bear on interaction with the host society depends not only on the differential contexts of immigrant reception but also on the nature of the networks themselves. As Lindo argues, networks that more closely replicate premigration networks can be expected to have a more conservative influence than networks developed between coethnics after migration. Secondly, premigration networks may differ widely in economic orientation – depending on factors such as class composition, level of development of the country of origin and urban experience. A third point is that the cohesiveness of networks may have different effects on different members. As Crul (2000) argued elsewhere, boys may profit from cohesive networks, while the school and occupational careers of girls may suffer, because conformity to traditional roles of women is more easily enforced. The contrast between the findings by Lindo and by Crul on Turkish youth may perhaps be explained in part by the time interval between the two studies, even though that was rather short. Partly under pressure from their children, parents are increasingly realizing the importance of education for social mobility. Moreover, as immigrants reside longer in the new country, their social networks are less likely than before to consist of people from the same region of origin, and to the degree that they still do, these tend to grow less conservative.

The question remains: does culture make a difference? To address it we need to look once again at what is understood by culture. The authors of the case studies in this volume use somewhat different implicit or explicit definitions. Some, such as van Niekerk, are referring first and foremost to normative and cognitive orientations. Lindo is reluctant to use such notions. He finds no evidence in his research material for something like Ogbu's notion of *folk theories of success* and he sees no reason to hypothesize their presence. His focus is on patterned social behaviour rather than on values or cognitive aspects. He argues that some patterns of behaviour characteristic of large parts of the Turkish community in the Netherlands interfere with the school careers of young Turks, but he doubts whether these patterns of social behaviour should be called culture. Notwithstanding these and other variations in how 'culture' is conceptualized, most if not all authors seem to agree on a number of points relevant to this issue. Although Weber believed that the Protestant ethic cannot be interpreted as a historically necessary result of previous economic relations – and must therefore be conceived as autonomous – there is a great reluctance among the authors represented here to see culture as an autonomous force. Culture is viewed by all as socially embedded, as related to present or previous social, political and economic relations. This is not to say that it is easy, or even possible, to trace all cultural patterns back to their 'origins'. It is simply not necessary in many cases to hypothesize that aspects of culture relevant to social mobility are more or less autonomous, such as values supposedly related to centuries-old religious traditions. At the same time, such explanations can often not be entirely ruled out either. Illuminating in this respect is Perlmann's analysis. His new, meticulous analysis of quantitative data shows that Jewish economic success – the fact that they reached middle-class status in greater numbers and within a shorter time span than other immigrant groups – cannot simply be explained by the fact that they possessed the relevant manual skills. The role of such skills was less important than the evidence available up to now had suggested. Experience in trade, and possibly a preference for it, played a role as well. Though Perlmann does not exclude even broader, more Weberian explanations, he does not find it necessary to appeal to them in order to explain the observed behaviour. The Greek case bears out Perlmann's analysis and is perhaps even more marked. Manual skills were virtually absent among Greek migrants, and trade, though part of the collective experience, was not part of their personal history, since they were overwhelmingly of peasant background.

It may be useful to see 'culture' as a sensitizing concept that can help draw our attention to a number of interrelated issues pertinent to the study of social mobility of immigrants and their descendants. At this point it seems appropriate to state what I mean by 'culture'. For a long time I have been using a definition proposed by the Swedish anthropologist Löfgren, though there are many variants that might do just as well. Löfgren (1981: 30) has defined culture as 'the common world of experiences, values and knowledge that a certain social group constitutes and reproduces in their daily life.' Three remarks about this definition are in order. First, it does not restrict the concept of culture to ethnic or national units. This may seem obvious to many readers, but it should be realized that such restrictions are indeed often made in discussions of culture versus structure or class, when class culture is subsumed under the notion of class.[15] Secondly, in this definition, tradition and homogeneity do not take precedence a priori above change and heterogeneity. Finally, Löfgren formulates his definition in terms of collective consciousness. Some argue that by defining culture in this way, based on symbols, meaning, ideas, values or other mental constructs, one denies the interrelatedness of culture and behaviour or culture and social structure (Goody 1994; see also Lindo's contribution). To me that is a *non sequitur*. By distinguishing between these sets of oppositions, I am making an analytic distinction, not an empirical claim. I would argue, in fact, that in order to study the empirical interrelatedness of culture and behaviour or social structure, we need to distinguish between the two.

As a sensitizing concept, culture draws our attention to a number of perspectives on the migrant situation that may help us to better understand patterns of differential social mobility. These may be designated as follows.

Culture as idiosyncrasy

Werbner argues that culture cannot *explain* the difference, since it *is* the difference. And it is true: as I have observed, culturalistic 'explanations' tend to be tautological, declaring that cultures are different because they are different. One can also maintain, however, that culture draws our attention to the aspect of historic specificity of a given case. As Gestalt psychologists would point out, the whole is more than the sum of its parts. Cultures are specific historical configurations.[16]

Culture as the sedimentation of experience

Metcalf *et al.* (1996: 128) have argued that opportunity structures are too often defined in objective terms, as if they can be defined independently of the way they are perceived by the actors.[17] The ways people perceive a situation and react to it, however, are not given by that situation, but are also influenced by their individual and collective experience. Culture is the term that refers to the collective part of this experience. The notion of 'experience' refers back to what was experienced. Culture may thus partly be understood as a product of factors such as a previous location in a specific class system, state system or natural environment, or rather all of these combined. Vermeulen and Venema, for example, focus attention on the role of the state in premigration experience. The notion of experience underlines once more the importance of a historical perspective, not in the sense of an exclusive focus on the past, but in the sense of taking into account developments over time.

A crucial question that still remains is to what extent the sedimentation of past experience may lead people such as the long-term unemployed to underestimate their opportunities for upward mobility, resulting in what Sansone in this volume calls self-exclusion. What Gans formulated in 1970 as the most important question in the study of culture and poverty is still just as important today (Wilson 1997: 66–86): how quickly will the poor be able to alter their behaviour in new circumstances and what obstacles originate from past experience?

Culture as agency

Culture is often presented as an agent that could do things. I have already criticized such a reification of culture. But this should not obscure the fact that the notions of culture and agency are interrelated. 'Agency versus structure' is a pair of opposites very akin to 'culture versus structure'.[18] So although Weber's Protestant ethic is usually cited as an example of the structure–versus–culture debate, it is sometimes presented in terms of structure versus agency (see note 10). The interrelatedness of culture and agency makes more understandable the moral overtones of relating social mobility to culture. But cultures are not simply products of free choices, and cultural beliefs and values seldom if ever change in response to moral revivals such as the one advocated by Harrison. Moreover, explanations exclusively in terms of external conditions have moral implications, too. They portray people as mere products, if not victims, of external circumstances,[19] thus denying them their role as actors. This runs the risk of denying people their responsibility and even their identity.

Culture and social structure as intricately linked

Beliefs, symbols and values are intrinsic to social interaction. Social relations would be meaningless without them. By the same token, there is no culture outside social structure.[20] This immediately clarifies why cultures can never be homogeneous. Groups and individuals have different positions and relations within an overall social structure or 'society'. There is a broad range of cultural variation within 'cultures' which relates to these differentiations. Cultures are not characterized by a replication of uniformity, but by the organization of difference.[21] Though we can analytically distinguish culture from social relations, the two are inextricably linked.

This is most evident, perhaps, in studies of families and gender, where the two can sometimes scarcely be distinguished.

To emphasize that social structure and culture are intimately interrelated is not to argue that the one can be derived from the other. It does, however, have a number of implications. If differences in social mobility between two groups can largely be explained by structural factors, that does not prove that cultural differences play no role of significance. The structural differences can also be viewed as an indication that cultural differences are likely to exist. There is no a priori reason why the structural would be the most fundamental. However, if the structural factors are then held constant, it is not so likely that cultural factors will provide important *additional* explanations. It follows from this that it may be a good research strategy to focus first on the noncultural aspects of the explanation, if only for the simple reason that these are more easy to establish. This is clearly the approach taken in many of the contributions to this book. In historical research in particular, it tends to be difficult to find independent data on the ethos of a group.[22]

In my introduction, I have argued that culture is a notion that can at once lead us astray and sensitize us to issues that are crucial to the study of social mobility. In this respect the concept of culture does not differ fundamentally from other central concepts in social science. Concepts always lead us in certain directions, away from certain important aspects and towards others, into some traps and away from others. It does seem, however, that the dangers now loom especially large in the case of the culture concept. It may well be sensible to avoid the word as much as possible. At the same time, we should realize that little is gained by merely avoiding the term. While that might reduce the risks of falling into culturalist traps, the traps themselves do not depend on the word *culture*. Moreover, by avoiding that combination of letters we also run a certain risk of losing what we have gained by using it. We can do without the word culture, but not without the insights it has contributed to sociocultural analysis so far. To me, finding an updated notion of culture for studying differential social mobility would have two important benefits. First, an adequate notion of culture – that is one which avoids the culturalistic traps – sensitizes us to how important the histories of immigrant groups are for an understanding of our subject matter. Second, it makes us aware of the moral implications and dilemmas involved in studying differential social mobility.

Notes

1. See also Carrithers 1992, Handler 1988 and Keesing 1994.
2. This is a common argument in American debates on the culture of poverty.

3. 'What we cannot understand is respectfully assigned to the mysterious residual category of culture' (Marcus and Fischer 1986: 38). Particularly in quantitative research, culture is often used to interpret the unexplained variation in comparisons of groups defined by ethnic origin.

4. This point has been made by quite a number of people. I will give only one example: 'I might add that the cultural and normative explanations often rest on a deceptive form of circular reasoning, not at all uncommon in race and ethnic studies. Why are two groups different with respect to a certain characteristic or dependent variable? Presumably, they differ in their values or in some norm. How do we know that they differ in their values or norms? The argument then frequently involves using the behavioural attribute one is trying to explain as the indicator of the normative or value difference one is trying to explain. A pure case of circular reasoning!' (Lieberson 1980: 8).

5. This is not to imply that culturalist explanations can be found only in the study of minorities or 'others'. Such explanations do not even require the word *culture*. For example, in Brubaker's (1992) well-known study of the German and French conceptions of nation and their relationship to those countries' policies and politics of citizenship for immigrants, the author concludes that the two concepts of nationhood are deeply rooted, robust and have altered little over a long span of time. This is offered as the *explanans*, rather than (assuming for the moment its validity) as the *explanandum*.

6. Greenstone (1991) has likewise pointed out how the ideas of culture and rationality tend to be applied as antitheses in the debates about the culture of poverty and the underclass.

7. Holton (1992: 191) writes about trust: 'The strategic importance of trust in the analysis of economy and society is that it appears as an aspect of economic culture at the heart of economic relations, rather than as a mode of cultural expression, so to speak, outside the economy but impacting upon it.'

8. Harrison's arguments apply both to these Asian countries and to immigrants from these countries. He contrasts this to Latin American countries and immigrants from that region, especially Mexicans. So Harrison is not arguing that all immigrants initially have an ethos that promotes success.

9. Werbner reminds us that Sombart had already examined the relationship between luxury and capitalism in the early 20th century (cf. Lehmann 1993).

10. In an interesting article on *The Protestant Ethic*, Poggi has observed, paraphrasing Barrington Moore: 'it remains unsettled whether *The Protestant Ethic* was an important breakthrough or a blind alley.' He adds: 'Even an "untenable Protestant ethic" remains something of a breakthrough and sets high standards for alternative answers to its own questions.' One way it does this is by drawing attention to the processual nature of the relationship between action and structure (1993: 299).

11. On social mobility research and some of the criticisms of this research tradition, see for example Bertaux and Thompson 1997b, Erikson and Goldthorpe 1992, Strauss 1971 and Thompson 1997.

12. Note that many would consider values and attitudes as belonging to the realm of culture, while relegating skills and contacts to political economy and class.

13. On this issue see for example Gans 1996 and 1997, Lieberson 1996, Perlmann and Waldinger 1997, Rumbaut 1997.

14. Most of the contributions in *Pathways to Social Class. A Qualitative Approach to Social Mobility* by Bertaux and Thompson (1997a) discuss the role of the family.

15. Löfgren (1981) used the quoted definition of culture to study class culture in a project entitled 'Culture and class: a study of social and cultural change in Sweden c. 1880–1980'.
16. This is the position taken by Perlmann in *Ethnic Differences*, at the end of his chapter on the Italians: 'All the preceding explanations ultimately direct attention away from any characteristics of life unique to southern Italy and toward broader sorts of explanatory frameworks relevant to pre-migration life: social class position, the economic order, religion, familiarity with schooling. At the same time, these and other factors – political arrangements for example – may have come together in a unique way in southern Italian culture. That culture, then, may have had an independent force beyond its sources' (1988: 118).
17. The passage I refer to here reads: 'Waldinger *et al.* (1990) have suggested an approach which combines the economic with ethnicity perspectives. Their interactive approach is built on two dimensions: opportunity structures and characteristics of the ethnic group. While this is a theoretical advance, it does not take the idea of 'interaction' far enough. It still assumes that 'opportunity structures' can be cultural neutral and can be defined independently of ethnic group norms and attitudes – an assumption challenged by our study.'
18. Alternatively, we can understand agency in terms of specific persons or groups, in different positions of power, acting upon the totality of social structure and culture.
19. Cf. Gilroy 1992 on anti-racism. Gilroy warns his readers that anti-racism seems very comfortable with the idea of blacks as victims. The older critiques of Althusser's structuralism also come to mind here.
20. The emphasis on culture as intrinsic to social relations or 'human actions' can be found, for example, in Goody 1994, Holton 1992 and Williams 1989.
21. Wallace (1966) was one of the first to elaborate this point. More recently the viewpoint that cultures are not homogeneous but 'distributive' is rather common (for example Barth 1989, Borofsky 1994, Goody 1994).
22. There are, for example, serious problems of operationalization in historical research on Weber's theses regarding the Protestant ethic (Voert 1994: 21–31).

References

Abu-Lughod, L., 1991, 'Writing against culture', in: R.G. Fox (ed.), *Recapturing Anthropology. Working in the Present* (Santa Fe, New Mexico: School of American Research Press)

Banfield, E.C., 1958, *Amoral Familism. The Moral Basis of a Backward Society* (New York: The Free Press)

Barth, F., 1989, 'The analysis of culture in complex societies', *Ethnos* 54: 120–42

Bertaux, D., and P. Thompson (eds), 1997a, *Pathways to Social Class. A Qualitative Approach to Social Mobility* (Oxford: Clarendon Press)

Bertaux, D., and P. Thompson, 1997b, 'Introduction', in: D. Bertaux and P. Thompson (eds), *Pathways to Social Class. A Qualitative Approach to Social Mobility* (Oxford: Clarendon Press)

Bidney, D., 1953, 'The concept of culture and some cultural fallacies', in: D. Bidney, *Theoretical anthropology* (New York: Columbia University Press)

Borofsky, R., 1994, 'The cultural in motion', in: R. Borofsky (ed.), *Assessing Cultural Anthropology* (New York: McGraw-Hill)

Brubaker, R., 1992, *Citizenship and Nationhood in France and Germany* (Cambridge: Harvard University Press)

Carrithers, M., 1992, *Why Humans Have Cultures. Explaining Anthropology and Social Diversity* (Oxford: Oxford University Press)

Castles, S., and G. Kosack, 1973, *Immigrant Workers and Class Structure in Western Europe* (London: Oxford University Press)

Crul, M., 2000, De Slentel tot Success: Over Hulp, Keuzes en Kansen in de Schoolloopbanen van Turkse en Marokkaanse Jongeren van de Tweede Generatie (Amsterdam: Het Spinhuis).

Ellis, R.J., and M. Thompson (eds), 1997, *Culture Matters. Essays in Honor of Aaron Wildavsky* (Boulder: Westview Press)

Erikson, R., and J.H. Goldthorpe, 1992, *The Constant Flux. A Study of Class Mobility in Industrial Society* (Oxford: Clarendon Press)

Foster, G., 1965, 'Peasant society and the image of the limited good', *American Anthropologist* 67: 293–315

Fukuyama, F., 1995, *Trust. The Social Virtues and the Creation of Prosperity* (New York: The Free Press)

Gans, H.J., 1970, 'Poverty and culture. Some basic questions about methods of studying the life-styles of the poor', in: P. Townsend (ed.), *The Concept of Poverty. Working Papers on Methods of Investigation and Life-styles of the Poor in Different Countries* (London: Heinemann)

Gans, H.J., 1996, 'Second-generation decline. Scenarios for the economic and ethnic futures of the post-1965 American immigrants', in: N. Carmon (ed.), *Immigration and Integration in Post-Industrial Societies. Theoretical Analysis and Policy-Related Research* (Basingstoke: Macmillan)

Gans, H.J., 1997, 'Toward a reconciliation of "assimilation" and "pluralism". The interplay of acculturation and ethnic retention', *International Migration Review* 31: 875–92

Giddens, A., 1976, 'Introduction', in: M. Weber, *The Protestant Ethic and the Spirit of Capitalism* (London: Allen & Unwin)

Gilroy, P., 1992, 'The end of anti-racism', in: J. Donald and A. Ratansi (eds), *'Race', Culture and Difference* (London: Sage)

Goody, J., 1994, 'Culture and its Boundaries. A European View', in: R. Borofsky (ed.), *Assessing Cultural Anthropology* (New York: McGraw-Hill)

Greenstone, J.D., 1991, 'Culture, rationality, and the underclass', in: Chr. Jencks and P.E. Peterson (eds), *The Urban Underclass* (Washington: The Brookings Institution)

Handler, R., 1988, *Nationalism and the Politics of Culture in Quebec* (Madison: The University of Wisconsin Press)

Hannerz, U., 1989, 'Culture between center and periphery. Toward a macroanthropology', *Ethnos* 54: 200–16

Harrison, L.E., 1992, *Who Prospers? How Cultural Values Shape Economic and Political Success* (New York: Basic Books)

Holton, R.J., 1992, *Economy and Society* (London: Routledge)

Keesing, R.M., 1994, 'Theories of culture revisited', in: R. Borofsky, *Assessing Cultural Anthropology* (New York: McGraw-Hill)

Leacock, E.B. (ed.), 1971, *The Culture of Poverty. A Critique* (New York: Simon and Schuster)

Lehmann, H., 1993, 'The rise of capitalism. Weber versus Sombart', in: H. Lehmann and G. Roth (eds), *Weber's Protestant Ethic. Origins, Evidence, Contexts* (Cambridge: Cambridge University Press)

Lewis, O., 1966, *La Vida. A Puerto Rican Family in the Culture of Poverty – San Juan and New York* (New York: Vintage Books)

Lieberson, S., 1980, *A Piece of the Pie. Blacks and White Immigrants since 1880* (Berkeley: University of California Press)

Lieberson, S., 1992, 'Socio-economic attainment', in: D.L. Horowitz and G. Noiriel (eds), *Immigrants in Two Democracies. French and American Experience* (New York: New York University Press)

Lieberson, S., 1996, 'Earlier immigration to the United States. Historical clues for current issues of integration', in: N. Carmon (ed.), *Immigration and Integration in Post-Industrial Societies. Theoretical Analysis and Policy-Related Research* (Basingstoke: Macmillan)

Löfgren, O., 1981, 'On the anatomy of culture', *Ethnologia Europaea* 12: 26–46

Marcus, G.E., and M.M.J. Fischer, 1986, *Anthropology as Cultural Critique. An Experimental Moment in the Human Sciences* (Chicago: The University of Chicago Press)

McClelland, D., 1961, *The Achieving Society* (New York: The Free Press)

Metcalf, H., T. Modood and S. Virdee, 1996, *Asian Self-Employment. The Interaction of Culture and Economics in England* (London: Policy Studies Institute)

Nikolinakos, M., 1973, *Politische Ökonomie der Gastarbeiterfrage. Migration und Kapitalismus* (Hamburg: Rowohlt)

Nikolinakos, M., 1975, 'Notes towards a general theory of migration in late capitalism', *Race & Class* 17: 277–88

Perlmann, J., 1988, *Ethnic differences. Schooling and Social Structure among the Irish, Italians, Jews, and Blacks in an American City, 1880–1935* (Cambridge: Cambridge University Press)

Perlmann, J., and R. Waldinger, 1997, 'Second generation decline? Children of immigrants, past and present. A reconsideration', *International Migration Review* 31: 893–922

Poggi, G., 1993, 'Historical viability, sociological significance, and personal judgment', in: H. Lehmann and G. Roth (eds), *Weber's Protestant Ethic. Origins, Evidence, Contexts* (Cambridge: Cambridge University Press)

Roosens, E.E., 1989, *Creating Ethnicity. The Process of Ethnogenesis* (Newbury Park: Sage)

Roosens, E.E., 1998, *Eigen Grond Eerst? Primordiale Autochtonie. Dilemma van de Multiculturele Samenleving* (Leuven: Acco)

Rumbaut, R.G., 1997, 'Assimilation and its discontents. Between rhetoric and reality', *International Migration Review* 31: 923–60

Shanin, T., 1978, 'The peasants are coming. Migrants who labour, peasants who travel and Marxists who write', *Race and Class* 19: 277–88

Sombart, W., 1911, *Die Juden und das Wirtschaftsleben* (Leipzig: Duncker und Humblot)

Sowell, T., 1981, *Ethnic America. A History* (New York: Basic Books)

Steinberg, S., 1989, *The Ethnic Myth. Race, Ethnicity and Class in America* (Boston: Beacon Press) [1981]

Strauss, A.L., 1971, *The Social Contexts of Social Mobility. Ideology and Theory* (Chicago: Aldine)

Thompson, P., 1997, 'Women, men, and transgenerational family influences in social mobility', in: D. Bertaux and P. Thompson (eds), *Pathways to Social Class. A Qualitative Approach to Social Mobility* (Oxford: Clarendon Press)

Valentine, C.A., 1968, *Culture and Poverty. Critique and Counter-Proposals* (Chicago: The University of Chicago Press)

Voert, M.J. ter, 1994, *Religie en het Burgerlijk Kapitalisme. Een Onderzoek naar de Relatie tussen Religieuze Overtuigingen en Opvattingen over Arbeid, Consumptie en Eerlijkheid* (Nijmegen: Instituut voor Toegepaste Sociale Wetenschappen)

Waldinger, R., H. Aldrich and R. Ward (eds), 1990, *Ethnic Entrepreneurs. Immigrant Business in Industrial Societies* (Newbury Park: Sage)

Wallace, A.F.C., 1966, *Culture and Personality* (New York: Random House)

Waters, M.C., and S. Lieberson, 1992, 'Ethnic differences in education. Current patterns and historical roots', *International Perspectives on Education and Society* 2: 171–87

Weber, M., 1976, *The Protestant Ethic and the Spirit of Capitalism* (London: Allen & Unwin) [1920–21]

Williams, R., 1989, *Culture* (London: Fontana) [1981]

Wilson, W.J., 1997, *When Work Disappears. The World of the Urban Poor* (New York: Vintage Books)

Wolf, E.R., 1982, *Europe and the People Without History* (Berkeley: University of California Press)

2

Introduction: The Persistence of Culture versus Structure in Recent Work. The Case of Modes of Incorporation

Joel Perlmann

The preceding chapter has highlighted the way in which cultural explanations have often been contrasted with structural ones. Here I will argue that recent work on ethnicity and immigration, while introducing new formulations, is more fruitful than simply trying to banish culture or structure, and is more fruitful than simply trying to assign weights to the importance of each, does not entirely break free of these older obsessions, even if the formulators would like to do so.

The formulations of William Julius Wilson (1987 and 1996) and of Douglas Massey and Nancy Denton (1993) provide an example; as their work is often discussed in terms of these issues, I mention them only in passing. For all the important freshness and originality for which their formulations have been justly hailed, and for all their disagreements, both Wilson and Massey/Denton insist that distinctive and destructive cultural patterns derive ultimately from structural features – both at the level of the individual's work and residential opportunities, and at the level of the concentration of the poor in particular neighbourhoods. Yet, notwithstanding their insistence on the ultimate structural sources of any cultural behaviour patterns, both formulations leave unresolved the discomforting question of how much survival power the cultural patterns have when the structural constraints change. I think that both Wilson and Massey/Denton themselves believe that cultural change will follow relatively rapidly from structural change; but my point is that neither formulation about the origins of a cultural pattern really allows one to make strong predictions about how quickly cultural change would follow from structural improvements.

In this chapter, I want to consider in more detail a different effort to bypass the structure/culture contrast, that of Alejandro Portes and his colleagues on modes of incorporation and segmented assimilation. This body of scholarship has been very influential in recent years and attempts to provide a more fruitful approach than simply juxtaposing culture and structure; and indeed, one reason for the formulation of these newer approaches may have been to surmount constraints inherent in the older structure versus culture approaches. For the sake of simplicity I focus almost entirely on the discussion of modes of incorporation as it appears in the second edition of Alejandro Portes and Ruben Rumbaut's *Immigrant America* (1996), which I think is a self-conscious and subtle effort to summarize an evolving body of remarkable research and reflection.

To review, then. Much early work on ethnicity tried to show that differences in ethnic group behaviour could be explained by appeals to differences in attitudes, outlooks and values that were thought characteristic of different groups. Other, typically later, work stressed the empirical limitations and internal contradictions of these cultural explanations – or still worse faults, such as self-congratulation, patronization, and arguments that were disturbingly parallel in nature to older biologically-based racial theories. The critiques of the cultural interpretations focused on the behaviour of ethnic groups as a reaction to discrimination in the wider society and especially on ethnic behaviour as a result of structural location, and most especially the social class location of ethnic group members. A long tradition in explaining differences in ethnic behaviour has wavered between, or tried to weave together, these competing forms of explanation, cultural and structural. In empirical terms, the challenge often takes the following form. Measures of social structural characteristics are taken – father's occupation, number of siblings, years of schooling and so on. If measures of cultural values can be obtained, those can be added to a multivariate analysis; if measures of cultural values are not found (and this is all too often the case) then the residual ethnic difference observed in ethnic behaviour – that is, the difference in ethnic behaviours remaining unexplained when structural characteristics of individuals in different ethnic groups had been taken into account – needs to be interpreted.

Interpreted as – as what? One interpretation is discriminatory behaviour against one or more of the ethnic groups involved. I do not discuss this interpretation further here because it is not relevant to the connections between the use of culture and the use of modes of incorporation as explanatory frameworks. However, what I say below could be extended easily enough to include the use of discrimination in interpreting the residual in the same way that culture is used as an interpretation of the residual. Portes and Rumbaut (1996) dismiss one possible way to interpret the residual when they cite the work of Barry Chiswick who refers to the result as 'the ethnic effect'. As Chiswick might have meant to imply, and as *Immigrant America* stresses (1996: 81–4), to say that the residual is associated with the ethnic group is tautological; to say that the residual is proof of cultural differences between ethnic groups is a highly questionable theoretical leap; but it is a leap consistent with the residual. A more modest interpretation – but still a leap – is that at least some of the residual can be explained in this way.

This is as far as many discussions of the explanations for ethnic differences go. One further step in the logic of explaining ethnic differences is worth mentioning before turning to *Immigrant America*, namely the relevance of contextual factors as opposed to individual-level factors. At the individual level, we might compare second generation Mexican and Korean immigrants and take into account the fact that the Koreans are far more likely to have had parents who were professionals and parents who were petty proprietors than are the Mexicans. If we then compare second generation Mexicans and Koreans whose parents were in roughly the same social class positions, we eliminate the impact of this difference in individual level characteristics, but not the difference in the contexts within which the Mexican and Korean second-generation members will grow up. There are many ways in which being part of a community of professionals and petty proprietors is different from being part of a community of immigrant labourers – even if the class position of individual families from each group is taken into account. These differences in contexts could well be both structural and cultural in nature (Perlmann 1988: 108–12, 211–13).

One can appreciate, I hope, what the modes of incorporation offers to someone who approached ethnic behaviour in the manner I just described; the modes explain why individual-level social structural characteristics do not capture all that needs to be explained about ethnic differences, and give a meaning to the 'residual ethnic difference' observed in multivariate analysis of individual-level data. The concept of the modes elaborates the notion that the social context is important in ways the individual-level data cannot capture – elaborates, specifies and systematizes that previously vague 'notion'.

So the residual ethnic difference need not be attributed to a distinctive cultural characteristic distinguishing one group from another; rather, the residual may reflect differences in the benefits that particular contexts offer individuals. I will first show briefly that approaching the modes of incorporation as an alternative to the limits of individual-level explanations (including cultural explanations) is exactly how *Immigrant America* in fact introduces their value and then raise some questions that still remain for someone sensitized – oversensitized? – to the question of 'independent' effects of cultural influences upon behaviour.

The modes are introduced in Chapter 1 of *Immigrant America* and are typically referred to as a rough and preliminary typology (rather than a full explanatory theory).[1] However, the powerful presentation of the modes, as an explanation of ethnic differences in socioeconomic outcomes and as a way of transcending the limits of individual-level analysis, is left to Chapter 3, entitled 'Making it in America'. The first half of Chapter 3 comprises a survey of the evidence on immigrant (and in some cases later-generation) socioeconomic attainments – especially in education, occupation and income. And in connection with each of these measures of attainment, the survey includes a subsection presenting a review of multivariate evidence from individual-level analyses. The point is always the same: the controls for individual-level variables do not explain the 'ethnic effect' at all well. *Education*: 'These persistent differences suggest the existence of broader cultural or social factors, not captured by the analysis of individual variables that affect the collective performance of each group' (Portes and Rumbaut 1996: 66). *Occupation*: 'As in the case of education, these factors [that is, microlevel factors] do not account entirely for differences in occupation among either individuals or nationalities, a result that suggests again the presence of broader cultural or structural forces' (ibid.: 71). *Income*: 'This low ability of predictive models based on individual variables to explain differences within and across immigrant groups indicates, once again, the need for an alternative and more encompassing explanation. This task must necessarily focus on factors other than those employed by prior studies, incorporating variables at a broader level of analysis' (ibid.: 82). The very next words comprise the title for the second part of the chapter: 'Explaining the Differences: Modes of Incorporation'. Shortly thereafter comes the elaboration: use of these modes 'is a way to overcome the limitations of exclusively individualistic models of immigrant behaviour (...) [The different modes] can help explain differences (...) among immigrants who are statistically "equal in a host of individual characteristics"' (ibid.: 83). From here the authors detail what it is about each mode that gives it explanatory power.

The first serious use of the modes, then, is as a solution to the persistent observation of a large ethnic residual (or unexplained difference) from individual-level analysis that might otherwise tempt the observer into leaping to the argument that independent cultural differences among groups explain the residual. I now want to stress how far we can push the corollary that living in different modes can effect not only the structural opportunities available to a person but also the attitudes, values and outlooks common in people from different groups. The crucial domain of life that distinguishes one mode of incorporation from another – at least in regard to 'making it' (and in fact, for all uses of the typology) – is the premigration social-class position prevalent in each immigrant group, and still more the distinction between waves of working-class immigrants and waves of immigrants that include enough higher-class members to help create a distinctive socioeconomic environment. And class origins create differences in cultural conditions of working-class and higher-class immigrant communities:

In addition [to the economic features of the labour migrant mode], there is often a kind of collective expectation that new arrivals should not be 'uppity; and should not try to surpass at least at the start, the collective status of their elders. (...) Ethnic-network assistance comes at the cost of ethnic pressures for conformity and the latter often reenforce employers' expectations about the "natural" position of the minority in the labor market. These dynamics help explain the self-perpetuating character of working class immigrant communities. [In the opposite kind of community the dominant feature is] that the support of ethnic networks is not contingent on acceptance of a working-class lifestyle or outlook.

(ibid.: 87)

Terms such as 'life style' and 'outlook' suggest that the working class 'pressures for conformity' are often internalized; these internalized characteristics, then, can become features observable at the individual level of behaviour. Furthermore, the members of such a 'working-class community', those immigrant groups characterized by a working-class mode of incorporation, are typically working class themselves, or at least members of a working-class community prior to immigration too, in the country of origin. Thus it would seem that these theoretical formulations about the context of working-class communities at least open the door to, and perhaps anticipate, differences in 'life style' and 'outlook' that could be observed at the individual level; differences that would precede immigration.

If we gave a test that measured motivation in arriving immigrants, a test that measured say a belief as Nathan Glazer (1955: 1722–3) might have phrased it 'that the world is open' to their initiative then these formulations of *Immigrant America* can be interpreted as predicting, I think, that we might well find that labour-migrant immigrant nationalities would score lower on such a test than higher-class migrant nationalities. I mention this hypothetical test because Portes and Rumbaut, comment derisively at the end of this chapter that

> Afterwards, apologists of successful groups will make necessities out of contingencies and uncover those 'unique' traits underlying their achievements; detractors of impoverished minorities will describe those cultural shortcomings or even genetic limitations accounting for their condition. Both are likely to affirm that in the end, "if there is a will, there is a way".
>
> (1996: 91–2)

Fair enough; we have all heard such tiresome self-congratulation and denigration; and we all know how destructive of empathy they can be – empathy for those facing real structural barriers to a decent life. Nevertheless, I want to insist that the discussion of life style and attitudes in *Immigrant America* predicts, or at the very least allow for, the possibility that, there is more of 'a will' in the middle-class compared to labour-migrant 'life style and outlook' – and that the greater 'will' is in fact part of the 'way' found later.

I think the authors might say, not that I have misunderstood but rather 'yes; so what?'. That is, cultural differences related to upward mobility may indeed emerge from differences in modes of incorporation, but such cultural differences stem ultimately from social class positions (class differences following and very likely also preceding migration). As such, these cultural differences should be understood as mere by-products of what really matters: the structural realities that lie behind the modes of incorporation. Again, fair enough; yet within this 'broader context' within which we can see the distant structural origins of cultural patterns, there is room in the narrow context of American life to see much room for differences in behaviour unrelated to differences in immediate structural context or structural incentives. *Immigrant America* in fact admits some discussion of such cultural differences in the passages I quoted; moreover, it is important to see that once the door has been opened to this sort of explanation, it is possible for others to utilize the same explanatory typology in order to throw the door open wider to cultural differences derived from the modes. My point here is simply that there is plenty of room within the formulation of modes to explore issues of differences in cultural baggage – at least baggage related to premigration class origins.

What, then, of other sorts of cultural differences, those that do not arise from the modes of incorporation? The sort of such cultural explanations cited as examples in *Immigrant America* typically date back to Weber's idea of the Protestant ethic. That is, in order to pose a theoretically interesting challenge, cultural theories must derive from aspects of experience that are not rooted in social class location and typically must derive from the domain of ideas. Here is an old example: in explaining American Jewish socioeconomic achievement, Nathan Glazer (1955) referred to premigration class background but also to various other sorts of cultural legacies. One of those cultural legacies he believed to have been derived directly from the religion of the Jews.

> Max Weber argues that they originated in a certain kind of religious outlook on the world, the outlook of Calvinism. There is no question that Judaism emphasizes the traits that businessmen and intellectuals require, and has done so since at least 1500 years before Calvinism. We can trace Jewish puritanism at least as far back as the triumph of the Maccabees over the Helenized Jews and of the Pharisees over the Sadducees.
>
> (ibid.: 1723)

I assume that this 'Jewish Puritanism' would qualify as an example of the kind of cultural explanation critiqued in *Immigrant America*; it is based in ancient religious differences, raised post-hoc, found to coexist with all sorts of other (structural) group advantages, and so on. Another example is cited in my chapter later in this volume, economic historian Simon Kuznets'

argument (1975) that a legacy as a particular kind of oppressed minority mattered, created a 'distinctive' individual and communal 'human capital'. My
point is simply to argue that such historical specifics could indeed lead to
influential differences in values, habits or outlook that may not derive from
the class base of a group's mode of incorporation, but from some other historically specific features of group's premigration life – and that it is hard to
see why historically specific features of one kind should be regarded a priori
as plausible (class origins, minority status) and features of other types implau-
sible ('Jewish Calvinism'). The point is not, of course, whether Kuznets is
right to stress the impact of minority status on human capital. Rather, the
point is to ask what the place of such an historically distinctive feature would
be in the modes of incorporation typology. The answer, I think, is that such a
feature has no place in that typology (that, after all, is what makes it a typology and not an historical narrative). Can such features – historically specific
and, in this case, cultural in nature – be added to the explanatory discussion
in *Immigrant America*? Of course, but to do so will inevitably complicate the
goals of a typology and the explanatory framework that rests on the typology.

I don't answer, as a better historian might, 'well then, to hell with the
typology'. However, I do want to be reassured that the modes are going to
dispose of much of the mess of ethnic diversity. To put it differently, if
there are historically specific features of premigration life that are relevant
to a full explanation, and if these are not captured in an explanation that
rests on the typology of the modes of incorporation, *how much* of the
whole of ethnically diverse behaviour do the modes in fact capture? Here I
want to stress the question of empirical tests. The section of Chapter 3 in
Immigrant America called 'Explaining the Differences' might more fairly be
entitled 'Explanatory Hypotheses that Might Explain the Differences'. The
first part of the chapter shows only that much remains unexplained by
individual-level social structural characteristics; the second part of the
chapter offers the elaboration of modes of incorporation. But this elaboration only shows that the modes can form the basis for a plausible and well-
developed explanatory hypothesis; that is not the same as empirical
validation of that hypothesis. In fact, *Immigrant America* does not offer an
assessment of how well the modes explain what they are called on to
explain. To say that the residual from individual-level analysis establishes
the impact of the modes on ethnic behaviour is to appropriate the residual
ethnic difference to support the modes – just as the residual was earlier
appropriated as support for the 'cultural values' explanation for behaviour.

There are some empirical techniques waiting in the wings, namely tests
for contextual effects. Some of these tests are very sophisticated and have
data requirements that probably cannot be met; others are cruder, but
applying them should at least be suggestive. In their paper Portes and
Macleod (1996) test for the power of school context using sophisticated
methods. Their Florida and California sample includes 42 schools.

They use the proportion of children receiving free lunches at the 42 schools as a measure of each school's SES context. In a similar way, one could consider measuring aspects of the ethnic context that are hypothesized to be critical to the modes of incorporation. Here the data requirements may become prohibitive; Portes and Macleod, for example, do not have adequate numbers of children in 42 nationality contexts as they do in 42 schools. But maybe a dozen nationality contexts; eight? It may be that the number of nationality contexts is too small to apply the sophisticated HLM methods that they use to measure school contexts. But work with cruder, yet still suggestive methods would be helpful; I used such tests very briefly (1988) and George Borjas (1992) has used them much more extensively. If what matters is the proportion of entrepreneurs in the group, why not take the proportion of entrepreneurs among the gainfully employed as a measure (is that measure so much cruder than taking the proportion of the student body getting free lunch as a measure of average SES?). A continuous variable, the proportion of entrepreneurs in a group, could be substituted for the ethnic dummy variables and results (variance explained and coefficients for ethnic groups) compared using this variable in a model rather than using the ethnic dummy variables in a model. I see no reason why such a test would be impossible; but if for some reason it is impossible to test the modes explanatory power directly – to test whether they will explain the residual ethnic difference – the implications of that impossibility would surely deserve close consideration.[2]

The discussion so far pertains especially to the immigrant generation, although most of what has been said could apply to the second generation as well. Yet the social context influences the development of the second generation in some ways that are generationally distinct. The new chapter in *Immigrant America*'s second edition on the second generation is, I think, the most complex in the book; the process described, as I understand it, is this. Forms of acculturation are offered as a new typology here, a typology for understanding the second generation. The parents' mode of incorporation has a good deal to do with which kind of acculturation will occur. And then the types of acculturation, once established, interact with several features of the social context within which the youth live. The specific features of the social context mentioned in the book are: the way the host society treats relevant phenotypes, the job structure and the geography of settlement. The geography of settlement in turn derives partly from the modes of incorporation. So: modes partially determine both acculturation and social context, and the interaction of acculturation and social context in turn provide the framework for our tentative expectations regarding which segment a youth will assimilate into.[3]

Now in this scheme some groups preserve or modify premigration cultural forms that serve as a buffer to over-rapid acculturation – the Vietnamese Church, the Sikh emphasis on family and tradition, the Cuban private schools, seem ways to maintain premigration cultural patterns. Still, here culture, at least in the formulation in *Immigrant America*, does not mean distinctive premigration legacies of outlook that are especially conducive to making it in America. Rather, the implication is that all groups are about equal in terms of the sorts of cultural elements discussed in the chapter. At any rate the theory ignores any possible ethnically-distinctive differences among cultural legacies: the theory is not about (for example) whether Confucianism or Buddhism works better than Catholicism as a buffer against the dangers of acculturation. Nor is the point for Portes and Rumbaut that some parts of the cultural baggage of Confucianism or Buddhism will be remarkably well-suited to American life and that part of the cultural baggage will be unpacked. I stress this distinction in the uses of 'culture' because Min Zhou's review of segmented assimilation in the *International Migration Review* (1997) does seem to stress the importance of ethnically-distinctive differences in the internal characteristics of the cultures serving as buffers. Thus Zhou comments (in the context of stressing that cultures are in fact transplanted selectively),

> For example, most of the Asian subgroups (...) whose original cultures are dominated by Confucianism, Taoism, or Buddhism often selectively unpack from their cultural baggage those traits suitable to the new environment, such as two-parent families, a strong work ethic, delayed gratification, and thrift.
>
> (1997: 994)

This passage can be read to mean that virtually any old-world culture can be drawn on for those values (a reading close in spirit to formulations in *Immigrant America)*, or that Confucianism, Taoism and Buddhism are especially good cultural baggage to unpack (a reading closer to Glazer's 'Jewish Puritanism' cited earlier, and close to what is treated with derision in *Immigrant America*). I don't see why the elaboration of modes of incorporation and segmented assimilation in *Immigrant America* necessarily *must*, on theoretical grounds preclude the second reading of Zhou's formulation, but the view in this second reading is at a minimum excluded from the typology, and at a maximum alien to the spirit of the book's discussion of cultural explanations. For *Immigrant America*, then, more or less any old-world culture could act as a buffer against the destructiveness of ending up in the inner city ghetto cultures of resistance. If so, however, why is the Vietnamese Church strong and some other church (for example, the Mexican) weak? One important reason is that the Vietnamese are not a working-class community, but (at least partly) an 'entrepreneurial' community.

Still, we may ask, are Vietnamese Church arrangements typical of every entrepreneurial immigrant church, or of most, or of only a few entrepreneurial immigrant Churches? Surely the churches of entrepreneurial groups are likely to vary; what then accounts for the strength of the Vietnamese Church in particular? Part of the answer must be found in the nature of church history in the country of origin; at least that was the case with regard to the loyalties of labour migrant groups to church institutions at the turn of the century – compare the Italians and the Poles, for example. Thus again we are veering back toward the historical specificity of cultural baggage.[4]

In sum, then, the modes of incorporation (and the related concept of segmented assimilation) bypass the structure/culture contrast, and may well prove a fruitful way to weave cultural themes back into the discussion of immigrant and ethnic achievement. On the other hand, the use of the modes, and of context rather than merely individual-level analysis does bypass rather than somehow resolve the issue of cultural influences. The scheme leaves the door open to discussions about cultural differences related to historical differences in premigration class position, and it does not provide a basis for including such discussions and ruling out premigration cultural legacies of other types. Moreover, the empirical need to validate the importance of the contextual advantages raises precisely the problem found in the older cultural explanation: the residual differences not explained away by controlling for the structural 'usual suspects' is not clear-cut evidence for the impact of the contextual advantages and disadvantages of the modes – it requires a leap to interpret the residual that way. And finally, in dealing with the concept of segmented assimilation, other features of historical background that cannot be easily squeezed into the typology of modes seem central, features that would normally be considered cultural differences. Although differences such as support for the community church are not differences in habits and attitudes directly relevant to socioeconomic achievement, one could imagine an argument that such is the indirect outcome of support for the community church. Once again, Portes and his collaborators may argue that this is precisely their point here; and mine is that the opening to the historically specific in this way is also an opening to the cultural legacy generally.

Notes

1. In a later article Portes (1997) makes the distinction explicit ('typologies are not theories' and the modes are a typology). However, I do not think the distinction is important for my purposes here; rather, as I emphasize below, the relevant section of *Immigrant America* is called 'Explaining the Differences'. Whatever form of 'explanation' is intended there is the form of explanation I am discussing here.
2. One might think that a related sort of test arises in connection with the impact of working within an ethnic enclave, compared to working elsewhere. If the wages

of otherwise statistically comparable individuals are higher in the enclave, that would be of interest. Nevertheless, that cannot be the end of the demonstration of the power of the modes (even leaving aside differences between an enclave and a mode of incorporation). We should still ask, *how much* of the difference in income across an ethnic divide can be explained by considering the contextual effect. If Cubans working in the enclave on average earn more than Cubans outside the enclave, is the difference large enough to explain most of the residual difference that was found among 'statistically comparable' Cubans and Mexicans in individual-level analysis? Such a test also ignores the additional complexity of whether selection for an enclave job reflects some unmeasured personal characteristics relevant to income.

3. See especially Portes and Rumbaut 1996: 247–53. A logically prior issue about context and origins also arises. The modes are enlisted to help us make sense of the differences among immigrant outcomes not captured by individual-level characteristics of immigrants. But over time, some effects of context should have been transferred to the individual level, to the parents' social class position – and captured in individual-level variables such as occupation, education, and income. Contextual effects upon the immigrant parents at time 1 are found reflected in the parents' individual-level attributes at time 2. Are we in fact still in need of the contextual level (or perhaps even more in need of it) when we consider the second generation? The answer may well differ across the modes of incorporation and across specific ethnic groups.

4. Perlmann and Waldinger (1997) and Perlmann (1998) examine the theme of cultural diffusion as it arises in connection with segmented assimilation (see also Waldinger and Perlmann 1998).

References

Borjas, G.J., 1992, 'Ethnic capital and intergenerational mobility', *Quarterly Journal of Economics* February 107d: 123–50

Glazer, N., 1955, 'Social characteristics of American Jews, 1654–1954', *American Jewish Yearbook* 56: 3–41

Kuznets, S., 1975, 'Immigration of Russian Jews to the United States. Background and structure', *Perspectives in American History* 9: 35–126

Massey, D.S., and N.A. Denton, 1993, *American Apartheid. Segregation and the Making of the Underclass* (Cambridge, Mass.: Harvard University Press)

Perlmann, J., 1988, *Ethnic Differences. Schooling and Social Structure among the Irish, Italians, Jews, and blacks in an American City, 1880–1935* (New York: Cambridge University Press)

Perlmann, J., 1998, *The Place of Cultural Explanations and Historical Specificity in Discussions of Modes of Incorporation and Segmented Assimilation*, Working Paper, The Jerome Levy Economics Institute

Perlmann, J., and R. Waldinger, 1997, 'Second generation decline? Children of immigrants, past and present – A reconsideration', *International Migration Review* 31(4): 893–922

Portes, A., 1997, 'Immigration theory for a New Century. Some problems and opportunities', *International Migration Review*, 31(4): 799–825

Portes, A., and D. Macleod, 1996, 'The educational progress of children of immigrants. The roles of class, ethnicity and school context', *Sociology of Education* 69(4): 255–75

Portes, A., and R. Rumbaut, 1996, *Immigrant America*, 2nd edn (Berkeley: University of California Press)

Portes, A., and M. Zhou, 1993, 'The new second generation. Segmented assimilation and its variants among post-1965 immigrant youth', *Annals* 530: 74–96

Waldinger R., and J. Perlmann, 1998, 'Second generations. Past, present, future', *Journal of Ethnic and Migration Studies* 24(1): 5–24

Wilson, W.J., 1987, *The Truly Disadvantaged. The Inner City, the Underclass, and Public Policy* (Chicago: University of Chicago Press)

Wilson, W.J., 1996, *When Work Disappears. The World of the New Urban Poor* (New York: Alfred A. Knopf)

Zhou, M., 1997, 'Segmented assimilation. Issues, controversies and recent research on the new second generation', *International Migration Review* 31(4): 975–1008

3

What Colour 'Success'? Distorting Value in Studies of Ethnic Entrepreneurship*

Pnina Werbner

Does culture make a difference?

The movement of migrants, traders, settlers and refugees across international and cultural frontiers (by no means a dislocation unique to the 20th century) repeatedly raises the question of how such peoples 'integrate', 'assimilate' or 'accommodate' to a new social and cultural setting. The answer is often put in terms of the symbolic resources such itinerants bring to bear on their new environment; of whether 'culture makes a difference'. Yet this apparently innocent, indeed pragmatic, question, unintentionally masks an implicit assumption that some cultures may be better, more valuable, more *successful* than others in some profound moral sense.

A key aim of modern anthropology has been to reject this assumption by repeatedly demonstrating that cultural value is relative: that cultures can only be made sense of in their own terms, and that moral ideas and practices are embedded in culturally specific, historically determined relations of production and sociality. When cultures are juxtaposed, explanations about the success or failure of a particular culture risk essentialist assumptions about closure, and a universal, fetishized notion of 'success'. Yet a stress on the fluidity, hybridity or openness of culture should not blind us to the fact that ideas about value, 'success' or 'failure' do exist in most cultures and depend on localized notions of value (Werbner 1997: 6).

A more limited interpretation of whether culture makes a difference is to ask whether cultures may be more or less successful in adapting to modernity. This is the familiar Weberian question. According to Weber, the Protestant ethic determined the entrepreneurial success of the Puritans who laid the foundations of modern capitalism. The values placed by the nonconformists on frugality, asceticism and saving, along with their belief that wealth was a sign of redemption, were the motor that fuelled the industrial revolution. This symbolic and cultural system, Weber argued, enabled the Puritans to deny affective, particularistic obligations, and to act purposively and rationally in the pursuit of profit and the accumulation of capital (Weber 1930). He thus identified an 'elective affinity' between Puritanism as a cultural system and industrial capitalism.

The present chapter considers some of the pitfalls of this Weberian hypothesis as it has come to be applied to studies of ethnic entrepreneurship. My aim is to expose false presuppositions about the universal meaning of value for moderns which underpin invidious comparisons of economic 'success'. To disclose these, I examine a series of case studies of Jewish, South Asian, Caribbean and African American entrepreneurs in Britain and the USA. Essentialist comparisons of this type also fail, I argue, to recognise the creative, changing dimensions of ethnic economic culture, the fact it is not simply an extension of some fixed, originary symbolic system. Third, I will argue in line with the work of consumption theorists that at the very heartland of capitalism, frugality, saving and impersonal rationality may not be the magic door to capitalist success. Nor, and this is my final point, are the people who create highly esteemed collective social and cultural value in our society always commensurably rewarded for their talents, a fact that throws in to doubt simple financial definitions of 'modern' success.

Failure

There is a kind of repetitive litany running through the ethnic entrepreneurship literature in line with the Weberian question. Why are some ethnic groups (Jews, Japanese, Koreans) so successful in accumulating wealth while others (such as blacks) have failed? An international version of this question, one which itself failed to anticipate the Pacific Rim economic meltdown or US boom of the late 1990s, reflected on why America was failing as an economic power (Harrison 1992). Whereas the failure of blacks in the ghetto was attributed by Harrison to the perpetual legacy of slavery, and the success of Asians and Jews to their upholding of Jewish and Confucian versions of the Protestant ethic – the failure of America, once the land of the Puritans, was attributed to the corrupting influence of television (ibid.).

Some British researchers too have agonised as to why Indians appear to be more successful than Pakistanis or Afro-Caribbeans. Sometimes the question is put in religious terms – why are Hindus more successful than Muslims? Such invidious questions, however well intentioned, leave us to ponder what might be the intrinsic nature of Pakistanihood, or blackness, or Muslimness, which leads to failure. From here to assumptions about the essential biological, mental or cultural inferiority of blacks or Muslims the route is short. In Perlmann's words, as cultures are ranked, there is a 'blurring [of] the distinction between values conducive to upward mobility and 'better' values' (1988: 7). We need to remember, however, that the people seeking cultural reasons for what they define as 'ethnic' failure are not consciously racists. They are genuinely puzzled by the apparent success of some ethnic groups. If Chinese or Japanese or Jews succeed everywhere, they reason, there must be some cultural causal explanation for this global phenomenon.

But even a shift in emphasis to structural causalities of success or failure is unsatisfactory, I propose. One of the implicit dangers of this line of argument is the assumption that success is to be measured by the degree of assimilation into the capitalist, industrial order of modernity. Success is defined in economistic terms – the most successful ethnic groups are those which statistically have the highest incomes, own the largest firms, occupy the best jobs. The least successful are those with low incomes or with high rates of unemployment. The unit of analysis is the individual. The measure of success is a single, common yardstick of value, ultimately translatable into hard currency. Such studies take for granted that value in our society has a financial, quantitative measure. Yet this assumption, we shall see, falsifies the full complexity of our modern, Western notions of value. These, I shall argue, are rooted as much in nationalist patriotism and aesthetic romanticism as in capitalism. They thus imply a notion of success which has collective as well as individual meanings.

The privileging of quantitative measures is true even of more serious works that interrogate the relative impact of class or 'structure' versus 'culture' in determining the successful mobility of ethnic groups in the West. This is at the heart of arguments by Steinberg (1981), Light and Rosenstein (1995), Waldinger (1996) and indeed Perlmann himself (1988). In Britain, the recent Fourth Ethnic Survey of Ethnic Minorities gives a fine-grained analysis of the structural factors affecting success rates of different ethnic minorities (Modood *et al.* 1997). So far, however, these arguments too have relied heavily on macro-statistics of aggregated *individual* cases, seen as isolable units of enumeration. Each individual in such statistical samples is defined by past or current occupation, income and education as well as ethnic origin. More subtle interpretations take account of family structure (Perlmann 1988). Nevertheless, all these analyses take for granted a definition of success and failure as the achievement of assimilation into the higher income, professional or managerial echelons of Western industrial society.

Defining success

To move the argument further, we need to consider in more abstract theoretical terms what we mean by success and failure. Very generally, I propose to define success as the competitive achievement of prestige or honour, and of the symbolic goods signalling these, within a specific regime of value. Success may be collective or individual, but even individual success depends on a context of sociality which elicits, facilitates and finally recognizes success as success. Big men in Mount Hagen, Papua New Guinea, depend on their wives, clansmen and partners for pigs and other goods in order to stage a successful Moka ceremonial. They depend on their competitors to acknowledge that success. They share with their rivals the view that large quantities of pigs and shells are, indeed, a measure of success. The glory achieved and the debts incurred by a successful Moka are simultaneously personal and male-collective, even as they obscure the crucial contribution of women to the event (Strathern 1971, Strathern 1988: 146–64 and 255).

The example makes clear what success *is*; it is determined by particular regimes of value. These define the goals to be desired, the rules and context of their achievement, and the competitive tournaments of value in which their successful attainment is displayed (see Appadurai 1986: 4 and 20–1). We may say that success is always relative to the definition of value in a particular social and cultural context. A world renouncer might be judged successful by his extreme poverty and asceticism; a capitalist by profits, turnover and shareholdings. Seen historically, it might appear that a radical divide in the constitution of value regimes occurred with the rise of modernity and capitalism. Whereas before, value (and hence success) were culturally embedded in traditional spheres of exchange and power, capitalism, according to this view, introduced common yardsticks of exchange which made it possible to measure and convert value (and hence success) quantitatively, across and between cultural domains; to alienate goods and labour and to accumulate fluid forms of capital. The movement is often seen as one from personalized gifts to alienable commodities (Mauss 1966). The present essay begins by tracing recent debates in anthropology on the limitations of this hypothesized transition before moving on to consider some critical evaluations of Pierre Bourdieu's work on the production of cultural value in capitalist societies (Bourdieu 1984 and 1995). Both Bourdieu's own work and that of his critics challenge the idea that value in the context of modernity has been universally commoditised.

Constituting value

A classic anthropological example of the way value is socially constituted is that of Kula, a gift exchange system practised in the Massim circle of islands off the coast of New Guinea. As ceremonial Kula objects circulate their 'fame' increases in direct relation to the succession of famous chiefs who temporarily own them (Malinowski 1922: 510, Munn 1986). Some of the most famous objects are known to have been circulating for more than a hundred years. In Mauss's terms, the objects exchanged personify all their prior owners and this becomes one measure of their value (Mauss 1966). By the same token, the successful capturing of such a valuable enhances the fame of its present owner even as it further enhances the value of the ceremonial object owned. Famous Kula valuables tend also to be especially beautiful, a factor which further increases their attraction and hence value.

At first glance it may appear that noncommoditised gift economies of this type are entirely remote from the way value is fixed in modern capitalist societies. Recent discussions in anthropology have stressed, however, that even where gift economies predominate, some goods may also be alienated as commodities through barter, for example (Thomas 1992: 35 ff. and 81). Objects typically have a 'social biography' – they may go through a succession of different transformations at different historical moments (Appadurai 1986); so too commodities may be converted into gifts and vice versa (Gregory 1982: 166–209) or be ambiguously both gifts and commodities, as in the case of the gold jewellery given as dowry to South Asian brides (Werbner 1990a: 291, 333). In modern capitalist societies, Carrier has argued, the gift economy persists in the domestic domain, even if the objects exchanged are purchased on the open market (Carrier 1995; see also Werbner 1990a and 1996a). Thomas, writing about 20th-century Fiji, suggests that ideas about gifting may be consciously preserved in opposition to what is perceived to be a commodity economy imposed from above (1992: 197–8). Miller (1987: 12 and 190 ff.) has argued that even ordinary everyday consumption in Western capitalist societies can be interpreted as a creative act of personal or group reincorporation or 'sublation', overcoming the alienation of the mass cultural market economy. Drawing on French structuralist traditions, Marshall Sahlins has analysed the semiotics of fashion and consumption in America (Sahlins 1976). For Baudrillard, the efflorescence of consumption objects in late capitalism has become a play of signs, entirely remote from any use values they originally may have had (see, for example, Baudrillard 1989).

In somewhat different ways, all these writers stress the potentially hybrid juxtaposition of value regimes, despite and alongside the global spread of capitalism. The value of objects, even mass produced objects, is, in this view, not entirely fixed by their exchange value on the open market. What such analyses also make clear is that objects may be placed ambiguously in several quite different regimes of value simultaneously. This means that the individuals or groups that produce or manufacture such objects may be ambiguously defined as successful from one perspective and as failures from another. Very fine musicians, for example, may be successful in the professional judgement of colleagues while failing to obtain commensurate financial rewards for their talent.

We may say that personified gifts of the kind exchanged in Kula acquire an 'aura' of their transactors, not unlike the aura attaching to a work of art. Walter Benjamin defines aura as 'The authenticity of a thing (...) the essence of all that is transmissible from its beginning, ranging from its substantive duration to its testimony to the history it has experienced' (1973: 215). The aura of an art object, for Benjamin, is its uniqueness, its originary combination of genius, tradition and ritual. I cite his views, because they also exemplify the sort of statements which uphold the modern emergence of an autonomous art sphere, a separate regime of value with its expert critics, aesthetic canons of taste, prophets and priests. The separation of this aesthetic 'field' from the mass popular market is identified by Pierre Bourdieu as a crucial feature of modernity. To be recognized as uniquely valuable, new works of art (including novels, dramas and music) must go through a process of consecration (Bourdieu 1995: 120–5; see also Lash 1993: 193) – by critics, museums and professional academies.

Both Western and Primitive works of High Culture, to be deemed successful, must have a social biography, starting from their original producer or context of production and tracing their movements through various owners until, in the case of the most distinguished objects, their final purchase by state and national museums. With each new owner the value of the object is enhanced, its 'fame' increases and its authentic uniqueness is further underlined. In line with this 'artefacts' may become 'art' (on the movement see Clifford 1988, chapters 9 and 10). The owner of a consecrated object gains fame through association with it.

By contrast, the value regimes of cheap, mass produced cultural goods, which may imitate or draw upon innovations in the art field but which cater to popular tastes, are subject to the exigencies of the market rather than to autonomous canons of taste (Bourdieu 1984 and 1995: 125–31). Bourdieu posits a homology between distinction in aesthetic appreciation and class. The struggle over the value of symbolic goods is, ultimately, a class struggle waged by elites claiming exclusive cultural and economic capital and with it the right to own, recognize and impose particular aesthetic canons upon the masses.

Yet the success of a class fraction is not identical to the success of individuals within it. Indeed, both Bourdieu and Becker (1982) recognize that the struggles over value are as much internal as external to a particular field of aesthetic production. Hence, one problem with the assumption of a homology between taste and class, a problem especially pertinent to the present discussion, is that by definition, in order to exist, a cultural 'field' must include both successes and failures: success is a relative term and is always defined competitively. Yet success in the field of art is an elusive quality. Unsuccessful artists are often discovered posthumously. Popular art is recovered as High Art, with profits accruing to the Brahmins of taste rather than the original creative artists. Great works are demoted as banal. Actors, novelists, poets, might be recognized only within small circles of like-minded aficionados. Their products might sell intermittently and they might sink into oblivion. At the same time, seen collectively, the cultural capital produced by a particular circle of artists, musicians, novelists or actors might achieve international acclaim. Their glory might be appropriated and claimed by their city or nation and embody that nation's cultural distinction. Success, rather than being an individual achievement, then, is often defined collectively – as the establishment and reproduction of a new value regime and its association with a particular 'place' or 'community'.

The autonomy of institutionalized, expert aesthetic spheres of value which Becker, Bourdieu and Habermas (1983) recognize as a crucial feature of modernity has been questioned by Nestor Canclini. Canclini argues that such models do not

> help us to understand what happens when even the signs and spaces of the elites are massified and mixed with those of the popular (...) when museums receive millions of visitors and classic or vanguard literary works are sold in supermarkets, or made into videos.
>
> (1995: 17)

The aggressive intervention of commercial, advertising and marketing forces in the art sphere has rendered the value of works of High art ambiguous, since often enough commercial judgement fails to coincide with expert judgement (ibid.: 32–3); yet it is only commercial choice that can ensure for the artist public recognition and financial survival (ibid.: 37). Commercialization has meant that selective works of art have now become a privileged area of capital investment, so much so that museums can no longer afford to exhibit them because of prohibitive insurance costs. This fetishization of creative works is matched by the enormous profits made by popular cultural artists and film stars. When value regimes cut across each other notions of success and failure are necessarily rendered ambiguous.

Collective value

In his critical review of Bourdieu, Lash (1993: 205) suggests that beyond invidious distinctions, competitive classifications of symbolic value are *ways of constituting collective identity*. In consumption terms, this is expressed in new life styles. But Lash's insight raises further issues which neither he nor Bourdieu address: a cultural product may be valued for its aesthetic achievements within an autonomous art field or for the price it commands (the assumption being that these will be homologous); but it might also be valued, as I have hinted already, in being an objectification of an *aesthetic genre associated with a collectivity*. This collectivity could be a highly valued one such as the nation or a significant ethnic group within the nation. In Hegelian or Durkheimian terms, once 'culture' becomes an emblematic objectification of the group, it achieves a transcendent value *beyond its market value*. Indeed, it may not even have a clear market value. This is reflected in the fact that much High and even popular culture in Europe today is state subsidized. Novelists, artists, musicians, actors, athletes, as well theatres, orchestras, galleries, museums, sports stadiums – can rarely survive without one form or another of substantial state or local state (or, in the 1990s, state lottery) support. Such support is also increasingly being afforded to 'folk', experimental or communal cultural events.

Let us take a concrete example from Britain. Ten years ago the Arts Council of Great Britain organized a travelling exhibition of carnival masque costumes from the Notting Hill Carnival, a street festival which takes place annually in London. These quite magnificent costumes of imaginary butterflies, African queens and birds of paradise are gigantic and elaborate affairs, built on wire frames and decorated with sequins. Each costume is a work of art. Each takes almost a year to make and its creation is the product of a collective effort by an expert carnival masque designer and a team of amateur tailors and other helpers. Abner Cohen, the anthropologist who studied the Notting Hill Carnival, describes the complex network of groups and committees that plan the carnival floats and dancing masque groups and make these costumes throughout the year (Cohen 1993). They are used for one brief day of glorious display before being dismantled and their materials reincorporated into next year's designs.By con trast to these unique, but highly ephemeral creations are the clothes manufactured and sold by postwar Pakistani settlers in Manchester in markets throughout England, Scotland Wales and Ireland. These fashion clothes are manifestly cheap and poorly made. Most are based on imitations rather than original designs. They too are meant to have an ephemeral and relatively short life. They are sold in markets to teenagers, the impoverished and the unemployed who cannot afford to shop in high street stores.

Which is more valuable: the carnival costume or the cheap garment manufactured by Asians in Manchester? In reality, the question is a meaningless one because the two objects are not comparable. They exist within different regimes of cultural value. The carnival costume is not a commodity. In this respect, it is priceless. The garments manufactured by Pakistanis are cheap commodities manufactured in the hundreds of thousands. Value resides not in a single garment but in its thousand-fold multiple. Antirelativists make the mistake of comparing the incommensurable, that is, objects or practices plucked out of their context of production and exchange. Statistics often suppress or mask such incommensurables. But there is an important sense, I want to suggest, in which we might be able to compare the carnival masque costume and the Pakistani-manufactured garment: seen analytically, both are the product of collective effort by migrant settlers.

According to Scott Lash, Bourdieu's approach can be traced to Max Weber's sociology of religion, recast as a framework for understanding artistic and cultural products as an economic market, based on the emergence of charismatic innovators and sacralising routinisers (Lash 1993). Lash, however, fails to see that in another sense, Bourdieu's approach is far closer to the interpretation of capitalism suggested by Weber's contemporary and adversary, Werner Sombart (1967): whereas Weber attributed the rise of capitalism to the rational frugality of the puritan sects, Sombart argued that modern capitalism was fuelled by the growth in demand for luxury goods in Europe during the age of imperial expansion. He also saw Jews rather than Protestants as crucially instrumental in this expansion (Sombart 1962). Moreover, Sombart recognised the complex structure of the luxury industries, built around chains of suppliers and producers. A later study, by Howard Becker (1982), of art 'worlds', similarly shows that the production of a work of art relies crucially on a hidden collaborative network of artisans, suppliers and distributors. Both Becker's and Bourdieu's studies make clear that the nature of the symbolic objects produced critically shapes the structure of the culture industries that produce them. It makes sense to argue, then, that such objects should be the starting point for an analysis of the politics of value within a cultural economy of success and failure.

The organization of art worlds helps illuminate the study of ethnic and immigrant entrepreneurs, I propose, because such entrepreneurs tend to concentrate predominantly in the mass culture industries. Each segment, or sector, of these industries has its own unique structure, depending on the goods produced; but they share in common a tendency towards vertical disaggregation, a feature that opens up numerous spaces for undercapitalized petty entrepreneurs at different stages of the production and distribution process. Over time, as my research in Manchester has demonstrated (Werbner 1990a and 1990b), ethnic movement into particular niches in an industry generates cumulative ethnic know-how and credit relations, and these become the basis for the formation of ethnic enclave economies. Many positions within these enclaves rely on artisan or marketing skills which do not require formal training beyond casual apprenticeships. It is from these ethnic enclave economies, I shall argue here, that certain individuals rise to fame and fortune. Such 'successful' individuals may thus be conceived of as the tip of an iceberg; they mask the networks of small businesses beneath them upon which their fortunes are built.

In line with the view proposed here that value is a collective achievement, the present paper regards the formation of such ethnic enclave economies, composed of networks of small businesses, as a key measure of 'success'. Outstanding individuals rise on the back, so to speak, of these networks which are usually geographically dispersed. The chapter thus rejects a common notion in the literature that defines ethnic economic enclaves as territorially concentrated clusters of businesses. Instead, ethnic enclave economies are best grasped, I propose, as *networked* spaces embedded in particular *industries* which focus around the production and distribution of particular types of *objects*. Part of this production or distribution may well be clustered in 'industrial districts', but this is only the most visible sector of a wider network of interconnected firms. 'Success' and 'failure' in such circumstances obviously have collective as well as individual meanings.

Bootstrap capitalism and immigrant pioneers

Bootstrap capitalism, capitalism which starts with little more than a bootstrap and lifts itself from the bottom upwards, is almost always a collective effort. In the case of South Asian settlers, the early beginnings were extremely modest. According to biographical narratives I collected, the first known migrants to Manchester arrived penniless shortly before the Second World War. It was a time of severe recession and they worked as door-to-door peddlers. Ironically, it was the war that gave them their first opportunity. They were enlisted to ammunitions factories and during the lunch breaks they sold their female coworkers nylon stockings. The fortunes of these early pioneer traders were thus built on nylon stockings.

After the war they were joined by relatives and friends from Pakistan and India. They initiated these newcomers into market trading by giving them credit and goods, while they themselves became wholesalers. They provided the newcomers with accommodation and loaned them money to buy their own houses. Many market traders also obtained credit from Jewish wholesalers who at that time dominated the clothing trade in Manchester. Jews themselves had started off as peripatetic market traders; Marks and Spencer had a penny stall on Market street in Manchester. Manchester had, since its foundation, been the commercial hub of a large hinterland with a consequent demand for service and retail industries – and hence also for self-employed entrepreneurs.

The economic niche captured by Asian settlers was one being vacated by earlier, Jewish entrepreneurs.[1] Like in the case of Jews, however, the clothing ethnic enclave economy and its expansion were built, first, on credit rather than on savings, and second, on social network links, on chains of entrepreneurs, or 'entrepreneurial chains' (Werbner 1990a and 1990b). As newcomers entered into the petty manufacturing or market trading of garments, established traders expanded into wholesaling, importing or large scale manufacturing. As the clothing enclave expanded, a few people made fortunes; most people managed to survive and make a living.

For a long time Indian and Pakistani clothing traders in the city were barely visible. Market traders operate from their homes where they store their goods and they travel widely over a large area. Traders based in Manchester had stalls in markets all over Greater Manchester, in the Lake District, in Wales and Scotland. None of the economic surveys on which statistics are based can identify these peripatetic traders. They constitute an invisible presence, part of a subterranean economy. In 1975, when I first started my research, the Asian clothing enclave economy barely seemed to exist. Ten years later, Asian traders had taken over whole tracts of urban space surrounding the city centre as the number of clothing wholesalers and manufacturers increased exponentially (see Werbner 1990b). Today some of these wholesalers are in decline, but the markets continue to flourish.

During this time Asians continued to manufacture and sell relatively cheap clothing at very cheap prices. They occupied the bottom end of the fashion trade. Yet they sold their clothes widely, to ordinary Englishmen and women. Some Asians opened delicatessens, restaurants, jewellery or sari shops catering specifically to the needs of the ethnic community. They carved out an ethnic niche for South Asian cultural commodity products sold to local Asian settlers. But the vast majority of migrants did not operate within the restrictions of the ethnic niche. Instead, they operated within the ethnic enclave economy which manufactured and sold clothing and related goods to outsiders, beyond the ethnic group.

Once the clothing enclave was established, it created a need for a support network of new kinds of services: for accountants, solicitors and transporters; for travel agents, insurance brokers and taxi drivers; for plumbers, electricians and decorators; for fashion designers and clerical workers. Later, as Asians in Manchester moved into knitwear and bought costly computerized knitwear machinery, there was also a demand for computer programmers and technicians. As some Asians made a lot of money, they began to buy luxury goods – flashy cars, large suburban houses. Asian hotels opened to accommodate buyers in the trade. Pharmacies, newsagents, takeaways, fancy goods merchants were added. All these services built up very gradually. They constituted an economic penumbra servicing the ethnic niche and ethnic enclave economy.

Asians businesses were by no means uniformly successful. Undercapitalized and often run by inexperienced traders and manufacturers, hundreds of small businesses collapsed or went into liquidation. Asian millionaires rose and fell. But the gradual expansion of the enclave and its penumbra continued. Its viability throughout was based on extensive internal credit relations between traders; and this required a certain level of trust. Asians upheld the enclave by prioritising ethnic social networks in business as they did in leisure. The ethnic enclave economy expanded through both credit and a collective accumulation of experience and know-how, and this, despite the intense competition which existed between coethnic traders. Rivalry needed to be managed alongside trust: Asians never formed a solidary group but on the contrary, they engaged in cut-throat competition with one another (see also Panayiotopoulos 1996).

Ethnic enclave economies versus ethnic economies

I stress the way businesses clustered around particular goods. The nature of the goods traded in, I want to argue here, is as significant in shaping the enclave as the social networks through which these goods flow. Recent discussions of ethnic entrepreneurship have questioned the utility of retaining the concept of an ethnic 'enclave' economy. Light, for example, in a series of articles, argues cogently that in measuring rates of ethnic employment generated by ethnic entrepreneurship, the *spatial* clustering of ethnic businesses is irrelevant. Far more important, he proposes, is the absolute number of ethnic employers, employees and self-employed provided with jobs by coethnics. This aggregation of workers and employees, scattered over a wide range of different industries, he defines as the 'ethnic economy'. The notion is pitched against the stress on spatial conglomeration as the key feature of ethnic business success. An oft-cited example is the heterogeneous clustering of Cuban businesses in Miami's 'Little Havana' (see Light *et al.* 1994 and 1995). The economies of scale that such ethnic enclave economies allow have been linked, according to one reading of the argument, to spatial proximity.

Light's aim is to move beyond the focus on such spatial concentrations. The problem, however, with his own analysis of the generalized ethnic 'economy' is that it fails to identify and explain the processual principles governing the entry of ethnic groups into entrepreneurial activities, the causal chains which lead to the expansion of their businesses and the dynamics of growth that enable the financial success of the lucky few. To arrive at an understanding of these generative processes of entry, expansion and success requires us to shift our gaze from spatial and statistical parameters to a focus on the specific objects that particular industries are organized to produce. Ethnic entrepreneurs tend to cluster in one or two such industries and it is this clustering which is more usefully referred to as the 'ethnic enclave economy'. An ethnic enclave economy is object-focused. It manufactures and markets particular types of goods. Within such ethnic enclave economies, entrepreneurs rely on their ability to retain connections *across* space through networking and movement. Some parts of an industry may be spatially concentrated (often manufacturing or wholesaling) while other parts of it (design, retailing) may be widely dispersed. Ethnic entrepreneurs may capture only a stage in the production or distribution process. Hence, against the focus on spatial clustering, anthropological accounts of trading networks in West Africa, for example, (see Cohen 1969, Eades 1987) have traced the production and flows of specific goods such as cattle or kola nuts across and between bounded spaces, and the competition to gain a foothold in different production stages of a trade or industry.

Ethnic enclave economies (or ethnic 'niches' as they are sometimes called) are more like transnational companies than shopping malls: they respect no boundaries. Rather than models of territorial aggregation, a more useful approach would seem to be that of Actor Network Theory which stresses the agency of objects in the determination of cultural and social production (Callon and Law 1995, Latour 1993). The nature of the goods manufactured and sold (in the present example, clothing and knitwear) has a determining effect on the shape and organisation of distribution networks, on spatial concentration and dispersal, and on the trajectories of growth of the ethnic enclave economy. The enclave is a web shaped by the flow of specific (related) goods, services and credits through it.

In the case of the Manchester clothing and garment industry, some of the profits in the trade were channelled into new forms of investment and in particular, rental property. Cheap inner city properties could be used as collateral for bank loans and were turned into flats let out to students, social service recipients or young professionals. Asians in Manchester became a class of landlord. This business enterprise too was relatively invisible and unlikely to be enumerated by censuses and surveys. In the meanwhile, the Asian restaurant and food trade in Manchester expanded enormously, as the English abandoned mashed potatoes and pork sausages in favour of spicy curries and continental flavours. Hence another generative process might be traced in the Asian food industry which over time became more complex – the opening of hundreds of grocery stores selling halal meat became the base for the emergence of food wholesalers and manufacturers, making anything from frozen samosa and Asian savouries to chutneys, along with big food importers of spices and basmati rice. Some of these firms began to sell their goods to supermarket chains. The new firms too needed servicing – they needed solicitors and accountants. So, despite the fact that many of the grocery stores were relatively unprofitable, they formed the base upon which large firms and white collar professionals relied for their custom.

The significance of this narrative is that when we gaze at that cheap market garment, we need to treat it with a good deal of respect. Because a whole world of Asian work and trading and profit came to be based upon it. Above all, what it created was the possibility of self-respect, autonomy and independence, despite endemic racism and the collapse of British manufacturing. In Asian terms it represented a shift from *nawkri*, servitude in wage labour, to *izzet*, honour and respect through self-employment. But is this a success story?

Collectively, Pakistanis in Manchester have used profits from business not only to invest in extravagant life styles but in good works: the building of mosques, donations to the home country, voluntary activism. One of the larger clothing wholesalers in the city devotes his time these days to running the Imran Khan Hospital Benefit Appeal (see Werbner 1996b). He has made little attempt to expand his business. His honour cannot be measured simply in terms of his profits and turnover. The process may be seen as one of collective conversion back from commodities into gifts.

Let us go back to our carnival masque costume. It too, we have seen, is the product of social networks and collective effort. Not only that. The

Notting Hill Carnival today is reputedly the largest street festival in Europe. It attracts millions of people every year who come to marvel at the costumes and dancing and join in its festivities. It takes over whole areas of London which belong, for a single day, to some of the city's poorest and most underprivileged residents. During carnival the streets of London belong to the people.

Carnival has not in the past been a great commercial money spinner. Abner Cohen reports on arguments among carnival organizers as to whether it should be commercialised. The artists and musicians have consistently argued that the pulling power of carnival comes not from overt political demonstrations or efficient marketing but quite the contrary, it derives from the aesthetic pleasure and freedom that carnival affords (see A. Cohen 1991 and 1993). Moreover, Afro-Caribbeans are a group that collectively suffers from very high, endemic unemployment rates. So can we say that the West Indian community in Britain which stages the Notting Hill Carnival and others like it is a success story or a failure?

Bootstrap capitalism and the culture industries

Although this may not seem immediately self-evident, bootstrap capitalism, capitalism from the bottom upwards, is based on the possibility of selling packaged culture. Immigrants with no capital rely heavily on the only capital they can gain access to or even invent – cultural capital. And to build up from nothing to something they need another kind of capital that only social relations can create – symbolic capital. Against Bourdieu (1984: 511), it is worth highlighting the fact that these two forms of human capital remain quite distinct even in capitalist, industrial societies. Symbolic capital is the moral reputation a person gains as an honest and fair trader and dealer – a person of honour. Cultural or subcultural capital, by contrast, is knowledge about how to package and sell a particular form of culture. Modernity and postmodernity have been marked by the enormous efflorescence of the culture industries. Fashion and jewelry, entertainment and food, houseware and toys, music, art, poetry, journalism, computer software, films, furniture, even electronic goods, are all packaged forms of culture.

In an age where design impacts on all commodities, there are, as Baudrillard (1989) reminds us, no purely utilitarian goods left. Reality has been displaced by hyperreality. In such a context it is not frugality, rationality and saving that make for capitalist success but an aesthetic appreciation of the hedonistic pursuit of luxury, and the cultural imagination needed to tap this quest. Hence, rather than Weber's protestant ethic, it may be something quite different – and opposed – which is the secret elixir of entrepreneurial success in the modern world.

In an illuminating account of East European Jewish immigration to the United States, *Adapting to Abundance*, Andrew Heinze, following Veblen

(1899) and Sombart (1967), describes the expansion of the luxury industries in the USA, imported by German immigrants. It is they, he argues, who above all helped build modern America as we know it today:

> Contrasting sharply with the reserved demeanour of native-born Americans, the German love of song, sport and celebration endowed city life with beer gardens and bowling alleys, as well as musical, literary, dramatic, and gymnastic clubs that transplanted German culture to America. In opposition to the Sabbatarian movement of American Protestants, Germans instituted the custom of Sunday picnicking. The efforts of commercially adept brewers and artisans made for a German presence in the mass-marketing of beer, furniture, pianos, lithographs, and eye-glasses. By the end of the [19th] century, the names of Pabst, Anheuser-Busch, Stingray, Prang, and Bausch and Lomb, among others, were widely known.
>
> (1990: 184)

It was into this atmosphere of luxury, enjoyment and plenty that Jews arrived to New York City in their hundreds of thousands from the impoverished shtetls of Eastern Europe and the Pale of Russia. Whereas there they were limited as traders and middlemen to selling a few basic items of food and clothing, they found in America an abundance of cultural products that could be packaged and sold. Not only that. Heinze argues that it was through the consumption of luxury goods that these East European Jews saw themselves becoming true Americans. They could not change their heavy accents or improve their command of English overnight, but they could own a piano and a fur coat, and go to the movies or on summer vacations like true Americans.

At the turn of the century there were almost a million-and-a-half Jews in New York City. Most had arrived penniless with their families. Many became street peddlers, peddling a range of luxury goods at marked down prices. The streets of the Lower East Side were transformed daily into a vast emporium of cultural goodies. Jews dominated the New York clothing, fur and jewelry trades. They published their own Yiddish newspapers and opened their own theatres. Like other immigrants, they became entertainers and comedians. They capitalized on the dark Jewish humour of the European ghetto, to make Americans laugh. And, from being the promoters of high culture to the Austro-Hungarian and Habsburg empires, set apart from the masses by their sophistication and civilization, in New York, Heinze tells us, Jewish musicians and artists embraced and created American popular culture. Tin pan Alley, as the popular music industry was called, was dominated by Jews (Heinze 1990: 140–1).

Another book, also on American Jewry and the entertainment business, *Blackface, White Noise* by Michael Rogin (1996), analyses crossover forms of vaudeville in which white Jewish comedians like Al Jolson blacked their faces and appropriated black culture in a parodic and carnivalesque celebration. Rogin exposes the ambivalence of blackface as an artistic genre which both stereotyped black people, who were virtually barred at that time from the entertainment industry, while bringing their music and dance into the mainstream. Jews both imitated black culture and, in their advocacy of the American creed of equality and freedom, joined civil rights movements attacking racism. It was through this ambivalent appropriation of black culture and jazz and its amalgamation with nostalgic European klezmer and light classical music, that popular American music emerged. Some of greatest American popular song writers of the time, such as Irving Berlin and George Gershwin, were Jewish.

Looking at that era through politically correct lenses, as Rogin does, the author fails to capture its politically incorrect effervescence. It was a moment in which immigrant entertainers and comedians of all nationalities parodied and stereotyped each other and everyone else – from snobbish Yankees to greenhorn Italians to Jewish wiseguys, drunken Irish or dumb negroes. The legacy of this humour has been retained in the films of Charlie Chaplin and the Marx Brothers as well as in Al Jolson's *The Jazz Singer*. Ethnic and cultural stereotypes were the stuff of comedy. What immigrant New Yorkers had discovered was that culture was there to be packaged, sold and consumed. The more attractive or entertaining the package, the better the market. A good deal was sold from peddlers' carts or in small, cheap theatres and clubs. All that was needed for success was a bit of flair, imagination and good luck.

I stress all this because when we hear of the Jews who founded Macy's or Sears-Roebuck, giant American department stores, and major networks such as CBS or NBC (Heinze 1990: 6–7), or of the Jewish film moguls who invented Hollywood, we have to bear in mind that these men did not emerge out of nowhere. They were already embedded in the ethnic-dominated culture industries and they rose out of the ranks of businessmen whose companies, like theirs, were small-scale and relatively unprofitable. The story of Hollywood is particularly instructive. By 1915, Heinze tells us,

> … four outstanding Jewish immigrants had laid the foundation for powerful movie enterprises (…) Adolph Zuker and William Fox, who came from Hungarian shtetls in the 1880s to become the leaders of Paramount Pictures and Fox Pictures, Carl Laemmle, who immigrated from Southern Germany in 1884 and founded the Universal Studio in 1912, and Samuel Goldwyn, formerly Goldfish, a Warsaw native who came to America around 1895 and emerged as one of the most successful producers in the business after 1913.

(1990: 207)

These men all came to America without money or formal education. To understand their rise it has to be seen in the context of the American urban entertainment industry in which, by around 1905, there were, in New York alone, one hundred-and-twenty-three small movie houses, known as nickle theatres or nickleodeons (ibid.: 204). Most were in Jewish and Italian immigrant neighbourhoods. It was from these modest beginnings, as owners of nickleodeons, that the movie moguls rose, first by challenging the monopoly of the American film industry at the time, and circumventing it by importing long, two-hour silent movies from Europe. They added entertainment and music to these silent movies, and built plush theatres for the nickle-paying masses. From there, it was a short step into film production and they began to take command of the dramatic content of the films they marketed (ibid.: 209). But it was the discovery of the financial potential of charismatic film personalities that ultimately turned Hollywood into one of the USA's largest export industries. Packaged film stars, to whom the Jewish entrepreneurs willingly paid exorbitant salaries, quickly became the brand names that appealed to millions (ibid.: 210).

The point I am making is simply this: capitalist success in our modern and postmodern world is not a matter of saving and frugality. It is a matter of being part of a social network which understands what luxury, desire and hedonistic consumption means and provides it to the masses at affordable prices. People write about the Japanese miracle as though it was simply a matter of hard work and paternalistic attitudes towards the work force; and they ignore the exceptional Japanese aesthetic talent in the field of technological design, or their sensitivity to the luxury desires of consumers (see Lash 1993: 207).

But are Jews in America successful? What does it mean to be successful in our society? If we measure success in simple, economistic terms we come up against the fact raised already that some of our most valued cultural activities are grossly underpaid, at least in Britain. Both composers and rank-and-file orchestra musicians earn less than primary schoolteachers. Good artists often feel lucky if they sell one painting a year. Talented actors live from hand to mouth; so do poets and novelists. In Britain the theatre is currently threatened with partial collapse as young talent is blocked by the inadequacy of state subsidies. In 1998, in the midst of an economic boom, national operas and provincial orchestras have come under threat of closure. For every Yehudi Menuhin or Daniel Barenbaum whose recordings sell in the millions, there are thousands of underpaid and unknown Jewish fiddlers and pianists who play in orchestras and teach to make ends meet. For every famous pop group in Manchester or Liverpool like Take That or Oasis there are thousands of similar pop groups whose young musicians dream of making it but never do. Mostly, their youthful members live on the dole, with musical gigs few and far between (S. Cohen 1991). There is a thriving South Asian music industry in Britain which includes talented musicians, vocalists, studio owners, promoters, and retailers, and is supported by local Asian radio, television and newspapers. Yet Asian tapes and discs sell at ludicrously low prices and most musical bands have to rely for a living on other jobs. Now and then there is a breakthrough: Apache Indian, a British Indian singer has set up his own charity, following an enormously successful tour of India (see Back 1996). Is the Asian music industry a success or is it a failure? From the point of view of Asian consumers the story is one of success. Yet Asian musicians subsist on the margins of the pop industry.

Purely economistic measures simply do not work in estimating value and success, even in our own society. The Jewish entrepreneurs who made Hollywood may well have been failed actors, musicians or writers. Hence the question of success and failure leads only to stereotyping and invidious comparisons.

Statistical failures

Most writing on ethnic entrepreneurship is based on census and survey statistics. How would struggling market traders and Asian musicians be classified in these statistics? No doubt, many of them would fall into the unemployed category since their earnings are intermittent and they often operate in the black, informal economy.[2] But as we have seen, vast edifices are built around such invisible, struggling small enterprises; whole industries emerge. Yet however inaccurate, statistics are essential modern tools in devising policies against discrimination and disadvantage. The recent Fourth National Survey of Ethnic Minorities paints a depressing picture of high unemployment rates and low earnings for Bangladeshis, Pakistanis and Afro-Caribbeans, even we allow for a good deal of disinformation (Modood *et al.* 1997, chapter 4). It also reveals a steep rise in self-employment and a correlation between earnings and educational qualifications. These obviously hold out the promise of future mobility (ibid.: 120). At the same time statistical surveys often obscure or fail to illuminate the generative and expansionary logic of ethnic enclave economies and hence of the foundations of ethnic 'success' since the focus of such statistics is, ultimately, the individual entrepreneur as a single quantifiable unit.

An example of this may be drawn from statistics in Britain on the relative achievements and failures of different South Asian national and religious communities. Based on a survey of Asian businesses in Bradford, Muhammad Rafiq (1992) highlights the relative smallness of Muslim-run, by comparison to Hindu and Sikh, businesses. He thus obscures the more important finding that Asian business in Bradford is in a state of flux following the virtual collapse of the Yorkshire wool industry. With dozens of new businesses emerging every year, there are signs that clothing and food industries are being established as viable enclaves and that these are, in fact, dominated by Muslims. Although their businesses are still very small, being recent creations, it is upon a multiplicity of such small businesses that large industries and empires are built. Passing premature judgement on the business acumen of Muslims in Bradford fails to grasp the generative trajectories of their ethnic enclave economies.

Three analyses of survey statistics on British Pakistani performance in the UK (Anwar 1996, Ballard 1996, Metcalf *et al.* 1996) highlight the arbitrary nature of statistical interpretation. Roger Ballard, an anthropologist, finds that

> the Census results provide emphatic confirmation of the extent to which [Pakistanis] have (...) managed to circumvent [the] constraints [of racism and discrimination] to achieve a considerable degree of upward mobility.
>
> (1996: 148)

By contrast, Muhammad Anwar (1996) highlights a mixed picture of relative Pakistani success *and* failure. In London, for example, Pakistani children are high achievers, whereas in Birmingham they are low achievers (1996: 133). Their unemployment rate is very high but so too is their self-employment and employer rate. Finally, the team of researchers at the Policy Studies Institute (Metcalf *et al.* 1996) concludes on the basis of a survey of around 150 entrepreneurs that Pakistani businesses are less successful than Indian businesses in almost every respect; unlike Indians, Pakistanis, they argue, are driven into business to escape racism. Yet these assertions are based on relatively tentative and ambiguous findings which contain many indicators of both success and failure.

Other surveys paint widely contradictory pictures. In a survey of Oxford Asian retailers and restaurant owners, Shaila Srinivasan found few differences between Pakistanis, Indians and Bangladeshis, virtually all of whom had achieved a reasonably high standard of living and uniformly expressed very considerable satisfaction with their level of earnings (1995: 11 and 92–5). Rather than being 'pushed', the entrepreneurs had 'jumped': they chose to become businessmen in order to raise both their economic and social standing' (ibid.: 84). As in Manchester, Asian entrepreneurs in Oxford had chosen to diversify into rental property (ibid.: 95). Srinivasan thus presents us with a picture of Asian middle-class prosperity typified by high levels of social integration into British society, along with a continued fostering of South Asian cultural values. Her survey, based on interviews she herself conducted, is persuasive, in that she was introduced to all her interviewees personally and indeed knew some quite well. A different survey of small Asian and Afro-Caribbean retailers, by Jones, McEvoy and Barrett, while criticizing invidious comparisons (1992: 179), nevertheless leads the authors to the opposite conclusion that such status aspirations are mystifications which disguise continued self-exploitation (ibid.: 185). The Afro-Caribbeans firms in this sample were small and struggling (ibid.: 197). Virtually all the enterprises surveyed avoided the use of banks (ibid.: 199). By contrast, a survey by Curran and Blackburn (1993) revealed very high use of banking among Greek-Cypriots and Bangladeshis, with Afro-Caribbeans receiving more loans from local authority sources. Ethnic entrepreneurs across the board surveyed consulted banks and enterprise agencies as well as accountants and solicitors frequently (ibid.: 54–61 and 68–82). Afro-Caribbean businesses had larger turnovers than those of Bangladeshis (ibid.: 24). Despite finding evidence of 'surprising' superior family support for Afro-Caribbeans (ibid.: 80), Curran and Blackburn tend nevertheless to accept the stereotype of Afro-Caribbeans as having a 'lower level of social integration' (ibid.: 103 and 111). However, like Srinivasan they also found no mention of racial discrimination as the reason for entering small business (ibid.: 124).

Clearly, differences in sampling elicit radically divergent pictures of the state of ethnic entrepreneurship in Britain. But even more than this: statistical interpretations can only be understood in the context of a *politics of representation*. What needs to be deconstructed, in other words, in such statistical analyses, is the politics *behind* the interpretation. Roger Ballard is quite explicit in stating his aims: to step 'beyond the patronising vision of black people as nothing but helpless pawns' (1996: 147), a vision, as we have seen, represented here by Jones, McEvoy and Barrett. This assertion of the agency of minorities also motivates, Ivan Light argues (Light forthcoming, Light and Rosenstein 1995), migration network approaches, critical of globalisation theory's deterministic explanations of international migrant labour movements.

Muhammad Anwar (1996), by contrast, is primarily motivated by policy issues – his statistics are mobilised as evidence of the need to improve educational and health services to immigrants. Future banking policy is also a key feature of Curran and Blackburn's survey. Srinivasan focuses on the issue of social and cultural integration into British society and denies major differences within the Asian business community. By contrast, the motive of the PSI survey, in stressing the failure of Pakistanis and Bangladeshis, is implicitly to highlight the possible negative impact of anti-Islamic cultural racism. Muslims are forced by Islamophobia to go into business; Indians choose to do so.

This kind of implicit politicization of research becomes evident, explicitly, in the press releases accompanying such surveys. Ballard's report, part of a larger survey, was advertised in the press under the headline: 'Asians have a Jewish future while Afro-Caribbeans have an Irish Future' (Bennetto 1996, Peach 1996, Travis 1996), thus compounding one stereotype by another. Such stereotypes abound in the press which regularly conducts surveys of Asian millionaires. There are now more than 300 Asian millionaires in Britain, one report claims, and their combined buying power is more than £ six billion (Cusick 1996). Asians are said to own 50 per cent of independent retail outlets in the UK and 80 per cent of independent newspaper and tobacco shops in London (Lyon and West 1995: 409). All this implies an obvious success story. But the press headlines responding to the PSI survey results challenged this fable of success: 'End of the Corner Shop?' screamed one report. 'Young Asians not interested in shopkeeping' (Chohan and Rasvi 1996). The English press lamented the death of the Asian/English cornershop, drawing implications from the PSI report which it never intended. Corner shop owners confessed to reporters that they hoped their children would be doctors and lawyers, not shopkeepers. But is the Asian corner shop really such a failure? One press analyst (Ahmed 1996) dismissed this claim with the warning that you cannot rely on the press or, for that matter, on spurious research surveys. The truth is, he proclaimed, that 'reports that small Asian businesses are doomed are ridiculous.'

The fact that corner shops are profitable concerns, noted in Srinivasan's research (1995) is borne out by another convincing ethnographic study of Asian newspaper and tobacco corner shops in London (Lyon and West 1995). They are, it seems, owned by Gujerati Patels, members of the Patidar caste, and they are evenly distributed spatially throughout London. Many of them have high turnovers and are extremely valuable: 45 per cent of the shops, the researchers found, were worth £200 000 or more (Lyon and West 1995: 414). There is trend, however, towards the purchase of professional properties as 'children of pioneer/parent Patels have begun to enter (...) professional businesses in recent years' (ibid.: 415).

Patels have clearly uncovered a very profitable niche that no-one knew was there. They are an upwardly mobile Indian caste which, historically, has gone into trading wherever its members settle overseas, although corner shops would appear to be a local British discovery. So perhaps the cultural explanation of entrepreneurship holds after all? Why was it not West Indians who discovered the profitability of the corner shop?

Who fails?

This returns us to the so-called problem of black business failure and the reasons for it.[3] My own aim here is not to answer this question but to deny its very validity. Black people have historically allowed their cultural talent, creativity and originality to be appropriated and commodified by others. For many years they were prevented by the exclusionary forces of racism from taking command of their intellectual property. Jazz, the Blues, Soul, Spirituals – where would 'America' (and the world) be without them? Perhaps no single ethnic group has contributed more of value, directly and indirectly, to global popular culture, to music and sports, than have black

African Americans and Afro-Caribbeans. Yet great artists like Billy Holiday or Bessie Smith died penniless and alone. The million dollar profits generated by black creativity were raked in by non-black agents, promoters and record companies.

This has all changed now. African American and British blacks know the value of their culture as packaged commodity and they guard their collective intellectual property from intruders and potential appropriators.[4] In a recent study of rap music in Los Angeles and New York, Dipanita Basu (1996) found that, notwithstanding the legacy of slavery, the violence and the poverty of the black ghetto, African American rappers have used hip hop culture as a lever to fame and fortune. Around this cultural form they have developed what I call a 'culture of entrepreneurship' (Werbner 1990a). They market not only rap but graffiti graphics, fashion and style. They own their own studios and record shops, and use their own musicians, DJs, cameramen, editors, mixers and producers. A whole network of secondary businesses and professional occupations has arisen around hip hop and rap, and it is almost entirely controlled by African Americans. This is because, Basu found, despite the global reach of rap, its inventiveness is based on a deep sense of localism. It tells of the hood (that is neighbourhood) in its own distinctive style, and because it is based on this very specific sense of localism, which is constantly changing and inventing itself anew, no-one seems able to copy it. It belongs in the hood, that violent ghetto neighbourhood, and even the most successful rappers must keep returning to the hood, Basu found, for inspiration. They must keep their old networks alive even after they are rich and famous (see Basu and Werbner 1998).

The culture of entrepreneurship African Americans are developing, evident also in the recent revival of Harlem as a cultural centre, is not a legacy of the past, just as their culture of origin was not the determining legacy of Pakistani settler entrepreneurship in Manchester, or even of Jewish entrepreneurship in New York City at the turn of the century. Social and communication networks, willingness to take and extend credit, cheap materials and production processes, perceived demand for cheap goods, racism, joblessness, an appreciation of culture as a commodity to be packaged and sold, all combined to create this culture of entrepreneurship.

Conclusion

So does culture make a difference? In the first instance we need to recognise that culture *is* the symbolic differences created by distinctive relations of sociality which arise in the context of migration or shared experience of poverty and even violence. The culture of entrepreneurship created by Pakistanis in Manchester was not in any simple sense a legacy of peasant farming culture in the Punjab. It was born in Manchester, by single men collectively suffering the indignities of peddling, or working long hours together in factories, while also sharing lodgings and food. If there was trust, it derived from those new experiences of migration and the enduring social networks they generated.

This is not a culturally deterministic explanation as some have assumed (see Waldinger *et al.* 1990). Cultures of entrepreneurship are not givens; they are invented traditions. At most, they are empowered, as the case of the Patidars highlights, by the knowledge that such inventiveness utilized by coethnics elsewhere has paid handsome dividends. But the actual goods produced and the networks supporting this production are always historically contingent, local inventions. Nor does this approach ignore problems of racism or economic restructuring. On the contrary, my aim has been here to explain the complex processes of communication, exchange and competition which allow immigrants not only to survive, but to expand into business in great numbers, in a strange land, with out any prior experience. Through trading preferentially with one another, penniless immigrants are able to create culturally constituted economic value.

To study ethnic entrepreneurship, then, requires a prior understanding and knowledge of the types of industries particular ethnic groups have penetrated in numbers. By tracing the goods or services marketed and produced in these industries (chutneys, garments, rap songs), one can begin to uncover the intra-and interethnic networks of supply and credit that enable the flow of goods within the industry. An appreciation of the various constraints embodied in the manufacture or movement of these objects allows us to gauge the shape of an industry and its developmental trajectories. These in turn reveal the economy of value and the economic rationality of entrepreneurs, as well as the opportunities they perceive for expansion or diversification. Much of this rationality is not particularly 'ethnic'. Indeed, more insightful studies, such as that by Ward (1991) or Curran and Blackburn (1993) highlight the fact that researchers' prior understanding of economic sectors allows for a superior interpretation of survey findings. Clearly then also, sampling is a decision that needs to be informed by prior fieldwork within an ethnic community. Shopkeeping is the most visible part of most industries. Even rap songs have to be marketed. But petty retailing is only a starting point for research. In itself, it is often the least revealing. As a Jewish cloth wholesaler once told me: 'If I can sell one thing, I can sell anything.' But the goods marketed and the services consumed have a career and a history. Their hidden narrative will very likely disclose a world of ethnic business, sociality, and competition. The spatial clustering of firms has itself to be problematized. With all the research on Little Havana, for example, (see Portes and Bach 1985), it remains quite unclear why such diverse Cuban businesses concentrate together, selling so many different types of goods. By focusing on such goods and the challenges, opportunities and values they embody, we can begin to move away from invidious comparisons between ethnic groups or their cultures. Within any industry there are areas of profitability and creativity, as well as boredom, routinized work and low profits. But as I have argued here, the most profitable objects/services are not always the most highly valued in the wider society, or considered to have the greatest lasting collective value. Nor can status and honour be objectively measured as external to the group.

The collective creation of value is thus my preferred measure of success, whether this be a carnival masque costume, a cheap garment or a rap song. The point is that value is always relative to the context of sociality in which it is produced. This feature of value is one that has been repeatedly recognised by anthropologists and sociologists, from Mauss and Malinowski to postcolonial ethnographers of marginality and exchange. The chimera of success thus exists first and foremost in the eyes of coethnic interlocutors who strive competitively to gain or create collective symbols of scarcity, honour and excellence.

Notes

* This chapter was first published in *The Sociological Review* (August 1999). Permission to republish the text is gratefully acknowledged. I am grateful to Hans Vermeulen and Joel Perlmann for their penetrating criticisms. Fieldwork and in-depth interviewing among Asian and Pakistani immigrant settler entrepreneurs in Manchester was conducted during 1975–79, and during 1987–89 with support from SSRC and ESRC UK grants. It has been updated periodically since with short forays in to the field and continuous contact with members of the community. The fieldwork consisted of participated observation in factories and markets, communal events, and observation of traders on their shopping rounds. The research also probed the relation between entrepreneurship and family or community mobilisation and networks. Much of this has been published in Werbner (1990a).

1. In terms of so-called 'interactive' models of entrepreneurship, Manchester was a high-demand economic environment, while Asian migrant settlers were predisposed towards entrepreneurship, initially for lack of opportunities in waged employment and later because the early pioneers had established a foothold in the clothing trade which required very little start-up capital and even less knowledge and skill (for a sophisticated analysis of interactive theories, see Light and Rosenstein 1995).

2. On the informalization of the clothing industry among Greek—Cypriot manufacturers see Panayiotopoulos 1996.

3. Exceptionally, in a recent article, Ram and Deakins (1996) praise the initiative, drive and productivity of young Caribbean entrepreneurs in Britain. Their results could just as well have elicited the opposite prognosis.

4. It has been argued that the political battle over the canon in the US has not so much enhanced the value of Third World cultural products, but of African-American works whose sales have rocketed as their place in the curricula of various disciplines has come to be established.

References

Ahmed, T., 1996, 'Why Asian shops will stay open all hours', *Eastern Eye* Friday 13 September, p. 9

Anwar, M., 1996, *British Pakistanis. Demographic, Social and Economic Position* (Warwick: Centre for Research in Ethnic Relations, University of Warwick)

Appadurai, A. (ed.), 1986, *The Social Life of Things* (Cambridge: Cambridge University Press)

Back, L., 1996, *New Ethnicities and Urban Culture* (London: UCL Press)

Ballard, R., 1996, 'The Pakistanis. Stability and introspection', in: C. Peach (ed.), *Ethnicity in the 1991 Census*, Vol. II (London: HMSO)

Basu, D., 1996, *Localism and Authenticity in the US Hip Hop Industry*, paper presented to the postgraduate seminar in Sociology and Social Anthropology, Keele University, October 1996

Basu, D., and P. Werbner, 1998, *Bootstrap Capitalism and the Culture Industries. A Critique of Invidious Comparisons in the Study of Ethnic Entrepreneurship*, paper presented at the Research Council of Norway's conference on 'Immigrants and the Labour Market', Oslo, November 1998

Baudrillard, J., 1989, *Selected Writings*, edited by Mark Poster (Cambridge: Polity Press)

Becker, H.S., 1982, *Art Worlds* (Berkeley: University of California Press)

Benjamin, W., 1973, *Illuminations*, translated by H. Zohn (London: Fontana) [1955]

Bennetto, J., 1996, 'Asians emerge as the new money makers', *The Independent* Wednesday 12 June, p. 3

Bourdieu, P., 1984, *Distinction. A Social Critique of the Judgement of Taste*, translated by R. Nice (London and New York: Routledge and Kegan Paul)

Bourdieu, P., 1995, *The Field of Cultural Production* (Cambridge: Polity Press)

Callon, M., and J. Law, 1995, 'Agency and the hybrid collectif', *The South Atlantic Quarterly* 94(2): 481–508

Canclini, N.G., 1995, *Hybrid Cultures. Strategies for Entering and Leaving Modernity* (Mineapolis: University of Minnesota Press) [1989]

Carrier, J.G., 1995, *Gifts and Commodities. Exchange and Western Capitalism since 1700* (London: Routledge)

Chohan, N., and H. Rasvi, 1996, 'End of the corner shop?', *Eastern Eye* Friday 13 September, p. 4

Clifford, J., 1988, *The Predicament of Culture* (Cambridge Mass: Harvard University Press)

Cohen, A., 1969, *Custom and Conflict in Urban Africa* (London: Routledge and Kegan Paul)

Cohen, A., 1991, 'Drama and politics in the development of a London carnival', in: P. Werbner and M. Anwar (eds), *Black and Ethnic Leaderships in Britain. The Cultural Dimensions of Political Action* (London: Routledge)

Cohen, A., 1993, *Masquerade Politics. Explorations in the Structure of Urban Cultural Movements* (Berkeley: University of California Press)

Cohen, S., 1991, *Rock Culture in Liverpool. Popular Music in the Making* (Oxford: Clarendon Press)

Curran, J., and R. Blackburn, 1993, *Ethnic Enterprise and the High Street Bank. A Survey of Ethnic Businesses in Two Localities*, Research Report, Small Business Research Centre (Kingston upon Thames: Kingston University)

Cusick, J., 1996, 'Integrity, hard work, sweat and luck', *The Independent* Wednesday 12 June, p. 3

Eades, J., 1987, 'Prelude to exodus. Chain migration, trade and the Yoruba in Ghana', in: J. Eades (ed.), *Migrants, Workers and the Social Order*, ASA Monograph 26 (London: Tavistock)

Gregory, C.A., 1982, *Gifts and Commodities* (London: Academic Press)

Habermas, J., 1983, 'Modernity. An incomplete project', in: H. Foster (ed.), *Postmodern Culture* (London: Pluto Press)

Harrison, L.E., 1992, *Who Prospers? How Cultural Values Shape Economic and Political Success* (New York: Basic Books)

Heinze, A.R., 1990, *Adapting to Abundance. Jewish Immigrants, Mass Consumption and the Search for American Identity* (New York: Columbia University Press)

Jones, T., D. McEvoy, and G. Barrett, 1992, 'Labour intensive practices in the ethnic minority firm', in: J. Atkinson and D. Storey (eds), *Employment, the Small Firm and the Labour Market* (London: Routledge)

Lash, S., 1993, 'Pierre Bourdieu. Cultural economy and social change', in: C. Calhoun, E. LiPuma and M. Postone (eds), *Bourdieu. Critical Perspectives* (London: Polity Press)

Latour, B., 1993, *We Have Never Been Modern*, translated by C. Porter (London: Harvester Wheatsheaf)

Light, I., (forth.), 'Globalisation and migration networks', in: J. Rath and R. Kloosterman (eds), *Migration and Garment Industry in Europe and North America* (Amsterdam: University of Amsterdam)

Light, I., and C. Rosenstein, 1995, *Race, Ethnicity, and Entrepreneurship in Urban America* (Hawthorne, NY: Aldine de Gruyter)

Light, I., G. Sabagh, M. Bozorgmehr and C. Der-Martirosian, 1994, 'Beyond the ethnic enclave economy', *Social Problems* 41(1): 65–80

Light, I., G. Sabagh, M. Bozorgmehr and C. Der-Martirosian, 1995, 'Ethnic economy or ethnic enclave economy?', in: M. Hatter (ed.), *New Migrants in the Marketplace* (Boston: University of Massachusetts Press)

Lyon, M., and B.J.M. West, 1995, 'London Patels. Caste and Commerce', *New Community* 21(3): 399–420

Malinowski, B., 1922, *Argonauts of the Western Pacific* (New York: E.P. Dutton and Co.)

Mauss, M., 1966, *The Gift*, translated by I. Cunnison (London: Cohen and West)

Metcalf, H., T. Modood and S. Virdee, 1996, *Asian Self-Employment. The Interaction of Culture and Economics in England* (London: Policy Studies Institute)

Miller, D., 1987, *Material Culture and Mass Consumption* (London: Blackwell)

Modood, T., and R. Berthoud, 1997, *Ethnic Minorities in Britain. Diversity and Disadvantage* (London: Policy Studies Institute)

Munn, N., 1986, *The Fame of Gawa. A Symbolic Study of Value Transformation in a Massim (Papua New Guinea) Society* (Cambridge: Cambridge University Press)

Panayiotopoulos, P.I., 1996, 'Challenging orthodoxies. Cypriot entrepreneurs in the London garment industry', *New Community* 22(3): 437–60

Peach, C., 1996, 'A question of collar', *The Times Higher* 23 August, p. 17

Perlmann, J., 1988, *Ethnic Differences. Schooling and Social Structure among the Irish, Italian, Jews and Blacks in an American City, 1880–1935* (Cambridge: Cambridge University Press)

Portes, A., and R.L. Bach, 1985, *Latin Journey. Cuban and Mexican Immigrants in the United States* (Berkeley: University of California Press)

Rafiq, M., 1992, 'A comparison of Muslim and non-Muslim owned businesses in Britain', *New Community* 19(1): 43–60

Ram, M., and D. Deakins, 1996, 'African-Caribbeans in business', *New Community* 22(1): 67–84

Rogin, M., 1996, *Blackface, White Noise. Jewish Immigrants in the Hollywood Melting Pot* (Berkeley: University of California Press)

Sahlins, M., 1976, *Culture and Practical Reason* (Chicago: University of Chicago Press)

Sombart, W., 1962, *The Jews and Modern Capitalism* (New York: Collier Books)

Sombart, W., 1967, *Luxury and Capitalism* (Ann Arbor: the University of Michigan Press) [1913]

Srinivasan, S., 1995, *The South Asian Petty Bourgeoisie in Britain* (Aldershot: Avebury)

Steinberg, S., 1981, *The Ethnic Myth. Race, Ethnicity and Class in America* (New York: Athenaeum)

Strathern, A., 1971, *The Rope of Moka. Big Men Ceremonial Exchange in Mount Hagen, New Guinea* (Cambridge: Cambridge University Press)

Strathern, M., 1988, *The Gender of the Gift* (Berkeley: University of California Press)

Thomas, N., 1992, *Entangled Objects. Exchange, Material Culture, and Colonialism in the Pacific* (Cambridge, Mass: Harvard University Press)

Travis, A., 1996, 'Blacks move towards suburbs', *The Guardian* 12 June, p. 6

Veblen, T., 1899, *The Theory of the Leisure Class* (New York: B.W. Heubsch)

Waldinger, R., 1996, *Still the Promised City? African-Americans and New Immigrants in Post-Industrial New York* (Cambridge Mass.: Harvard University Press)

Waldinger, R., H. Aldrich and R. Ward, 1990, 'Opportunities, group characteristics and strategies', in: R. Waldinger, H. Aldrich and R. Ward (eds), *Ethnic Entrepreneurs: Immigrant Business in Industrial Societies* (London: Sage)

Ward, R., 1991, 'Economic development and ethnic business', in: A. Curren and R.A. Blackburn (eds), *Paths of Enterprise. The Future of the Small Business* (London: Routledge)

Weber, M., 1930, *The Protestant Ethic and the Spirit of Capitalism* (London: George Unwin)

Werbner, P., 1990a, *The Migration Process. Capital, Gifts and Offerings among British Pakistanis* (Oxford: Berg)

Werbner, P., 1990b, 'Renewing an industrial past. British Pakistani entrepreneurship in Manchester', *Migration* 8: 7–42. [Reprinted in: J.M. Brown and R. Foot (eds), 1994, *Migration. The Asian Experience* (London: Macmillan)]

Werbner, P., 1996a, 'The enigma of christmas. Symbolic violence, compliant subjects and the flow of English kinship', in: S. Edgell, K. Hetherington and A. Warde (eds), *Consumption Matters. The Production and Experience of Consumption*, Sociological Review Monograph (Oxford: Blackwell)

Werbner, P., 1996b, 'Fun spaces. On identity and social empowerment among British Pakistanis', *Theory, Culture and Society* 13(4): 53–81

Werbner, P., 1997, 'Introduction. The dialectics of cultural hybridity', in: P. Werbner and T. Modood (eds), *Debating Cultural Hybridity. Multi-Cultural Identities and the Politics of Anti-Racism* (London: Zed Books)

4

The Cultural Fallacy in Studies of Racial and Ethnic Mobility*

Stephen Steinberg

> *The recognized causes of poverty are in fact largely symptoms or results of poverty. They are, to be sure, potent to produce more poverty; they are evidences of a downward tendency and must be corrected; but they are not the 'underlying' causes.*
>
> (Brandt 1908: 643)

The central question of this volume – does culture make a difference? – seems at first blush to be totally innocent of politics. After all, to explore 'the interrelation between culture, identity and socio-economic position' is an unassailable line of sociological inquiry. Yet, for me, the pairing of 'culture' with 'socioeconomic position' is a red flag signalling a discourse that is fraught with problems and anything but politically innocent. And so, I would like to say at the outset, that if we are going to venture into an ideological mine field, we ought to do it with our eyes open. Let me explain.

Social science has long bathed in self-congratulation over its repudiation of scientific racism – the various doctrines that traced racial hierarchy to the genes. However, no sooner were these theories thrown into the proverbial rubbishbin than another theory arose that explained racial hierarchy in terms of culture. According to this theory, groups that languish on the bottom do so because they are saddled with aberrant or dysfunctional value systems that impede their social and economic mobility. Though projected as a new theory tailored to contemporary events, this theory was actually a throwback to ideas that held currency even before the ascent of social Darwinism and biological determinism in the late 19th century. When Europe began its colonization of Africa in the 17th century, the distinction between the 'civilized European' and the 'savage African' was invented to give justification to the domination of the one over the other.

Both the English who settled in North America and the Dutch who settled in the Cape of Good Hope shared a conception of 'savagery' which they applied to the native peoples they encountered. As George Fredrickson (1981: 7) writes in *White Supremacy*:

> These beliefs were not yet racist in the nineteenth-century sense of the term because they were not based on an explicit doctrine of genetic or biological inequality; but they could provide an equivalent basis for considering some categories of human beings inferior to others in ways that made it legitimate to threat them differently from Europeans.

Two distinctions were invoked to divide the human race into superior and inferior categories. One was between 'Christian' and 'heathen'; the other, between 'civil' and 'savage'.

This, of course, is the obsolete nomenclature of 17th-century Europe. However, to my ear it has disturbing resonance with the modern characterization of the poor and downtrodden as culturally and morally deficient. 'Sloth and immorality' are the terms that recur in early 20th-century discourse on poverty. Although contemporary social science has purged itself of such patently value-laden terminology, in its own way – as I argue in this chapter – it also posits culture and morality as reasons that the poor languish in poverty. How different are we, really, from our forebears who invoked heathenism and savagery to legitimate racial hierarchy? Indeed, I was tempted to entitle this article: 'Heathenism and savagery in the inner city'.

If this seems far fetched, one only has to consider Dinesh D'Souza's *The End of Racism* (1995). According to D'Souza, racism has its origins in the superiority of Western civilization. Europeans recognized the conspicuous 'civilization gap' between themselves and the primitive peoples who were to become their colonial subjects. For D'Souza, the entire biological paradigm, from 19th-century social Darwinism down to *The Bell Curve* (see Herrnstein and Murray 1994), has been an unfortunate mistake. Indeed, he wants to bring us back to the original paradigm that traced racial inequality to differences in 'civilization'.[1]

Although liberal intellectuals have had a field day trashing D'Souza's book, my contention is that his basic position, which traces ethnic inequality to differences in culture, is not fundamentally at odds with the position that is central to mainstream social science. D'Souza has only stated in bald terms propositions that receive more circumspect articulation among leading scholars in the field. Indeed, D'Souza's book is peppered with citations to a large canon of empirical studies that have probed the culture and morality of poor minorities. His transgression is not in advancing a new theoretical paradigm, but rather in carrying this paradigm to its logical conclusion and doing so with ruthless consistency. After all, if the chief problem in black America is their moral and cultural inadequacy, then does it not follow that their deliverance lies in their moral and cultural rehabilitation? Is this not the message we heard even from the Million Man March?[2]

Let us return to the history-of-ideas framework that I began with earlier. Notwithstanding the sensation that followed the publication of The Bell Curve, the triumph of liberal social science has been its repudiation of scientific racism. The new liberal orthodoxy on race affirmed the primacy of environment over genes, and established the ways in which race – and therefore racial hierarchy – is socially constructed. The emancipatory promise of the liberal paradigm is obvious, at least compared to the paradigm it supplanted, which treated racial traits as fixed and immutable, and provided justification for the rigid segregation associated with Jim Crow in the south. However, the liberal paradigm had at least two fateful flaws that permitted the evolution of a new brand of racism, one that was tailored to the racial realities of the postsegregation era.

The first flaw was to conceptualize and define racism in terms of attitudes rather than conditions.[3] It was of course recognized that blacks and whites differed in their life chances and living standards, but these differences were assumed to stem from racial prejudice: that is, from the distorted and malicious beliefs that whites had about blacks. Theoretical reductionism combined with methodological reductionism to produce scores of studies that sought to measure the extent and sources of prejudice in individuals, all with the ultimate aim of devising strategies for disabusing bigots of their benighted beliefs. Here, alas, was an incredible inversion of 'white social science'. The major paradigm involved a praxis that ministered to the oppressor rather than to the oppressed! The thrust of social research and social policy was directed, not at improving conditions for blacks, but rather at reforming attitudes among whites. Liberation for blacks would have to wait for whites to undergo a therapeutic transformation.

A second flaw in the liberal paradigm stemmed from the ambiguity surrounding the claim that racial differences can be traced, not to genes, but to 'environment'. Rarely was 'environment' construed in terms of structures of oppression that denied blacks elementary rights of citizenship and subjected them to systematic abuse on the part of all major institutions, including institutions of higher learning. Instead, 'environment' was construed as pertaining to the deprivations and the culture of blacks themselves, conditions that perpetuated poverty from one generation to the next. Once again, a flawed theoretical premise served as the undergird for an enormous body of research: scores of ethnographic studies scoured every aspect and detail of black families, neighbourhoods and communities in a misdirected search for the factors that explained black 'underachievement'. Though not necessarily by intent, these studies yielded a picture of social disorganization and cultural pathology that in effect located the sources of black poverty and marginality within the black community itself.[4]

Ironically, the same liberal sociology which had relinquished scientific racism to the trashcan of history, found itself resurrecting a victim-blaming paradigm that merely substituted culture for genes. This paradigm has received a series of iterations across the decades. In the 1950s the buzzword was 'cultural deprivation'. The liberal position, reiterated in scores of studies, was that the academic underachievement of minority children had its sources, not in the genes, but in the cultural deprivations associated with their homes, neighbourhoods and communities. The remedy, then, was to provide these culturally bereft children with the cultural materials and experiences that accounted for the academic success of their middle-class counterparts.

In the 1960s the 'culture of poverty' was added to the sociological lexicon. Oscar Lewis, who coined the term, argued that as a reaction and adaptation to their circumstances, the poor develop a distinctive way of life that is passed down from one generation to the next. In yet another leap of faith, Lewis held that children steeped in the culture of poverty would be unprepared to take advantage of opportunities even if they were to arise. The implication of this model was that poverty and racial disadvantage had become *self*-perpetuating.[5] In the 1980s the term 'underclass' was suddenly at the centre of academic discourse. Originally coined by Gunnar Myrdal to refer to groups that remain mired in poverty even during periods of economic expansion and declining unemployment, the term was now used to suggest that this subaltern class was not only materially deprived, but lived outside the prevailing normative order as well. Myron Magnet put it this way:

> Disproportionately black and Hispanic, they are still a minority within these minorities. What primarily defines them is not so much their poverty or race as their behavior – their chronic lawlessness, drug use, out-of-wedlock births, nonwork, welfare dependency, and school failure. *'Underclass' describes a state of mind and a way of life. It is at least as much cultural as an economic condition.*
>
> (1987: 130; emphasis added)

In the 1990s yet another formulation has come on stream, this time with a leftist twist. It is held that the poor develop an 'oppositional culture'. On this view behaviour that is conventionally regarded as aberrant, is actually a form of 'resistance' to hierarchy and domination. Unlike earlier models, resistance theorists place the cultural responses of the poor in a context of political economy. Nevertheless, they share the core assumption that oppositional culture and practices are not only a product of marginality, but play an active role in driving the poor deeper into poverty. In this way the poor become implicated in the social reproduction of inequality.[6]

It is important to note that all of these discourses have been assailed by critics who contend that they amount to a cultural blaming-of-the-victim, shifting responsibility for social inequality away from societal institutions onto the poor themselves.[7] Nevertheless, as the succession of models suggests, no sooner is the head of this theoretical dragon severed than it regenerates another. The nomenclature changes, but the core assumption is the same: that cultural deficiencies explain why the poor languish in poverty. In so many words, the suggestion is that these latter-day heathens and savages must learn to live by the codes that govern civil society – the very society that, with utmost civility, places a stigma of inferiority on its ethnic minorities; casts them into isolated ghettos, barrios, and ethnic slums; denies them access to jobs and opportunities that might provide them a channel of escape; then judges them for not playing according to the rules of a system that victimizes them; and as a crowning irony, castigates them for not displaying the cultural virtues and living by the moral codes that are assumed to govern the lives of their oppressors.[8]

Despite their claim of value neutrality, social scientists are implicated in the legitimation of this system of ideas. With grants from government and foundations, they are commissioned to penetrate the interior of the nation's ghettos and barrios, armed with the tools of their respective disciplines, to ferret out the reasons that these pariahs are not exemplars of middle-class virtue. With inculcated myopia, these field workers record the manifest reality: social disorganization, cultural pathology and patterns of self-destructive and anti-social behaviour. These men and women of science mean no harm. On the contrary, like the missionaries who once voyaged to distant colonies, they want to lift the downtrodden to a higher plane. The hard question, though, is whether they unwittingly place a stamp of scientific legitimacy on the idea that the groups on the bottom are condemned by their own cultural and moral deficiencies.[9]

It is not my intention to substitute the myopia of the person who cannot see the forest for the trees with the myopia of the person who sees only forest and cannot discern the complex process of reproduction that occurs within. It is easily demonstrable that the culture of the poor is different in important respects from the culture of the middle classes. Nor can it be denied that the poor develop cultural responses and defences that are dysfunctional in relation to such mainstream institutions as schools and job markets. Nor can it be denied that attempts to modify the culture and practices of the poor may have salubrious effects for the individuals involved. None of these caveats, however, warrants the claim that there is a causal relation between culture and poverty. The problem, fundamentally, has to do with the reification of culture.

Reification occurs whenever culture is treated as a thing unto itself, divorced from the material and social conditions in which it is anchored. In principle, there is little disagreement with this proposition: culture-of-poverty theorists, in their various rhetorical guises, acknowledge that the cultural patterns of the poor are 'adaptive' to the situations in which the poor find themselves and thus are ultimately rooted in social structure. However, a further theoretical claim is made, and this is where controversy begins. It is held that once culture comes into existence, it takes on 'a life of its own'. In other words, it is held that the culture of poverty exists as an independent and self-sustaining culture, one that not only constitutes a distinctive way of life, but also is capable of reproducing itself from one generation to the next. This is the 'cycle of poverty', so cherished in the social science literature. Reforming the culture of the poor, or so it is held, is key to breaking this vicious cycle.

But does culture really take on 'a life of its own'? This is the core assumption that deserves critical scrutiny. Granted, in terms of surface appearances, culture *seems* to have a life of its own. To repeat, we can readily observe the poor living by values and codes of behaviour that are divergent from those of middle-class society and this has been documented by scores of ethnographic studies. However, the counterargument, put forward in a smaller canon of studies, is that what *looks* like a shared culture is, on closer examination, similar responses of discrete actors to the exigencies and circumstances that define and limit their choices. This is not culture pursued for its own sake, or prized for its intrinsic worth. Properly defined, it is not a culture at all, but only defensive and reactive responses to structures of inequality as they impinge on the personal sphere of life. If it is a culture at all, it is a culture of last resort. Elliot Liebow had it right in *Tally's Corner* (1967). Liebow's subjects were streetcorner men who did not hold steady jobs, maintain monogamous relationships, or function as parents for their children. Nevertheless, Liebow rejected the idea that they had different values with respect to work and family, or that their behaviour signified a distinctive subculture. As he wrote:

> The streetcorner man does not appear as a carrier of an independent cultural tradition. His behavior appears not so much as a way of realizing the distinctive goals and values of his own subculture, or of conforming to its models, but rather as his way of trying to achieve many of the goals and values of the larger society, of failing to do this, and of concealing his failure from others and from himself as best he can.
>
> (1967: 222)

Liebow also offers this eloquent rebuttal to the claim that the poverty subculture is self-perpetuating:

> Many similarities between the lower-class Negro father and son (or mother and daughter) do not result from 'cultural transmission' but from

the fact that the son goes out and independently experiences the same failures, in the same areas, and for much the same reasons as his father.

(ibid.: 223)

In short, it is not culture, but racial and class hierarchy, that is reproduced from one generation to the next. Put another way, the culture of poor and marginalized groups does not exist in a vacuum. On the contrary, it is in constant and dynamic interaction with the matrix of political, economic and social factors in which it is embedded. The 'sin of reification' occurs whenever this culture is abstracted from this larger matrix, and assigned independent causal significance.[10] Does culture make a difference? Yes, but only in conjunction with the material and social factors in which it is anchored and on which it depends for its sustenance.

Like a flower cut away from its stem, culture stripped away from the structures on which it depends rapidly loses its resilience, and all too soon, its vitality. This is no less true of the privileged than it is for the disprivileged. Take a corporate executive – white, male, and affluent – who is a casualty of downsizing and unable to find a comparable job. How long does it take before he experiences a commensurate diminution of status and self-esteem? Before his marriage is strained to the breaking point? Before he takes refuge in whatever figurative 'streetcorner' is relevant to his status? What then can we expect of the racial pariahs who are cast to the fringes of society, where survival, much less self-respect, is a daily challenge? Shall we administer a psychological test? Shall we summon the ethnographer to record their cultural flailing as they pitifully attempt to salvage some shreds of their tattered selves?

On the other hand, if we scrupulously observe the injunction against abstracting culture from political economy, then we must also reject a praxis that would address culture alone, without addressing the matrix of political, economic and social factors in which it is embedded. Melioristic reform that addresses symptoms but neglects underlying causes is doomed to failure. This was precisely the conclusion that John Ogbu reached in his 1978 study of *Minority Education and Caste*, based on the study of caste-like groups in six societies (Israel, Japan, India, New Zealand, Britain and the United States). In all six societies under examination, Ogbu found not only similar patterns of academic underachievement, but also a similar cycle of social reforms that were notable for their failure to significantly improve educational outcomes. Ogbu reached the following conclusion:

[T]he lower school performance of blacks is not itself the central problem but an expression of a more fundamental one, namely caste barriers and the ideologies that support them. *The elimination of caste barriers is the only lasting solution to the problem of academic retardation.*[11]

Another anthropologist, Gerald Berreman (1991: 45–6), also writes:

> If I were asked, 'What practical inference, if any, is to be drawn from the comparative study of inherited inequality – of ascriptive social ranking?' I would say it is this: There is no way to reform such institutions; the only solution is their dissolution.

Berreman goes on to quote Kardiner and Ovesey who wrote, in their study *The Mark of Oppression*, that 'there is only one way that the products of oppression can be dissolved, and that is to stop the oppression' (1951: 387).

In the final analysis, the reification of culture not only constitutes bad theory, but it leads to ineffectual social policy as well. Its net effect is to shift the onus of moral and political responsibility for social change away from powerful institutions that could make a difference onto the individuals who are rendered powerless by these very institutions.

We social scientists need to take off our political blinders, and to refuse to play out our assigned role of placing a stamp of scientific legitimacy on victim-blaming ideologies. To say this, however, contradicts the cardinal assumption of this chapter: that agency is a poor match for structure. Not only are social scientists subject to the same ideological influences that operate elsewhere in society, but in their professional capacity, they are also subject to the wiles of powerful institutions – government, foundations, elite universities, publishing houses and professional organizations. These arbiters of 'knowledge' have a powerful influence on the direction and content of research. Whether by design or not, they determine which ideas are propelled to the centre of academic discourse and which are relegated to the fringes. At the present conjuncture, perhaps all we can hope for are critiques from the margins of our discipline that decry the subtle and multifarious ways in which social science functions as a servant to power.

Notes

* Another version of the text, entitled 'The Role of Social Science in the Legitimation of Racial Hierarchy', has been published in 1998, in *Race and Society* 1: 5–14.
1. See especially D'Souza 1995: 97–100 and chapter 12.
2. For a searing analysis of the politically regressive aspects of the Million Man March, see Reed 1995: 20–2.
3. This was shrewdly observed by Thomas Pettigrew at a 1966 American Academy Conference on the Negro American (see Pettigrew 1966: 312).

4. For a recent critique of urban ethnography, see Kelley 1997, chapter 1. Kelley begins by quoting a subject in John Langston Gwaltney's *Drylongso*, who says: 'I think this anthropology is just another way to call me a nigger.' Also, see di Leonardo 1998, chapter 2.

5. Lewis's original explication of the culture of poverty concept was in *La Vida* (1964: xlii–lii). See also Lewis 1966 and 1968.

6. 'Resistance theory' has its origin in the writing of Pierre Bourdieu (1977), Paul Willis (1977) and Henry Giroux (1983). For a recent application, see MacLeod 1995. In *When Work Disappears* (1996), William Julius Wilson embraces the assumptions of the resistance theorists. Wilson argues that, in response to persistent joblessness, ghetto residents develop a cultural repertoire and patterns of 'ghetto-related behaviour' that 'hinder rational planning' and otherwise prevent them from taking advantage of even the scarce opportunities that exist for work. For a critique of *When Work Disappears*, see Steinberg 1997: 72–83.

7. One of the few contemporaneous critics to challenge the 'cultural deprivation' model was Kenneth Clark. In *Dark Ghetto* he wrote: 'To what extent are the contemporary social deprivation theories merely substituting notions of environmental immutability and fatalism for earlier notions of biologically determined educational unmodifiability?' (1965: 131). For critiques of the culture of poverty school, see Gans 1993: chapter 20, Leacock 1971, Lewis 1967, Ryan 1976, and Steinberg 1989: chapter 4. For critiques of the underclass discourse, see Gans 1993: chapter 21, Katz 1989: chapter 5, Kornblum 1984, and Steinberg 1995: chapter 6.

8. The term 'civility' has recently emerged as a recurrent trope in political discourse. For an astute analysis, see DeMott 1996.

9. It bears repeating that I do not impugn the personal motives of social scientists, either individually or collectively. To say that social scientists are implicated in the legitimation of racial hierarchy is not to suggest this is their intent. It goes without saying that social scientists are not exempt from the sociological axiom that motive and function are often at odds with one another, and that behaviour can have unintended consequences.

   Let us consider another example outside the emotionally charged realm of race studies. Theorists who contend that schools are a mechanism in the reproduction of inequality do not presuppose that teachers *desire* this outcome. On the contrary, it is assumed that most teachers genuinely want to help their students escape poverty. If anything, the fact that teachers are *not* aware of the uses and values of their work, makes them all the more useful for propagating the myth that the schools are a 'great equalizer' and that children who fail have no one to blame but themselves.

10. 'The sin of reification' is Abraham Kaplan's term. To quote Kaplan (1964: 61): 'Reification is more than a metaphysical sin, it is a logical one. It is the mistake of treating a notational device as though it were a substantive term, what I have called a construct as though it were observational, a theoretical term as though it were a construct or indirect observable.'

11. Ogbu 1978: 357, italics in original. Ogbu has partially retreated from this position in subsequent research, as is evident from his later publications. To some extent, this shift of emphasis reflects a shift in method. In his more recent studies, Ogbu compared the educational performance of different minority groups within particular school settings. Such an approach obviously foregrounds the operational significance of cultural factors. On the other hand, Ogbu's methodology in

Minority Education and Caste involved comparisons of whole societies. This approach shifts the analytical focus to *systemic* factors: to caste itself, and the structures that engender inequality and that are served by these inequalities.

Essentially, this boils down to the much-debated question of the relative importance of structural versus cultural factors. In response to his own critics, Oscar Lewis resolved the matter as follows: 'The crucial question from both the scientific and the political point of view is: How much weight is to be given to the internal, self-perpetuating factors in the subculture of poverty as compared to the external societal factors? My own position is that in the long run the self-perpetuating factors are relatively minor and unimportant compared to the basic structures of the larger society' (quoted in Leacock 1971: 35–6).

References

Berreman, G.D., 1991, 'Race, caste, and other invidious distinctions in social stratification', in: N.R. Yetman (ed.), *Majority and Minority* (Boston: Allyn & Bacon) [1972]

Bourdieu, P., 1977, *Outline of a Theory of Practice* (Cambridge: Cambridge University Press)

Brandt, L., 1908, 'The causes of poverty', *Political Science Quarterly* 23: 637–51

Clark, K.B., 1965, *Dark Ghetto. Dilemma's of Social Power* (New York: Harper & Row)

DeMott, B., 1996, 'Seduced by civility', *The Nation* 263: 11–19

D'Souza, D., 1995, *The End of Racism* (New York: The Free Press)

Fredrickson, G.M., 1981, *White Supremacy. A Comparative Study in American and South African History* (New York: Oxford University Press)

Gans, H.J., 1993, *People, Plans, and Policies* (New York: Columbia University Press)

Giroux, H.A., 1983, *Theory and Resistance in Education. A Pedagogy for the Opposition* (London: Heinemann Educational Books)

Herrnstein, R.J., and Ch. Murray, 1994, *The Bell Curve. Intelligence and Class Structure in American Life* (New York: The Free Press)

Kaplan, A., 1964, *The Structure of Science* (San Francisco: Chandler Publishing Company)

Kardiner, A., and L. Ovesey, 1951, *The Mark of Oppression* (New York: W.W. Norton)

Katz, M., 1989, *The Undeserving Poor* (New York: Pantheon Books)

Kelley, R.D.G., 1997, *Yo' Mama's Disfunktional!* (Boston: Beacon Press)

Kornblum, W., 1984, 'Lumping the poor. What *is* the underclass?', *Dissent* September 1984: 295–302

Leacock, E.B. (ed.), 1971, *The Culture of Poverty. A Critique* (New York: Simon & Schuster)

Leonardo, M. di, 1998, *Exotics at Home* (Chicago: University of Chicago Press)

Lewis, H., 1967, *Class, Culture, and Poverty* (Washington: Cross-Tell)

Lewis, O., 1964, *La Vida* (New York: Knopf)

Lewis, O., 1966, 'The culture of poverty', *Scientific American* 215: 19–25

Lewis, O., 1968, 'The culture of poverty', in: D.P. Moynihan (ed.), *On Understanding Poverty* (New York: Basic Books)

Liebow, E., 1967, *Tally's Corner. A Study of Streetcorner Men* (Boston: Little Brown)

MacLeod, J., 1995, *Ain't No Makin' It*, 2nd edn (Boulder, Colorado: Westview)

Magnet, M., 1987, 'America's underclass. What to do?', *Fortune* 115: 130–50

Ogbu, J., 1978, *Minority Education and Caste. The American System in Cross-Cultural Perspective* (New York: Academic Press)

Pettigrew, Th., 1966, 'The Negro American', *Daedalus* 95(1): 287–441

Reed Jr., A.L., 1995, 'Black politics gone haywire', *The Progressive* 59(12): 20–2

Ryan, W., 1976, *Blaming the Victim*, revised edition, (New York: Vintage Books)

Steinberg, S., 1989, *The Ethnic Myth. Race, Ethnicity and Class in America* (Boston: Beacon Press)

Steinberg, S., 1995, *Turning Back. The Retreat from Racial Justice in American Thought and Policy* (Boston: Beacon Press)

Steinberg, S., 1997, 'Science and politics in the work of William Julius Wilson', *New Politics* VI(2): 72–83

Willis, P.E., 1977, *Learning to Labour* (Farnborough, Hants.: Saxon House)

Wilson, W.J., 1996, *When Work Disappears. The World of the New Urban Poor* (New York: Alfred Knopf)

5

Situational and Structural Rationales for the School Performance of Immigrant Youth. Three Cases

Margaret A. Gibson

The central concern of this volume is how to account for the variability in social mobility patterns among different immigrant groups and over time within an individual group. Are the differences due to cultural variables or to contextual variables, or, as Vermeulen and Perlmann ask in their introductory Chapters, can culture explain at least some of the differences? In this chapter I explore these questions by reviewing research from three studies that I have carried out with immigrant youth spanning the last 25 years. Each centres on the school performance of students at the secondary or high school level but with a view to the larger community and societal context for schooling and to the interaction among cultural and contextual variables that influence patterns of achievement.

The first study took place in the mid 1970s, on the island of St Croix in the US Virgin Islands, where I was conducting doctoral dissertation research on relationships between ethnicity, immigrant status, gender and student performance. The second study, which was carried out in the early 1980s, focused on Asian Indian immigrants settled in a California town I call 'Valleyside'. The school district was concerned because the number of Indian immigrants had grown rapidly over the previous decade, and there was a serious racial backlash occurring against the Indian children and their families. The third study took place in the same school district a decade later, focusing on the Mexican population. District administrators were disturbed by the generally poor academic performance of Mexican-descent high school students and requested that I carry out a study to identify factors impeding their success.

Although in none of the studies have I been able to follow students from school into the work force, the findings do give some indication of the social mobility strategies of the different groups and the role that schooling plays in this. The analysis will be guided by an interpretative framework that has evolved within the field of educational anthropology in the United States over the last two decades and that is set forth most fully in a chapter by John D'Amato (1993) on the factors that give rise to patterns of resistance or compliance in school by ethnic minority children. I shall adapt the framework to help explain why some immigrant groups or subgroups are more able than others to use schooling as a stepping stone to social mobility.

Anthropologists of education have long been interested in the relationship between ethnicity and school performance. During the 1970s and 1980s two major theoretical frameworks evolved to explain inter-group variability (Jacob and Jordan 1987, 1993). The first focuses on cultural factors, positing that discontinuities between home and school lead to miscommunication and even conflict between ethnic minority students and their teachers, which in turn contributes to poor patterns of school performance for minority students. The second framework emphasizes instead structural factors at the societal level that disadvantage minority groups who historically have been subjected to discrimination and denied equal employment opportunities. In consequence, adolescents from these groups

> develop attitudes of warranted cynicism regarding the social mobility functions of institutions like schools [and] practice a group wide 'oppositional culture' in dealing with the representatives of such institutions.
>
> (Ogbu, as cited by D'Amato 1993: 185)

Both frameworks have been found wanting, because, in the first instance, cultural differences between home and school do not necessarily lead to poor performance and in the second, social inequalities, even those historically rooted within the larger society, do not necessarily lead to cynicism, resistance to school authority, or lack of investment in schooling (Erickson 1987).

Based on his own fieldwork with Hawaiian youngsters and related ethnographic studies of student compliance and resistance within the classroom, D'Amato (1993) suggests that our analysis must consider both the structural and situational rationales that guide student behaviour in school. Structural rationales, in D'Amato's usage, stem from factors external to the school that cause students to 'play by the rules' or not. Among these is the instrumental value that children attach to schooling and the credentials it confers. For example, does the student believe that success at school will lead to a desired job or improved social status, or to recognition within one's family, community or peer group? Conversely, does the student believe that poor performance or behaviour at school will have negative consequences as, for example, in parental sanctions, lost status, or lost mobility opportunities? A student's structural rationales are generally, but not always, shaped by family and community forces, including a group's 'folk theories' about how to get ahead in society (Ogbu 1991, Ogbu and Simons 1998). These theories, in turn, are shaped both by cultural and contextual variables. D'Amato notes that students who have strong structural rationales for investing in schooling will usually go along with teacher routines and apply themselves to their work, even if they must tolerate extremely uncomfortable conditions at school related, for example, to clashes between their parents' values and those espoused by teachers, or to a racist social climate that permeates their day-to-day school experiences.

The circumstances are very different, however, for immigrant and ethnic minority students who have no adequate structural rationale for persisting in school. In such situations 'the children become aware of their power as a group' and will resist teacher authority unless they find sufficient intrinsic value in the schooling experience itself, which D'Amato suggests, usually hinges on the teacher creating a classroom culture which the students accept and that is compatible with the values embedded within their own peer group interactions (1993: 197 ff). Students who perceive intrinsic value in the schooling or classroom experience develop a situational rationale for behaving in school and complying with school or teacher rules for success.

Students who have neither a sufficient structural rationale nor a situational rationale for accepting school routines frequently band together to resist teacher authority and to take control as best they can of classroom interaction. Such students are also more likely to perform poorly and to withdraw from school early. On the other hand, where students find either intrinsic or extrinsic value in the schooling experience, or both, they will comply with teacher authority and persist in school. Not all groups have the same rationales for engaging in school work, but they must have some rationale to cause them to invest the effort required for school success, to put up with the boring routines, to deal with conflicts between home and school cultures, and, as is often the case for immigrant and other ethnic minority students, to endure the discomfort of prejudice and discrimination directed toward members of their group.

I shall employ this framework to guide the analysis of my three cases, seeking to explain not only the variability in school performance between the groups, but also to explore the variability that occurs within groups related to such factors as gender, social class and, in the case of immigrants, generation in new country. I seek to compare the rationales of the different groups and subgroups and, in turn, to explore how these rationales are influenced by both cultural and contextual factors. In so doing, I hope also to contribute to this volume's central question regarding whether variability in social mobility patterns is due largely to situational and structural factors or whether culture explains some of the difference. Following Vermeulen (1996: 8), I view culture as the 'collective consciousness' of a particular group based in its shared experiences, values and knowledge.

To the extent that my own field data permit, I shall also provide information on the premigration status of each group and its postmigration position within US society.

The West Indian case

The West Indian case focuses on the school performance of both immigrant and nonimmigrant West Indian children attending public schools in St Croix, one of the three inhabited islands that comprise the United States Virgin Islands.[1] Like other Afro-Caribbean societies, St Croix is characterized by its relatively small size, its colonial and slave experience, a population predominantly African in descent, and its continued dependence on a colonial power.[2] Efforts to Americanize St Croix, which along with St Thomas and St John had been purchased by the United States from Denmark in 1917, proceeded slowly prior to the 1960s, when St Croix's sugar plantation economy was replaced forever by one based on industry, tourism, tourist-related services and local government. Tourism and industry together brought full employment to St Croix, but at a cost to the native population, which rapidly became a minority in its own homeland.

By 1975, the island's population had surpassed 50 000, a growth of more than 300 per cent in the preceding 15 years (US Bureau of the Census 1973, US Department of the Interior 1976). The increase resulted from immigration to St Croix by 'continentals', the local term for both black and white Americans from the US mainland, by Puerto Ricans, who had moved to St Croix from the small islands of Culebra and Vieques, and by workers from non-US islands of the Caribbean. The latter came both as permanent residents and as temporary or 'bonded' workers, whose stay was dependent upon the existence of jobs that no US citizen or permanent US resident was available to fill. Regardless of their place of birth, in Antigua or Trinidad, St Lucia or Nevis, for example, and in spite of their shared African-Caribbean heritage, all immigrant West Indians were viewed by their Crucian hosts as 'aliens', a process of labelling that served both to bind them together and to set them apart from the native population.

Even children born in St Croix to noncitizen parents, and thus American citizens, had the 'alien' identity ascribed to them. I refer to this group collectively as 'Down Islanders', a term that reflected the immigrants' ancestry and origins in the islands located south of or 'down from' St Croix. This term, although heard less frequently than 'alien', was commonly understood. By the mid 1970s Down Islanders, at 44 per cent of the population, had become the single largest group residing on the island. Crucians totalled 27 per cent; Puerto Ricans, both first and second generation, 22 per cent; and continentals, 7 per cent. The recent wave of Down Islanders, like the Puerto Ricans before them, had come because jobs were more plentiful in St Croix than in their homelands. During the early 1970s, for example, when St Croix was enjoying relatively full employment, the unemployment rate in neighbouring Antigua was 40 per cent (Nordheimer 1973).

Employment niches

The rapid population growth and expansion of the private economic sector had been accompanied by an equally sharp rise in the size of local government. Within the native group there existed a small professional and business elite, but for the most part Crucians were employed in civil service jobs. From a scant 3 per cent of the work force in the 1940s, the local Virgin Islands government had grown by 1975 to 25 per cent of the total work force and more than 60 per cent of the native-born work force (Senior 1947, US Bureau of the Census 1985, US Department of the Interior 1976). White continentals controlled industry, tourist-related businesses and many of the island's other commercial enterprises. A growing number of the smaller businesses were owned and operated by Puerto Ricans. Down Islanders, for the most part, held jobs that natives shunned, mainly the service jobs connected with tourism, such as waiters, maids and clerks in the island's duty free shops, positions in the expanding continental-owned Hess oil refinery, and skilled and unskilled jobs in construction. The economic boom had brought shopping centres, resort hotels and housing complexes, but with them sharply inflated land prices, placing home ownership out of reach for increasing numbers of Crucians. The native elites had become richer, but the poor had become poorer, leading Virgin Islanders to note that tourism was a new form of slavery. Continental businesses had simply replaced the European planters (O'Neill 1972).

Ethnic relations

By local estimates probably 70 per cent of those who considered themselves Crucians had ancestors who had emigrated to St Croix from other Caribbean islands, and Down Islanders who had arrived in St Croix before the 1960s had generally been absorbed into the Crucian community. Crucians and Down Islanders share, to a very great degree, a common heritage, and cultural differences within each group are as great or greater than the differences between them (Dirks 1975, Green 1972). Family structure and patterns of childrearing are similar, for example, as is religious affiliation.

This easy acceptance of newcomers from other Caribbean islands changed during the 1960s and early 1970s with the rapid expansion of the population and with the increasing sense on the part of many Crucians that their island was being stolen from them (Moorhead 1973). Family ties and birth place became increasingly significant symbols of belonging and one frequently heard the expression '*mi bo'n hea*' [me born here] to signify one's identity as a native. Parents' and grandparents' birthplace in St Croix were also used to identify 'true Crucians' and to prove one's right to a job in the local government. As their number rose, Crucians came increasingly to see Down Islanders as 'invaders' and 'exploiters'. They resented the fact that Down Islanders sent their savings off-island rather than investing locally and they felt a growing sense that control over the social fabric of their homeland was slipping from them. Anti-immigrant cracks, such as 'aliens work like slaves', 'all they care about is making money', and 'they send it home and it doubles', were common. One elderly Crucian woman expressed her bitterness by saying: 'When I was young, I knew them all; if they did anything wrong, they were sent home. Now (...) they pee in your bushes and wear their hair all funny. They show no respect.' A younger Crucian noted similar resentment, saying 'aliens don't have any manners. Look at the way they walk (...), or drive a car!' Down Islanders, for their part, had little good to say about Crucians. Many described the natives as surly and rude, occasionally venting even stronger sentiments, such as 'crab has no head and so no brain; Crucian has a head and still no brain.' Or 'I can get along with white people better than Crucians. They're crazy, evil people, messing themselves up.'

School performance

Between 1970, when St Croix public schools were forced by court order to open their doors to the children of foreign workers, and 1975, the percentage of noncitizen children skyrocketed from 12 per cent (all children of permanent residents) to 40 per cent. Another near 30 per cent of public school students were of Puerto Rican descent. Crucians students were suddenly no longer the majority or even the largest single group. They had been displaced from their position of numerical dominance to that of a minority in their own schools. Moreover, given the Virgin Islands' status as a territory of the United States, the Crucian population had little power to control the flow of immigration into the island, whether from the mainland United States, from Puerto Rico, or from other Caribbean island nations.

I arrived in St Croix expecting to learn that Crucian children would be top performers in the public schools because they knew the local culture and had the advantage of being insiders. Likewise, I assumed that the immigrant West Indians would be disadvantaged by their family backgrounds and their status as outsiders. Although almost all public school children were of similar racial and class backgrounds, that is, poor and black, the immigrant parents had even fewer economic resources at their disposal and less schooling.[3] Furthermore, ethnic hostilities often spilled over into schools. For example, Crucian teachers constantly made disparaging remarks about Down Islander children, such as: 'The aliens have ruined our schools. So many of them are overage, and they can't even do second-grade work.' Crucian youngsters, in turn, made fun of non-native classmates, calling them names and telling them to 'go back' where they came from. One boy explained his reception as follows: 'They teased me and destroyed my belongings. (...) Crucians don't like aliens. If we know more than them, they try to beat us up.' As a result, Down Islander newcomers kept to themselves, noting that 'non-citizens stay away from other groups because they know they are not much liked. They feel unwelcome.'

Clear performance patterns emerged, but not those I anticipated.[4] Down Islanders, on the whole, were doing better in school than Crucians, and girls within both groups outperformed the boys.[5] The differences, although small during the early primary years, became readily apparent by junior high. Grades, track placement, annual promotion rates and school persistence provide evidence of these disparities. For example, at the junior high where I conducted participant observation, 84 per cent of the Down Islander girls 82 per cent of the Crucian girls and 73 per cent of the Down Islander boys were promoted from seventh to eighth grade. In sharp contrast, only 34 per cent of the Crucian boys were promoted. Moreover, of the Crucian boys retained in seventh grade, one in three dropped out of school immediately and most of the others failed to attend school with any regularity the following year. The situation was no different at the other junior high. Within the public school system, almost all the Crucian boys had left school by age fifteen or sixteen. The ethnic and gender differences in school performance continued through high school. An estimated 70 to 75 per cent of the Down Islander and Crucian girls graduated from high school. About 60 per cent of the Down Islander boys reached tenth grade and between 40 and 50 per cent finished 12th grade. In sharp contrast, only 20 per cent of the Crucian boys reached grade ten and possibly no more than 10 per cent received a high school diploma (Gibson 1991). No similar gender disparity existed in the private schools, which served the island's middle class.[6]

As I came to understand the economic and social setting, I also came to see that immigrants and natives viewed the opportunity structure very differently and had different 'folk theories' of getting ahead economically and socially. Their differing perceptions were reflected in the school response patterns of their children and to some extent at least in their children's structural rationales for remaining in school. Down Islanders were generally better behaved, more attentive in class and invested more time in their homework. 'Teachers like aliens', one Crucian boy explained, 'because they can get them to do what they say – kiss their asses.' Teachers, he said, tried to get Crucian students to comply but could not 'get away with it'. Classroom observation supported his views, particularly with respect to boys. Lower-class Crucian boys, for the most part, as they reached adolescence, were unwilling to follow the instructions of those teachers whom they viewed as bossy, declaring openly that 'slavery's done'.

Class distinctions clearly played a role in shaping student responses and behaviour, but social class alone does not explain why Crucian girls and boys performed very differently, or why Down Islander boys performed better than Crucian boys. As in other Caribbean societies (Patterson 1975, Wilson 1973), two separate, interrelated, generally gender-specific value systems were at work within Crucian society, each with its own standards for judging a person's worth. Women earned respect within a system that may be characterized as a culture of 'respectability', a creolized version of the culture of the European planter class, whereby lower-class women sought to improve their social position by mimicking the behaviours of the local elites. Young men, on the other hand, especially of lower-class background, adhered to a cultural system whereby a person's worth was measured by his peers rather than by the imposed European (or American) standards of respectability. Men, and boys as they moved into adolescence, were given recognition for the things they could do well – being good with words, showing toughness and generosity, as well as loyalty and leadership. This culture of 'reputation', according to Wilson (1973), is a creative response to the elusiveness of high-class status.

Thus, within Crucian society, just as adolescent girls were expected to be 'good' to demonstrate their respectability, boys had evolved an oppositional subculture in which they gained status by being 'bad', which generally meant challenging the values of those in positions of dominance, including their teachers (Gibson 1982). One young Crucian explained that 'a man earns a reputation by his ability to lead others, no matter the direction.' Another noted that

> Boys earn status by doing the silliest things. [They say] 'he bad, mon. He goin' on bad' [which is to say good], because he broke the rules, or beat up a bigger boy, or played his radio, broke a window or lit a brush fire.

Others offered similar explanations. By their junior high years (grades seven and eight) the Crucian boys' defiance of school rules became increasingly blatant. This was particularly true for those who had been assigned to the slowest sections of grade seven. Their rebellious actions, although decried by school authorities, earned them status among their peers. Not all Crucian boys attending public school openly resisted school authority or confronted the system. A few managed to earn a reputation by being quick with words, a good athlete or a talented musician. The large majority found it necessary, however, to demonstrate their opposition to the system. Some Down Islander boys, as well as some girls from both groups, also defied school authority, but the patterns of defiance and resistance were far more dominant among the Crucian males.[7]

While no Crucian parents wanted their sons to get in trouble at school or to be expelled for their poor behaviour, most with sons in public school appeared resigned to this eventuality. 'Boys all come to ruination', one father explained, but like other lower class parents he also felt his sons were treated unfairly by those in authority. One mother commented similarly: 'I know my son's not perfect, but it doesn't matter what he does. They say he's wrong.' She knew that her son had a quick temper, but she believed, too, that school authorities were always harassing him. She noted that 'we're just poor black people' and believed that the school principal, a very respectable Crucian woman with high status in the community, had a grudge against her family. Other Crucian parents described similar incidents. Social class hostilities and local resentments within the Crucian community, it seems, spilled over into school settings to the detriment of the Crucian boys.

Discussion

The school performance patterns for each group had been shaped not only by their historical experience of slavery and colonization and by the local economic context, but also by each group's particular situation in the host society and its relationship to the larger US society. White Americans, while comprising less than 5 per cent of the resident population, ultimately held control over much of the island's economy. Members of the Crucian elite had also profited from the economic expansion and the steep rise in land prices, but the large majority of Crucians had little to gain from the largely uncontrolled population growth.

Using the framework of situational and structural rationales for complying with school authority, we find variability along gender, ethnic and class lines. Crucian girls, for their part, generally enjoyed school, providing them with a situational rationale. It got them out of the house and offered an opportunity to socialize with friends. Most girls also saw schooling as instrumental to their goal of self-reliance. In other words they found extrinsic value in school credentials, which offered them a structural rationale for remaining in school. They recognized that a high school diploma had become a prerequisite for obtaining office work, including the government jobs they desired. Not all Crucian girls conformed to school rules, but those who misbehaved usually did so discreetly and avoided teacher punishment. Nor did all girls apply themselves to their studies, but as boys were quick to point out, girls could receive a diploma 'for never being absent'. Pregnancy was the main reason a young woman dropped out of school, but after the baby was born she could either re-enroll in high school or attend night school in order to complete requirements for her diploma.

Down Islander girls' rationales for completing high school were very similar. They saw it as instrumental to their goal of economic independence and a stepping stone to a better life. Moreover, since they expected Crucians to get preference in hiring, they believed they needed to be better prepared in order to compete in the job market.

Unlike their sisters, the lower-class Crucian males saw little value in putting up with the school routines. Assuming, as it seemed these boys did in their more optimistic moments, that they would get a blue collar government job based on their family connections or their personal reputations, as had been the case for their older brothers and fathers, school credentials had little instrumental value. Indeed a preponderance of the students interviewed, Puerto Rican, Down Islander and Crucian alike, concurred that Crucians get the 'better' jobs because 'people look out more for their own' and because 'they are from here and have the preference.' By the mid 1970s, however, unemployment was on the rise, anti-American and anti-white attitudes were becoming more prevalent and many Crucian boys felt uncertain about their futures. Government employment was growing scarce and most Crucian boys were unwilling to take low-level, non-government positions where continentals or Down Islanders would be their supervisors. These boys had little structural rationale for remaining in school. Likewise, they found little intrinsic value in school routines and much discomfort in the culture of respectability pressed on them by their middle-class teachers. They could earn more status with their peers by challenging the rules at school or by cutting class and hanging around with their friends. Moreover, these boys quite frankly admitted that they would turn to crime if there were no jobs for them to their liking. As they saw it, outsiders were stealing their island and they deserved their share. Moreover, an increasing number not only saw schools as unresponsive to their needs but as an instrument of their oppression (Moorhead 1973). By the mid 1970s crime was rising sharply, and many of the crimes were committed by young unemployed Crucian men and teenage boys.

The Down Islander boys were culturally very similar to the Crucian boys (Green 1972). Based on these similarities, there is good reason to suppose that they shared much of the Crucian boys' discomfort with a school culture and school routines that were at odds with their youthful male 'culture of reputation'. While the lower class Crucian boys bore the additional burden of having middle-class Crucian teachers look down on them because of 'who they were', the Down Islander boys were also looked down upon because they were aliens. How then can we account for the fact that the Down Islander boys were significantly less likely to be disruptive or to drop out of school during junior high? One explanation is that their families were more middle class, at least in their premigration status back home and this may have been true for a handful of the boys, but my field data indicate that in general the Down Islander families had even fewer resources to draw upon than the Crucians. A second explanation, and the one supported by my data, is that these boys had a greater structural rationale for remaining in school. In their home islands a high school education was neither free nor available to all students and their parents made it clear that they would have far better chances for getting ahead, whether in

St Croix or back home, if they finished high school while they had the chance. Many, although certainly not all, seemed to accept their parents' admonitions not to squander their chance for an education. A comparative perspective, or dual frame of reference (Suarez-Orozco 1989) also enabled their parents, and perhaps these young immigrant West Indian males as well, to evaluate their current situation in comparison to conditions back in their island homelands. While the Crucian boys appeared to share a growing sense of oppression and to share a conviction that what was justly theirs was being stolen from them, the Down Islander boys on the whole exhibited greater optimism about their future prospects.[8]

The Punjabi case

My study of Asian Indian immigrants, almost all from the Indian state of Punjab, calls attention to the dynamic nature of the immigrant group's success theories and educational strategies. More specifically, it examines the interrelationship between the cultural background of a group of Punjabi immigrants and their experiences prior to migration, the structure of the host community in which they have settled, including economic and social conditions, the Punjabis' particular situation in the US setting and the reciprocal influence of these forces on educational strategies and performance. As with the West Indian case, attention to gender differences in educational aspirations and achievement highlights the interaction between cultural and contextual variables.

The setting for the study is a small agricultural town in California's Central Valley. Settled initially at the time of California's gold rush, Valleyside grew slowly until the mid 1960s. Over the next 15 years the county population increased by approximately 40 per cent, to a total of 50 000. During this same period the Punjabi population living in and around Valleyside increased tenfold, to more than 6000 by local estimates. At the time of fieldwork (1980–82), Valleyside's population was about 71 per cent white, 12 per cent Punjabi, 12 per cent Mexican and 5 per cent other. The findings reported here come largely from participant observation and interviews with a focal sample of 42 Punjabi families, all with children attending their senior year at Valleyside High School, and from the academic records for all 232 Punjabis students in grades 9–12. A similar set of interviews, together with academic records, were collected from white Valleysider seniors and their parents (Gibson 1987, 1988a).

Employment niches

Most of the Valleyside Punjabis were followers of the Sikh religion and members, by birth, of a traditional landowning group in northern India known as Jats. A proud independent and self-reliant people, Jats are dominant in number and power in most villages throughout Punjab. Although those who had emigrated to Valleyside had only small to moderate sized holdings in Punjab (8–10 acres on average), they considered themselves and were considered by others, to be members of the highest ranking group within the social structure of their villages. Moreover, they had the security of owning their own land and were able to employ others to do the hardest manual labour. Those who immigrated to California came not so much to flee either low status or poverty as to maintain or improve their family's economic condition. They believed educational and economic opportunities would be far better for their children in the United States than in India. They also believed that they could adapt relatively easily to life in Valleyside because it is an agricultural community similar in a number of respects to village Punjab. They knew, too, that they could turn to family members already settled in Valleyside for assistance when necessary.

In 1981 only one third of the fathers in the focal sample had been in the United States for more than ten years another third for five to ten years and the final third for less than five years. Most had arrived in Valleyside with few salable skills apart from their farming savvy and with little or no cash. Many were in debt to the relatives who had helped pay for their air fares. Out of necessity, most had little choice on arrival but to take back-breaking work, usually for minimum wage, as farm labourers, generally pruning, thinning and picking peaches. A full-time farm worker at that time usually earned no more than $500 to $600 a month in the off season, yet even the most frugal families needed $1000 a month to meet basic living expenses. They counted on summer earnings, when women and children worked alongside the men for up to 14 hours a day picking peaches. The average annual income for a family who worked in the fields was under $15 000, including children's earnings. All Punjabi families struggled financially during their first years in Valleyside, but most, due to their frugality, hard work and custom of sharing homes among members of the extended family, had been able to purchase their own homes within five years of their arrival. Some had also purchased their own farms. By the early 1980s Punjabi farmers owned an estimated 50 per cent of the county's peach acreage (La Brack 1982a,b), plus additional acres of prunes, walnuts, almonds and pears.[9] Most of the farms were small and barely large enough to turn a profit, but a few families had become very successful, owning hundreds of acres of the tri-county's best orchards. It was mainly those who had arrived in Valleyside before 1970 who, by 1980, had been able to purchase even a few acres of land. Most of the more recent arrivals worked as farm labourers, usually for another Punjabi, although those with some knowledge of English had shifted from farming to factory work in nearby cities.

Ethnic relations

Although almost all of the Punjabis spoke of hostile actions directed at them or members of their families by white Valleysiders, it was the newcomers that suffered most. The old-timers, generally farm owners, were better established in Valleyside and were respected, albeit sometimes begrudgingly, for their agricultural skills and substantial influence in the county's largest industry. Newer arrivals were less acculturated to American ways and seemed not only to attract more attention but also to be more preyed upon by a minority of white Valleysiders, often teenage males, who were openly hostile to the Punjabis. During their interviews most parents chose to minimize the negative aspects of their relations with whites and to emphasize examples of positive interaction. Most also advocated a strategy of ignoring the hostilities, wishing to avoid a situation of response and counter-response. One man commented:

> Now if we started swearing at them, what is the point? If some white children pass by in a car and shout, 'Hey Hindu', and give us the finger, it would make things worse if we go after them in our car. If they abuse [us] and we abuse them, then we will have bad feelings amongst us.

Punjabis explained that the prejudice stemmed in part from the fact that they 'look different', 'live separately' and pursue a different 'style of living'. They assumed, too, that 'when you go to another country, you go there knowing that [prejudice] is possible.' Furthermore, those who worked as farmers and farm workers observed that majority-group hostilities towards them had little direct economic impact. The hostilities did, however, detract from the quality of the lives: 'You do feel it', one woman explained. 'If someone treats you badly, obviously you are going to be upset about it. The reason why we don't do anything is because it is their country.' Punjabi adults were shielded from the most injurious effects of prejudice not only by their strategy of separation but also by their positive sense of self-esteem, even cultural superiority, their egalitarian ideals, deeply rooted in the Sikh religion, and their strong sense of community.

For Punjabi young people, who had daily contact with white students and teachers at school, the situation was far different. Not only did they encounter sharp conflicts between their family values and those promoted by the school, but in one way or another Punjabi students were told constantly that India and Indian culture were inferior to Western and American ways. Punjabis students were criticized for their hairstyle, their diet, their dress, their language and their values. They were faulted for deferring to the authority of elders, accepting arranged marriages and placing family ahead of individual interests. And they were condemned most especially for not joining in majority-dominated school activities and for resisting as best they could the pressures to conform to the dominant culture.

Speaking Punjabi to one another was a case in point. White Valleysiders, students and teachers alike, said that if Punjabis would only speak in English then there would be more mixing and less friction between groups.

Punjabi students, including those fluent in English, noted on the other hand that it was the prejudiced attitudes and behaviour of the Valleysiders that deterred them from mixing and that they should not be faulted for speaking Punjabi with one another. Both in school and outside the Punjabi students encountered a climate of racial hostility that permeated their day-to-day experiences. Verbal jibes, such as 'you stink' or 'you goddamn Hindus', and milder forms of physical abuse, such as food throwing, were common. More offensive but less frequent incidents included white students spitting at Punjabis, sticking them with pins and throwing lighted cigarettes at them. Punjabi boys who wore their hair long and in a turban, in keeping with Sikh teachings, were constantly teased, as were the most recent arrivals from India whose dress and language set them apart. White students felt some safety in numbers, as the following comment from a white senior makes clear:

> Numbers mean power, and you get hundred Anglos and ten Punjabis, and you know that the Anglos can overpower the Punjabis. So they can say that my way of living is right and yours is wrong and get away with it.

Teachers and administrators, although disturbed by the situation, seemed unable or unwilling to turn things around. They dealt with the most blatant hostilities, but otherwise attributed the situation to white students' 'ignorance' and urged Punjabi young people to be 'understanding'. Punjabi students also knew from experience that if they defended themselves when verbally harassed they would be labelled as troublemakers, disciplined by school authorities and, quite likely, by their parents as well.

School performance

Only 30 per cent of the Punjabi students at Valleyside High had begun their schooling in the United States and only 12 per cent were US born; 60 per cent had been in this country for less than six years, some arriving after their fathers, who had wished to establish themselves in Valleyside before moving their families to the United States. Punjabi was the language of the home for all these young people and most spoke little or no English when they entered Valleyside schools. Only recently, moreover, had the schools begun to offer any special assistance to students with limited facility in English. The Punjabi parents, for their part, could offer their children little direct help. Few spoke English and fewer still were literate in English. Most had received only limited formal education themselves in India.[10]

In spite of the barriers, the US-born Punjabis and those who had arrived during the early elementary years (sometimes termed the 1.5 generation) generally persevered in school and managed to do reasonably well, taking on average as many college preparatory classes in high school as their white American peers. Those who arrived at a later age, however, generally fared far less well academically. Many remained in special classes for English language learners throughout their years in high school and never took the academic courses needed for college admission. Still, an estimated 85 to 90 per cent of all Punjabi students, including the freshest arrivals from village India, met at least the minimum requirements for high school graduation.

Although boys and girls finished high school in equal numbers, boys enrolled in more college preparatory classes. This gender difference related to the girls' expectations that their formal education would terminate directly after high school or, with parental permission, after two years at the local community college. Parental concerns stemmed, in part, from a traditional rural Punjabi belief that 'too much' education would make a girl too independent in her views and behaviour, thus tarnishing her reputation and quite possibly her chances for a good marriage. Parents were also reluctant to permit their daughters to live away from home in situations where they would lack close parental or extended family supervision.[11]

Discussion

In spite of their relatively high status in village India and the success of the earliest arrivals in purchasing their own farms, the parents in the sampled families shared few of the characteristics commonly associated in America with success in school. In addition to low incomes, little formal education and lack of familiarity with Western culture, most were also handicapped by a limited knowledge of English, and few were able to help their children with their schoolwork. How then can we account for the comparative success of these Punjabi Sikh students? The answer, I believe, lies in the interaction of cultural and contextual factors.

Sikhs have a long and self-conscious history of perseverance in the face of adversity, and they have developed effective strategies for preserving, honouring, and teaching this history. In India, where they comprise only 2 per cent of the population, they are accustomed to fighting to maintain their religious beliefs and identity while also pursuing their economic goals. In Valleyside it is no different. Moreover, the characterization of these rural Sikhs as having little education applies only to formal schooling and does not apply to their command over religious and scriptural knowledge, agricultural skills and traditional cultural values. The latter are crucial in fashioning their children's educational attitudes and success strategies. While book learning and school credentials have not, at least until recently, been considered necessary for those who farm in India, most Jat Sikh parents espouse great respect for education, as evidenced by the folk sayings that laced their interviews: 'The difference between an educated and an uneducated person is the difference between the earth and the sky', parents said, or 'education is the third eye', 'if you are blind yourself, how can you lead others?' and 'with only a simple education, one can expect only a simple job.' Farming, in their view, fit the category of a 'simple' job.

Parents recognized, however, that their own opportunities in the United States had been severely restricted by their limited schooling. Moreover, few of the parents, even those with the larger landholdings, expected their sons to farm. They recognized that their children wanted a more secure and remunerative livelihood than farming could offer. Parents and children alike viewed formal education as an investment in the future.

In village India, a Jat woman's labour is essential to the successful operation of a Punjabi farm, and women must work hard to manage the household and to promote the interests of their large extended families. It is not a job, however, that requires a great deal of book learning or the kind of independent thinking that is encouraged at the higher levels of education. In fact, a belief that too much education may make a woman 'snobbish' and 'spoiled' is characteristic of Punjabi Sikhs of rural background. In the new Valleyside setting attitudes were changing rapidly as parents came to see that a young woman's earnings outside the home could contribute substantially to a family's income and that an educated woman could obtain a far better job than one lacking formal education. Although many of the girls worried that their parents would insist on marriage immediately after high school, four-fifths of those in the focal sample actually went on to attend the local community college the year following their high school graduation.

While boys had more incentive than girls to pick high school courses that would lead to postsecondary education, the advice they received from their parents was very much the same: 'Obey your teachers.' 'Do your school work.' 'Keep trying harder.' 'Stay out of trouble. You're there to learn, not to fight.' On the whole, there was close congruence between parents' views and those of their children with respect to the value of formal education as an avenue to upward social mobility in the United States. Moreover, although the parents were deeply concerned about the racial hostilities at school and the nearly incessant pressures placed on their children to 'Americanize', they would brook no excuses for poor academic performance or poor behaviour at school. Young people knew that if they behaved inappropriately they would bear the consequences. 'The fields are waiting', parents warned, and this was no idle threat. Girls knew, too, that an arranged marriage would be imminent if their parents felt their behaviour might bring dishonour to the family's good name. All Punjabi young people could cite examples of culturally deviant students who had been withdrawn from school by their parents.

In terms of our framework of structural and situational rationales for complying with school rules for success, we see that both the boys and girls felt pressure to do nothing that would shame the family. This pressure came not only from their parents but from a well organized set of community forces that worked to keep young people within the Punjabi fold. Boys also felt considerable pressure to become economically successful and most viewed schooling as instrumental to their social mobility within the United States. They knew, too, however, that they could fall back on farming if they were unable to make it in some other career. For girls remaining in school meant forestalling the inevitable arranged marriage. It also provided a time to socialize with Punjabi girlfriends, to learn the ways of the dominant culture, many aspects of which had enormous appeal and to be at least somewhat away from the watchful eye of parents and other community members. The girls also hoped to obtain jobs that would require at least a high school diploma and most hoped to attend the local community college, perhaps as much to delay their marriage as to improve their job options. Ethnic hostilities at school were plainly upsetting to the students and distracted them from their studies, but their rationales for remaining in school, their closeness with their Punjabi peers, their sense of self worth, and their belief that if they applied themselves they could become successful, helped buffer the sting of the prejudice. Only a few Punjabi students voluntarily dropped out of school, finding conditions too difficult.

This Punjabi case has focused on how the educational strategies and school adaptation patterns of the student generation are directly and strongly influenced by cultural models of their families and ethnic community. It has sought to indicate as well that these models are by no means static. Punjabis in rural India did not invest heavily in formal education because it was of little instrumental value to those who remained on the family farm. In Valleyside, however, where credentials opened doors to opportunities that were unavailable to the parent generation, the values rapidly shifted. Not only were young men encouraged to pursue higher education and to take up careers apart from farming, such as business, law and engineering, but young women were encouraged as well to take up jobs outside the home. As parents came to see that higher education would be an asset for their daughters, they also shifted their views about young women attending college, in part it must be noted because of the pressures brought to bear by the young women themselves.

The Mexican case

Unlike the previous two cases, which focus largely on patterns of school performance in the first generation, the Mexican case includes almost equal numbers of students who were born in Mexico (first generation), born in the United States to Mexican-born parents (second generation), and born in the United States to US-born parents (third generation and beyond).[12] For purposes of analysis, the children who arrived from Mexico during their preschool or early primary years are also included in the second generation. The setting for this case is also Valleyside and the research sample included all 113 Mexican-descent students who were attending ninth grade at Valleyside High in March 1992.[13]

As in the Punjabi case, most of the immigrant parents found Valleyside a good place to live and to raise their children. One man explained: 'Myself, I feel very happy. It's a small town, very peaceful. All the neighbours are good to us. We get along well. It's also a good place for the schooling of my children.' Others noted that they felt comfortable in Valleyside, that it was 'like Mexico', and that 'there are a lot of Mexican people [here]'. Many commented that when they left Mexico life there was 'very difficult' and that they found it at least somewhat easier in Valleyside. Most of the Mexican-born parents had arrived in this country during the 1970s and 1980s, in greatest numbers from the states of Jalisco and Michoacan, but also from other states across northern and central Mexico. One man explained his situation on arrival:

> When we came to this country we had no one to help us. One can fall asleep under a tree, or in the car, anywhere, because one does not know anyone, and does not have money to get an apartment (...). One has to start from the bottom here.

Unlike the Punjabis, most of the Mexican parents had come on their own to Valleyside without the sponsorship of family members already settled in the area.

Most of Valleyside's Mexican population was struggling to make ends meet, and there was only a small and relatively new Mexican middle class. Within our sample of 113 students, three-fourths qualified for the government subsidized Free Lunch Program. US-born parents, on average, had more education and somewhat higher incomes than the Mexican-born parents and none worked in the fields as farm labourers, but few had jobs that would place them solidly in the middle class. The median income for families with a least one US-born parent was only $15 000 in 1992. This was the case even though two-thirds of these parents had graduated from a US high school or had received their high school equivalency diplomas.

For the immigrant parents conditions were even more difficult. Almost all worked as farm labourers and over half of their children were eligible for services through the federally funded Migrant Education Program.[14] Some had year-round work, others only seasonal jobs, in the fields and orchards around Valleyside, often employed by Punjabi farmers or working alongside Punjabi labourers, thinning, pruning and picking peaches. Most had had little opportunity to attend school in Mexico beyond the elementary level: two-thirds of the mothers and somewhat more than half of the fathers had finished six years of schooling or less. The annual income including children's earnings was under $15 000 for most of these families. A few of the parents observed that conditions in Mexico had improved since they had left and wondered if they were in fact better off in Valleyside. Several spoke of family members still in Mexico, generally siblings, who had completed university degrees and now had professional jobs. In general, though, most seemed to feel that they lived a little better in the United States, noting that in both countries options are limited to those without education. The difference, one man explained, 'is that even though it is hard [in the US], one lives like a *ricito* [middle class person] with a car, a television, a bed, which we didn't have there. There we slept on the floor.'

Some parents noted, too, that it was their lack of English, as well as lack of education, that kept them from leaving the fields. Many felt trapped and they wanted a better life for their children. Parent interviews were laced with admonitions and advice that they gave their children about school. The following comments were typical:

> I have always told my children that the people who don't study never become anything (...). Studies are the future of humanity and especially of the young people today.

> I tell her, 'It's good that you study, that you get a degree of some sort, because if you don't, you'll end up like us. You are going to go to the fields, where else?' And I ask her, 'Do you want to work in the fields?'

> We tell them, '[your education] is going to be your inheritance. It's the only thing, see? There's no more.'

> [Mother's advice to daughter] 'Look, if you want to have money in the future, you have to study (...). Do you want to be hanging from the sack the whole year?' [sack used for picking fruit from trees]

> I took her to the fields and I told her, 'Look, my daughter, you see those girls gathering peaches?' I said, 'Look, if you don't go to school, I am going to see you here.'

There was strong consensus among the immigrant parents that their children needed to stay in school and that with schooling they would be able to have a better life.[15]

School performance

With the collaboration of school officials, the research team was able to collect school transcripts for students each year they attended Valleyside High. Only 58 of the original 113 graduated with the Class of 1995 from Valleyside High.[16] Four more students received a high school diploma or an equivalency diploma from the local continuation high school. Graduation rates varied by generation, with the children of immigrants, that is, the first and second generation students, more likely to graduate with the Class of 1995 from Valleyside High (57 per cent) than the children of US-born parents, that is, those in the third generation and beyond (40 per cent).

This was the case even though the parents of third generation students spoke English and were familiar with the US school system.

Equally significant was the variability by gender. While two-thirds of all the girls graduated or received their equivalency diplomas, only half of the boys did. The differences are more striking when analyzing for both gender and generation: 69 per cent of the third generation and beyond girls compared to just 35 per cent of the third generation and beyond boys finished high school in 1995.[17] This gender difference may also be associated with students' track assignments on entering high school, since more of the boys (75 per cent) than girls (41 per cent) in the third generation and beyond were placed into remedial math and/or remedial English classes on entering ninth grade. Four years later only 39 per cent of the Mexican-descent students who had been placed into these remedial classes graduated from high school, compared to 82 per cent of the students placed in the regular and accelerated math and English classes and 50 per cent of those placed into ESL math and ESL English classes.[18]

Ethnic relations

In school the students encountered an instructional and social climate that disparaged Mexican culture. For example, at an abstract level, most teachers supported the desirability of Mexican students being bilingual and bicultural, but at a concrete level what teachers communicated was very different. Although teachers stated that there was no district-wide or high school policy that specified 'English only', students nonetheless received a loud and clear message that Spanish was not a valued language. Most teachers insisted on English only in their classrooms and half disapproved of the students speaking Spanish at school even when chatting with friends. Many also questioned the wisdom of Mexican students studying Spanish in high school, believing this would detract from time spent on English. Most believed, furthermore, that the Mexican parents were wrong to insist that their children speak to them in Spanish believing that they should embrace English as the language of the home.

In sharp contrast, almost all of the students believed they had a right to speak Spanish at school if they wished and, like their parents, they believed that being bilingual would help them be more successful in later life. Nearly half felt that it is necessary to speak Spanish well in order to be considered a 'real Mexican'. Parents were concerned about the teachers' negative attitudes, recognizing that their children could lose their desire to maintain and improve their Spanish if they were discouraged at school even from speaking it. Worse still, as several parents noted, their children had become ashamed or embarrassed to speak in Spanish. Negative attitudes about the use of Spanish at school, and even at home, had direct impact on how students felt about school, about the adults who taught them and in some cases about how they viewed their own identity and culture.

Although most of the Mexican students stated that their teachers encouraged them to do well in school, a clear majority also believed that some teachers were prejudiced against Mexicans and that this prejudice resulted in unequal and unfair treatment of Mexican-descent students both in the classroom and on campus in general. Many students commented on how all Mexican students get labelled as 'troublemakers' because of the actions of only a few. They noted, too, that Mexican students were generally disciplined more harshly than white students. Many believed that teachers favoured white students over them – paid more attention to them, treated them with more respect, gave them more academic support.

Relations between white and Mexican students also needed improvement, the students noted. In most of the cases that students described in their interviews, a white student would make a comment or a gesture that was perceived to be racist and the Mexican students would react. One student, who later transferred to the continuation high school, explained:

Some think that they are so rich (...). Like if we wear those kinds of Mexican shoes [*huaraches*], they call you 'Beaner' or 'You wetback'. They say things like 'Why don't you go back to your own country.' (...) They always say things like that, and it kind of hurts because like my dad told me before, 'Hey, we were here first. They just took our land.' And it's true. I think it's not fair for them to say that to us. They should accept us for who we are.

Many other students made similar comments, noting both that California used to be part of Mexico and that white students' gibes often related to a lack of awareness of what it means to be poor:

Like there was this one poor kid last year (...). He used to wear the same shirt all week, one shirt, and they called him 'dirt shirt'.

The white students (...) like when you get something new, they always have a comment to say like 'Where did you steal that?' (...) and then you'll say, 'Shut up white boy', or hit them or something.

In such a fashion an insensitive quip could rapidly escalate into a fight, and the Mexican student would be disciplined more severely because he threw the first punch.

Students noted that the anti-Mexican attitudes influenced their feelings about school and, in some cases at least, their behaviour in school. While all Mexican-descent students were affected adversely by a school climate that devalued their identity, the students who expressed the greatest unease were those who were tracked into remedial classes in ninth grade.[19]

Discussion

In several respects the Mexican and Punjabi cases are similar. Both sets of students were the targets of racist remarks at school. In both groups many had parents who felt trapped in minimum wage jobs as field labourers. Both said their parents encouraged them to do well in school. But the results were different for the two groups. The Punjabis persisted in school even in the face of the severe prejudice and cultural misunderstandings and, in the case of the more recent arrivals, even when they felt they were getting watered-down instruction in their ESL classes. The Mexican students, on the other hand, were more likely to drop out of school or transfer elsewhere when placed in low-level remedial classes or kept for a number of years in ESL classes. The Mexican students also were more likely to fight back when they felt they had been wronged by others, and they had gained a reputation for being troublemakers.

Neither group of students found a great deal of intrinsic value in their classroom experience, although those in the college preparatory classes may have felt more intellectually challenged and thus more rewarded by their efforts. And newcomers, for a time at least, found their ESL classes helpful in providing them with basic English skills. Students also enjoyed coming to school to socialize with their friends. For the Punjabis, this may actually have provided a quite strong rationale because they were expected to be at home under the watchful eye of their elders when not at school, girls in particular. In any case, it seems fair to say that neither group had, in D'Amato's sense, a compelling situational rationale for complying with school rules and investing much energy in their studies.

The variability between the two groups appears more closely tied to differences in the extrinsic value they attached to school compliance and persistence. The Punjabis parents had strong and effective systems in place for keeping the younger generation in line. Students knew that if they misbehaved at school they could expect to be punished by their parents. They knew, too, that poor behaviour would produce gossip in the community and that if they got too far out of line their parents would withdraw them from school. The Mexican students cited no similar sanctions. Punjabi young people at home and through the Sikh temple were also exposed to a steady diet of Sikh history, replete with stories of those who had prevailed in the face of adversity. These young people's sense of self and future opportunities were also bolstered by a collective consciousness that Jat Sikhs as a people have been successful throughout the world wherever they have settled. And most importantly, perhaps, these Sikh young people had numerous role models within their own Valleyside community of those who had become major players in the county's economy and who could find them jobs or render advice when they needed assistance. There was also wealth within the Sikh community that could be invested in education. Few of the Punjabi students mentioned that they must leave school to help support their families, while this was foremost on the minds of many of the Mexican students, perhaps most especially the boys whose families had most recently arrived.

The Mexicans differed from the Punjabis in other significant ways. They had come on their own to Valleyside and in most cases had no family or village mates to help them get established. Nor did they have the same type of cohesive community with attendant sanctions to keep young people within the fold. There was much greater cultural homogeneity among the Punjabis, most of whom had their roots within the small Doaba region of Punjab. The Valleyside Mexicans were a far more diverse group in terms of their backgrounds and there were no long-established strategies in place to maintain group unity or to foster group interests as in the Punjabi case. Nor was there a similar sense of shared peoplehood, as in the Punjabi Jat Sikh example. Neither did the Mexicans, as a group, enjoy the same high social standing in their towns and villages in Mexico that Jats enjoyed in village India. While some had been moderately successful in their jobs before bad economic times in Mexico had forced their migration, most were from quite modest backgrounds. Moreover, and again in contrast to the Punjabi case, there were no clear community leaders within the Mexican group to whom all looked for support and direction. When I began the Punjabi research, it was quickly made plain to me the persons I needed to meet with to garner community support for the study. There was no similarly well defined system of leadership within the Mexican community and no obvious persons who could offer support or deny access to the research team.

Generation was another factor of significance. In both cases the children of immigrant parents shared some of the optimism that is typical of immigrant groups, what we might characterize as an 'immigrant orientation to schooling' (Gibson 1995a). In the Punjabi case, there were only a handful of families who had been settled in California for two or three generations, most of whom had become economically successful and were looked to for leadership within the community. The Mexican case was different. Although one third of the Mexican students had parents, and often grandparents as well, who had been born and raised in the United States, most were struggling to get ahead, or even simply to make ends meet. At an abstract level these youngsters may have believed that education pays, but at a concrete level, for persons of backgrounds similar to themselves, they had all too little evidence of education's extrinsic value (Handsfield 1993). In D'Amato's terms, they had neither the situational nor structural rationales that would promote compliance with school rules for success.

Conclusion

Returning to the central question of whether the variability in school performance can best be explained by cultural variables or by contextual variables, it appears from the cases discussed that it is not so much one or the other as it is the dynamic interplay between the two, as immigrant groups respond to economic and educational opportunities both in the host country and in their countries of origin. To guide the analysis of the three cases I have utilized an interpretative framework that focuses on the rationales that influence student behaviour in school. I have suggested that for students to invest the effort required for academic success they need a strong or at least sufficient rationale for complying with school rules and doing what is expected of them. Following D'Amato (1993), I have distinguished two types of rationales. The first, termed structural rationales, are largely extrinsic to the schooling process itself and are most generally shaped by a student's family, community or ethnic group, including the group's 'folk theories' about how to get ahead in society. The second, termed situational rationales, stem from the intrinsic value which students find in the schooling experience itself. Students need one type of rationale or the other, or both, to 'play by the rules' at school.

In the cases reviewed in this chapter we find that some groups of students had far stronger structural rationales for persisting in school than others. In addition to ethnicity, we find that students' rationales were influenced by their gender, their social class and their generation in the United States. The immigrant Down Islanders believed by and large that educational credentials were a necessity if they were to be competitive in the job market, whether in St Croix or back in their home islands. Similarly, the Crucian girls, who wished to be economically independent, knew they needed a high school diploma in order to obtain entry-level jobs in the local government. For the Crucian boys, however, the diploma itself had little value. Moreover, they saw little connection between what they were learning in school and the blue collar government jobs they hoped to obtain. Like their older brothers and fathers, they expected to get a government job based on family connections, their status as native Crucians and their personal reputations. Once hired, they also expected that they would receive the on-the-job training in a particular trade.

For all West Indian students attending public schools in St Croix study, there was a sharp disjuncture between the formal school curriculum, which had been imported with little modification from the US mainland and the locally dominant African-Caribbean culture. At the time of field work more than half of the teachers had also been imported from the mainland United States and most had little understanding of the local culture. Crucian teachers, moreover, were largely from a different social class background than their pupils, and their behaviour exemplified a creolized version of European and American canons of respectability. In general, the girls felt more comfortable with the teachers than the boys and were more accepting of their authority. Boys, on the other hand, who were guided by the lower-class male African-Caribbean culture of reputation, found themselves frequently in direct conflict with many of their teachers. In sum, most Crucian boys found little intrinsic or extrinsic value in the schooling process itself and had little incentive to comply with teacher rules and expectations.

The Crucian boys' resistance to schooling was similar to that described in the literature on involuntary minority youth in the United States and working class white youth in Britain, males in particular (Ogbu 1991, Willis 1977).[20] These boys resented the outsiders who in their view had stolen their homeland and they refused to take jobs where outsiders would be their supervisors. They also resisted the authority of the native elites, including their Crucian teachers, whom they felt held a grudge against them because of their social class background. 'Slavery's done', these boys declared. Like other groups who see little structural rationale for accepting school routines (D'Amato 1993), these adolescent boys had a strong sense that they were constantly being put down by their teachers and treated like babies. In their own view they were young adults and too old to be 'bossed'.

The Down Islander boys were more willing to accommodate themselves to school routines than Crucian boys because they believed they needed school credentials to be competitive in the job market. They also harboured no similar resentments to the Crucian elite or to the continental business owners. Although in their own homelands they, too, had experienced domination and blocked opportunities for advancement at the hands of white oppressors and some members of the native elite, their migration to St Croix had changed this dynamic. The immigrant boys perceived the opportunity structure from a very different vantage point than the Crucian boys. Moreover, since few of these boys had permanent residence papers, they needed either to be in school or employed in order to legitimate their continued stay in the US Virgin Islands. They were grateful, therefore, for both the educational and employment opportunities available to them. There was variability within each group, of course, and not all the Down Islander boys applied themselves with diligence to their schooling, or were equally respectful of teacher authority, but classroom observations and interviews with the boys themselves, as well as their teachers, highlighted the differing school response patterns and mobility strategies of the two groups, one immigrant and one nonimmigrant.[21]

Turning to the two Valleyside studies, we find in the Punjabi case a group of students who had very strong structural rationales for persisting in school and staying out of trouble. If they misbehaved they could anticipate that their parents would withdraw them from school. Errant boys expected to be told that they had lost their chance for further schooling and, lacking credentials, sent to work in the fields. A girl whose behaviour was out of line could expect to be kept at home under the watchful eye of family members until her marriage could be arranged. Most Punjabi students also wanted to stay in school because it was their main opportunity to socialize with friends, to be exposed to American culture and to obtain the school credentials that would lead either to college or to a white collar job. For all these reasons they persevered even though they often experienced sharp conflicts within the classroom between Punjabi and American values and had to cope with a social climate where their religion, their culture and their identity were frequently misunderstood and even disparaged. In sum, their situational rationales for complying with school routines were weak, but their structural rationales were strong.

I find the Mexican case more difficult to explain, in part because the data which I gathered for that study are less complete. It is important to emphasize, however, that even though the Mexican and Punjabi immigrant parents occupied similar job niches on arrival in Valleyside – as farm labourers – their economic mobility strategies must be understood in terms of the structural niches they occupied in the old country. While most of the Punjabi Jat Sikhs had owned farms in India, had hired others to help work their land, had enjoyed high status as the elite of their villages, and had experience in maintaining a strong ethnic and religious identity in the face of assimilationist pressures, the Mexicans enjoyed no similar advantages. Moreover, once in Valleyside, the Mexicans formed no similar close-knit community that structured their children's activities. As in the Punjabi case, many of the Mexican youths were distinctly uncomfortable with the social climate at school.

They also felt that as a group Mexican students were unfairly disciplined and generally given less support by teachers. They saw plainly that white students and teachers viewed their culture as inferior to 'American' culture and their home language as inferior to English. Unlike the Punjabis, however, the Mexican youth enjoyed no sense of cultural superiority that helped to shield them from the full weight of racial hostilities. Nor did the Mexican youth face the very strong parental and community sanctions for misbehaviour at school or for apparent lack of diligence in school work that the Punjabis did. It seems that most Mexican students found little intrinsic value in their schooling experience; most also lacked a sufficiently powerful structural rationale to counterbalance the discomfort they felt with the social environment at school or to motivate them to invest great effort in their school work in spite of their discomfort. The exception to this were the students taking accelerated classes and the most recent arrivals, who, like recent arrivals from India, were separated for much of the day in ESL classes and who appreciated the intensive assistance they received with learning English.

Although these Mexican youths knew the difficulties of their parents' jobs and wanted something better for themselves, they lacked the Punjabis' optimism about their chances for the future. This was particularly true for the third generation youths, who appeared to have no clear group mobility strategies. For the most part, they also lacked role models within the Valleyside community of Mexicans who had been able to move ahead economically by persisting in school. Students tracked into remedial classes on entering high school appeared most vulnerable to the perceived assault on their identity at school and they readily banded together with peers to resist school authorities and their routines. A majority of the same students dropped out of school before completing 12th grade.

Such a result is not inevitable, however. As D'Amato (1993) suggests, classrooms can be reorganized to make education situationally rewarding for students. This is especially important for those students who lack a sufficient structural rationale for engaging academically at school. Classroom instruction and the larger school structures can also be reorganized to help validate rather than undermine students' identities and to provide students with the role models, tutorial assistance and the cultural capital required for school success. Further comparative research on immigrant school performance needs to take into account not only the cultural and contextual variables that originate outside the schools, but also the learning environments that exist for immigrant youngsters within the schools themselves.

Notes

1. For fuller discussion of the West Indian case, see Gibson 1976, 1982, 1991.
2. For more detailed discussion of the history and development of St Croix, see Dookhan 1974, Lewis 1972, and Lewisohn 1970.
3. I did not collect information on family income from the students in my three samples, but on the island's west end, where I carried out my field research, 45 per cent of all black families had incomes below the poverty level in 1979 (US Bureau of the Census 1984). In 1980 the median income was $7458 for all native-born black Virgin Islanders (includes St Thomas and St John, as well as St Croix), compared to $6533 for all immigrant black West Indians residing in the USVI (US Bureau of the Census 1985: table 90).
4. Findings come from three separate student samples. Sample A included all 273 students who were enrolled in grade seven in May 1974 at one of the island's two junior high schools. Sample B (N = 106) and Sample C (N = 75) were drawn from an ethnic census of all fourth and eighth graders enrolled in St Croix public schools in 1969 (Bramson 1969). Using both school records and interviews, I was able to follow these students' progress in school from 1969 to 1975.
5. Puerto Rican girls were also doing better than Puerto Rican boys, but less well than either the Down Islander or Crucian girls (Gibson 1976).
6. Almost all parents who could afford the tuition sent their children to one of the island's numerous private schools, many of which were church affiliated. Patterns of school persistence and achievement were reportedly far stronger in these schools, which served most of the continental children, one in five of the Crucian children and a smaller percentage of Puerto Rican and Down Islander children. Careful investigation of performance patterns at these schools was beyond the scope of my project, but conversations with teachers and parents indicated that the Crucian boys attending private schools generally did well academically, accepted teacher authority and remained in school through to grade 12.

7. In retrospect I realized that the types of student resistance and oppositional behaviour that I observed in St Croix in 1974–75 were strikingly similar to the behaviour of 'the lads' described by Willis (1977) in his now classic ethnography of working-class adolescent males in Britain.

8. The Down Islander boys who lacked permanent residence papers may also have been more reticent to turn to crime as an alternative, recognizing that a run-in with the law would likely result in their deportation.

9. The strategies used by Punjabis to acquire land and to build an ethnic enclave in Valleyside are discussed in Gibson (1988b).

10. Only recently has it become customary, even among Jats, for all sons to complete secondary school – ten years in India – and within our sample of parents a majority of the mothers and quite a few of the fathers were illiterate or semiliterate. More than one third of the mothers had no formal education and only one in ten had attended middle school or beyond. One fourth of the fathers had attended school for five years or less and fewer than half had completed secondary school.

11. In the 17 years since the original study, patterns have changed. Much like the longer settled Punjabi families in Britain, many Valleyside Punjabis now see that a daughter's education can lead her to better employment opportunities which, in turn, will aid the family and even enhance marriage arrangements (Bhachu 1985, Gibson and Bhachu 1988).

12. Support for this project has come from The Spencer Foundation, a University of California Presidential Grant for School Improvement, the University of California's Linguistic Minority Research Institute, UC MEXUS, and from the Bilingual Research Center, the Division of Social Sciences, and the Faculty Research Committee at UC, Santa Cruz.

13. Findings come from student questionnaires completed by all 113 students, semi-structured interviews carried out with 50 of the students and their parents, students' academic records, a faculty questionnaire and interviews with 30 teachers. All 113 students had two parents of Mexican descent. Another 12 students with only one parent of Mexican descent are excluded from this discussion. Five UCSC graduate students working on their masters theses assisted with the fieldwork.

14. Children whose parents have entered the country within the past three years for the purpose of working in the fields are eligible for services from the Migrant Education Program.

15. Most of the qualitative findings reported here are drawn from interviews with second generation students and their parents. Interviews with the third generation students and their US-born parents have not yet been fully analyzed.

16. Nine students were excluded from the analysis because they transferred to schools in other districts and we were unable to track their academic progress at their new schools.

17. Further research with larger samples and in additional locations is needed to test the generalizability of these findings.

18. Students with limited proficiency in English were assigned up to five periods of ESL (English as a Second Language) instruction each day, including classes in math, science and social studies, as well as English at various levels.

19. For fuller discussion of the findings emerging from the Mexican case see Gibson 1995a,b and 1998.

20. Following Ogbu, I use the term 'involuntary minority' to refer to groups incorporated into the host society involuntarily, most frequently by means of colonization, conquest, or slavery and assigned a subordinate position within it.
21. See Gibson and Ogbu (1991) and Ogbu and Simons (1998) for discussion of the immigrant/involuntary minority framework. The framework is helpful in explaining some of the variability between the two types of students, but it cannot explain the wide differences in school performance that exist either among different immigrant groups or within a single group (Gibson 1997).

References

Bhachu, P., 1985, *Twice Migrants. East African Sikh Settlers in Britain* (London: Tavistock Press)

Bramson, L., 1969, *An Ethnic Census of St Croix Schools. Appendix to R.O. Cornett, Plan for Higher Education on St Croix*, unpublished manuscript College of the Virgin Islands, St Croix, USVI

D'Amato, J., 1993. 'Resistance and compliance in minority classrooms', in: E. Jacob and C. Jordan (eds), *Minority Education. Anthropological Perspectives* (Norwood, NJ: Ablex)

Dirks, R., 1975, 'Ethnicity and ethnic group relations in the British Virgin Islands', in: J.W. Bennett (ed.), *The New Ethnicity* (St Paul: West Publishing)

Dookhan, I., 1974, *A History of the Virgin Islands of the United States* (Essex: Caribbean Universities Press for the College of the Virgin Islands)

Erickson, F., 1987, 'Transformation and school success. The politics and culture of educational achievement', *Anthropology and Education Quarterly* 18(4). Theme issue 'Explaining the School Performance of Minority Students', edited by E. Jacob and C. Jordan

Gibson, M.A., 1976, *Ethnicity and Schooling. A Caribbean Case Study*, unpublished PhD-dissertation, University of Pittsburgh

Gibson, M.A., 1982, 'Reputation and respectability. How competing cultural systems affect students' performance in school', *Anthropology and Education Quarterly* 13(1): 3–27

Gibson, M.A., 1987, 'Playing by the rules', in: G.D. Spindler (ed.), *Education and Cultural Process*, 2nd edn (Prospect Heights, IL: Waveland Press)

Gibson, M.A., 1988a, *Accommodation Without Assimilation. Sikh Immigrants in an American High School* (Ithaca, NY: Cornell University Press)

Gibson, M.A., 1988b, 'Punjabi orchard farmers. An immigrant enclave in rural California', *International Migration Review* 22(1): 28–50

Gibson, M.A., 1991, 'Ethnicity, gender and social class. The school adaptation patterns of West Indian youths', in: M.A. Gibson and J.U. Ogbu (eds), *Minority Status and Schooling. A Comparative Study of Immigrant and Involuntary Minorities* (New York: Garland Publishing)

Gibson, M.A., 1995a, 'Additive acculturation as a strategy for school improvement', in: R.G. Rumbaut and W.A. Cornelius (eds), *California's Immigrant Children. Theory, Research, and Implications for Educational Policy* (La Jolla, CA: Center for US-Mexican Studies, University of California, San Diego)

Gibson, M.A., 1995b, 'Promoting additive acculturation in schools', *Multicultural Education* 3(1): 10–12

Gibson, M.A., 1998, *Three Generations of Mexican-descent Students in a California High School*, unpublished manuscript, Department of Education, University of California, Santa Cruz

Gibson, M.A. (ed.), 1997, 'Ethnicity and school performance. Complicating the immigrant/involuntary minority typology', Theme issue *Anthropology and Education Quarterly* 28(3)

Gibson, M.A., and P.K. Bhachu, 1988, 'Ethnicity and school performance. A comparative study of South Asian pupils in Britain and America', *Ethnic and Racial Studies* 11(3): 239–62

Gibson, M.A., and J.U. Ogbu (eds), 1991, *Minority Status and Schooling. A Comparative Study of Immigrant and Involuntary Minorities* (New York: Garland Publishing)

Green, J.W., 1972, *Social Networks in St Croix, United States Virgin Islands*, PhD-dissertation, University of Washington

Handsfield, L.J., 1993, *Abstract and Concrete Attitudes among Mexican-descent High School Students*, Master's thesis, University of California, Santa Cruz

Jacob, E., and C. Jordan (eds), 1987, 'Explaining the school performance of minority students', Theme issue *Anthropology and Education Quarterly* 18(4)

Jacob, E., and C. Jordan (eds), 1993, *Minority Education. Anthropological Perspectives* (Norwood, NJ: Ablex)

La Brack, B., 1982a, 'Immigration law and the revitalization process. The case of the California Sikhs', *Population Review* 25(1/2): 59–66

La Brack, B., 1982b, 'Occupational specialization among rural California Sikhs. The Interplay of culture and economics', *Amerasia* 9(2): 29–56

Lewis, G.K., 1972, *The Virgin Islands* (Evanston, IL: Northwestern University Press)

Lewisohn, F., 1970, *St Croix under Seven Flags* (Hollywood, FL: Dukane Press)

Moorhead, M.C., 1973, *Mammon vs. History. American Paradise or Virgin Islands Home* (St Croix, VI: United People Party)

Nordheimer, J., 1973, 'Caribbean seeks way to give islanders share in tourism benefits', *New York Times*, 4 March

Ogbu, J.U., 1991, 'Immigrant and involuntary minorities in comparative perspective', in: M.A. Gibson and J.U. Ogbu (eds), *Minority Status and Schooling. A Comparative Study of Immigrant and Involuntary Minorities* (New York: Garland Publishing)

Ogbu, J.U., and H.D. Simons, 1998, 'Voluntary and involuntary minorities. A cultural-ecological theory of school performance with some implications for education', *Anthropology and Education Quarterly* 29(2): 155–88

O'Neill, E.A., 1972, *Rape of the American Virgins* (New York: Praeger)

Patterson, O., 1975, 'Context and choice in ethnic allegiance. A theoretical framework and Caribbean case study', in: N. Glazer and D.P. Moynihan (eds), *Ethnicity. Theory and Experience* (Cambridge, MA: Harvard University Press)

Senior, C., 1947, *The Puerto Rican Migrant in St Croix* (Puerto Rico: University of Puerto Rico, Social Science Research Center)

Suarez-Orozco, M.M., 1989, *Central American Refugees and US High Schools. A Psychosocial Study of Motivation and Achievement* (Stanford, CA: Stanford University Press)

US Bureau of the Census, 1973, *1970 Census of Population*. Vol. 1, *Characteristics of the Population*, pt. 55, Outlying areas, Virgin Islands. Washington DC

US Bureau of the Census, 1984, *1980 Census of Population*. Vol. 1, *Characteristics of the Population*, chap. C: General social and economic characteristics, pt. 55, Virgin Islands of the United States. Washington DC

US Bureau of the Census, 1985, *1980 Census of Population.* Vol. 1: *Characteristics of the Population*, chap. D: Detailed population characteristics, pt. 55, Virgin Islands of the United States. Washington DC

US Department of the Interior, 1976, *Annual Report of the US Government Comptroller for the Virgin Islands on the Government of the Virgin Islands, Fiscal Year ended June 30, 1975.* St Thomas, VI

Vermeulen, H., 1996, *The Concept of Culture in the Study of Immigrant Ethnic Groups*, paper presented at the conference 'Does culture make a difference', University of Amsterdam, 14–16 November

Willis, P.E., 1977, *Learning to Labour. How Working Class Kids Get Working Class Jobs* (Farnborough: Saxon House)

Wilson, P., 1973, *Crab Antics. The Social Anthropology of English-speaking Negro Societies of the Caribbean* (New Haven, CT: Yale University Press)

6

What the Jews Brought.
East-European Jewish Immigration
to the United States, c. 1900

Joel Perlmann

The story behind this article is well known: the East-European Jews came to the United States at the same time as many other European immigrant groups (between 1880 and 1920, see Table 6.1); yet the East-European Jewish immigrants and their offspring reached middle class status in fewer decades, or in fewer generations, than did other immigrant groups and their offspring. Explaining this phenomenon of rapid East-European Jewish upward mobility has been a staple product of American social science for at least two generations.[1] Indeed, this historical puzzle has received so much attention in discussions of ethnicity and mobility that any refinement of the arguments about Jewish upward mobility cannot help but bear on the way we think about ethnicity and mobility generally. More specifically, the case of the Jews has been prominent in American debates about structure and culture among the immigrants.

I was drawn to study the East-European Jewish immigration when I began to think about the variety of quantitative sources that might have been studied in earlier generations, but that could shed a good new light on the East-European Jewish immigration if these sources were subjected to analysis with the aid of a computer.[2]

I focus on a seemingly modest issue, the extent to which East-European Jewish immigrants to the United States were concentrated in each of two major sectors of economy. The first sector is manufacturing – especially in skilled trades such as tailoring, shoemaking or carpentry – and the second sector is commerce, in particular petty trade. This issue will not resolve all aspects of our puzzle, but it nonetheless does go to the heart of current social science interpretations of American Jewish social mobility.

One prevalent line of explanation for Jewish upward mobility, and I think really *the* prevalent line of explanation among social scientists today, stresses above all a structural fit in economic terms – that is, a fit between the immigrants occupational skills and the American economy. Or to put it another way, the distinctive Jewish economic mobility patterns in the United States, have had much to do with the premigration economic

Table 6.1   Jewish immigration to the United States: 1880–1924

Period	Number of Jewish Immigrants (in 000s)		% of Jewish Immigrants		Jewish Immigration as % of Total Immigration
	In Period (1)	Av. Per Yr (2)	From Russia (3)	From Aus.-H (4)	(5)
1881–89	204	23	68	26	4
1890–98	367	41	76	20	11
1899–1902	214	54	64	25	11
1903–07	615	123	78	15	12
1908–14	656	94	79	16	10
subtotal, 1881–1914	2057	61	76	19	9
1915–19	66	13	40	5	6
1920–24	287	57	38	28	10
1925–29	56	11	35	28	4
subtotal, 1915–29	408	27	38	24	7

Note: Nearly all of the pre-1914 Jewish immigration not accounted for in columns 3 and 4 was from Romania (4% of the 1881–1914 Jewish immigration, and 11% in 1915–24). The figures for the Russian and Austria-Hungarian Empires after 1914 involve estimation based on countries formerly part of the Empires.

Sources: Kuznets (1975: 35–126, especially table I) and US Bureau of the Census (1960).

position that the Jews had occupied earlier in Europe – that premigration economic position had provided the Jews with certain skills useful in the American economy. For centuries, the Jews had been concentrated in commercial occupations (typically petty trade), and (in eastern Europe especially) they had also been concentrated in artisanal crafts, crafts that were in the process of being transformed to more modern industrial working arrangements. Of these crafts, the most important was tailoring, but it was by no means the only important artisanal craft among Jews. Now, according to the prevalent social scientific argument that I am summarizing, it was the concentration in manufacturing handicrafts, in artisanal occupations, that was a special source of advantage to the Jews when they came to America – compared to a background of so many other groups in agricultural labour. Experience in petty trade may have helped too, just as other factors, like experience in urban places (or at least in small towns) rather than rural locales may have helped; but it was the manufacturing skills that were crucial. Manufacturing skills were transferrable skills and therefore, so the argument goes, former artisans were greatly over-represented among the Jewish immigrant arrivals. These artisan skills gave the Jews a crucial advantage compared to other immigrants who lacked such skills.

I could point to many formulations of this argument; but will just cite one example, by Calvin Goldscheider and Alan S. Zuckerman, *The Transformation of the Jews* (1984). This is an especially sophisticated book, based on very wide reading and impressive thinking about theoretical issues and about Jewish social history. Goldscheider and Zuckerman write:

> The migration [of East-European Jews to the United States] was selective on socioeconomic grounds. (...) There was a much higher proportion of skilled laborers (...) among immigrants than among the Jewish force in the Tsarist Empire. In addition, merchants and dealers were much less likely to emigrate during the first decades of mass emigration. They accounted for one third of the gainfully occupied Jews in Russia and 6 per cent of the immigrants. (...) Emigration occurred especially among artisans whose skills could be easily transferred abroad. (...) Fully two thirds of the Jews entering the United States had been engaged in manufacturing and mechanical pursuits in Europe, more than three fourths as skilled workers. (...) The selectivity of the Jewish migration fit into the particular labor and occupational opportunities in America and provided the Jews an enormous structural advantage over other immigrants in the pursuit of occupational integration and social mobility.
>
> (1984: 162–7)[3]

We have here a series of interlocking arguments: (1) East-European Jews had been concentrated in trade and handicrafts; (2) those in handicrafts were much more likely to emigrate; and (3) having emigrated, their artisanal skills gave them a crucial leg up in the American industrial economy. Now, in a word, I believe questions must be raised about the last two of these arguments. In particular, I am going to stress that the prevailing interpretation does not pay close enough attention to the tendency of East-European Jews to concentrate in commercial occupations, above all in petty trade.

We need to think about the concentration in trade in two ways. First, the phenomenon of occupational concentration is itself a topic that deserves our attention, because it amounts to a distinctive ethnic pattern of behaviour that needs to be explained. And vaguely pointing to 'industrial skills' will not adequately explain that move into trade. Second, the move into trade is not merely interesting because it is a distinct ethnic pattern; rather it is a crucially important pattern, since that move was the pivotal shift required for Jewish upward mobility. So to say that a vague appeal to industrial skills will not explain the move into trade is to say that the appeal to industrial skills will not explain a crucial feature of Jewish upward mobility.

However, the dominant trends in the social scientific and historical literature have tended to produce a curious and largely unconscious convergence of intellectual interests that led scholars to focus on the industrial skills rather than on the commercial orientation of the Jewish immigrants. First, when in 1907, Isaac Rubinow wrote authoritative summaries of the Russian Jewish economic situation and Jewish immigration to the United States, he was at great pains to contradict, and referred repeatedly to, 'the argument that the entire Jewish race is a race of traders and therefore exploiters', or 'the theory generally accepted both in Russia and in the United States that the European Jew is in the majority of cases a merchant, and only in America is transformed into a productive worker' (1907: 498, 500 and 506). He argued both that the percentage of Jews in industrial occupations was greater than popular conception would have it and that the immigration had been dramatically selective: a third of the Russian Jews but only 5 per cent of the immigrants were in commerce. Rubinow's work was later central to several influential papers by the economist and economic historian, Simon Kuznets. Kuznets extended Rubinow's analysis in several essays on these issues, most notably a magisterial book-length monograph, 'The Immigration of Russian Jews to the United States, Background and Structure', published in 1975. Through Rubinow and Kuznets, the argument worked its way into the work of social scientists interested in stressing the concrete skill advantages of the Jews – for example knowing how to use a needle and thread in a labour market demanding that skill. Social scientists could oppose this explanation based on skill advantage to the vague, self-congratulatory, and nostalgic mentions of cultural characteristics – traditions of learning, Jewish psychological traits, and so on – that formed a competing explanation for the East-European Jewish mobility patterns in the West.[4]

Added to this early defensiveness about the commercial characteristics of the Jews, and to the later emphasis on the explanatory power of the concrete skill advantages of the Jews, was the interest of labour historians and of social historians generally who had been strongly influenced by the concerns of the new labour history – historians as different as Herbert Gutman, Irving Howe and Susan Glenn, for example. These influential historians have written perceptively about both the strong working-class character of the East-European Jewish immigrants, the Jewish socialist movements of Russia that were brought to the United States and the long-standing political position of the Jews on the left.[5]

All three of these orientations have much more than a grain of truth to them – concern to correctly state the proportions of Jews not working in commerce (Rubinow, Kuznets), interest in the socioeconomic, rather than the cultural origins of Jewish social patterns (Goldscheider and Zuckerman), and the concern with Jewish immigrant labour history (Howe, Gutman, Glenn). I do believe, however, that they have tended to lead us away from an important reality, the considerable concentration of Jews in commerce – petty trade in this context – and therefore these orientations make it difficult to adequately explain the puzzle of the rapid Jewish upward mobility.

Now, as already mentioned, there has been another line of explanation (much less favoured today by most social scientists), that stresses cultural continuities between East-European Jewish life and Jewish behaviour in the new world. A classic formulation of this cultural argument is to be found in Nathan Glazer's survey, 'Social Characteristics of American Jews, 1654–1954' (1960). There Glazer stressed the significance of Jewish commercial involvement, although he does so as part of a far more encompassing cultural argument than the argument I suggest in this essay. Reflecting the social psychology of the early 1950s, Glazer was eager to show that psychological propensities that propelled the Jews into middle class life, and that these propensities had been reenforced over centuries of experience in Europe.

> The modern student of social phenomena cannot stop at psychological explanations. (...) Ultimately social explanations must resort to history and explain a present peculiarity by discovering an earlier one. We think the explanation for Jewish success in America is that the Jews, far more than any other immigrant group, were engaged for generations in the middle-class occupations, in the professions and in buying and selling. (...) The special occupations of the middle class – trade and the professions – are associated with a whole complex of habits. Primarily these are the habits of care and foresight. The middle class person (...) has been taught the world is open to him, and with proper intelligence and ability, and with resources well used, he may advance himself.
>
> (1960: 1722–4)

Glazer, goes on to cite other Jewish cultural legacies as well. Like Calvinism, he says, 'Judaism too, emphasizes the traits that business men and intellectuals require' (ibid.: 1723). Appealing explicitly to Weber here, Glazer argues that 'Jewish Puritanism' stimulated the success of the Jews in European trade (although he acknowledges the economic and political factors that operated to achieve the same outcome) and the religious culture, as well as the class-based culture, produced a 'mind-set' conducive to Jewish business and intellectual success in America.

I cite Glazer's arguments (now nearly half-a-century old) partly in order to give an example of a cultural, as opposed to a skills-based structural, argument. However, I also cite Glazer's argument in order to forestall a possible misunderstanding of my own goals here. For my purposes, it is not necessary to make the claims Glazer does – not to draw on so many elements of Jewish history, nor to assume that these elements created so many characteristics of a 'mind-set'. Rather, I argue that there were characteristics of economic behaviour that radically distinguished the Jewish immigrants from other immigrants in this period, particularly the rate at which the Jews made the choice to enter trade. And finally, the rapid economic improvement of the Jewish immigrants and their children is directly related to the concentration of the Jews in commercial rather than manual labour occupations in the first half of the 20th century (although I do not present any new evidence on this last point). This ethnically distinctive characteristic, the propensity to rapidly enter trade, cannot be adequately explained, I will argue, by simply referring to the Jews' ability to transfer concrete manufacturing skills into the American labour market. On the contrary, this characteristic of their behaviour suggests a continuity with an earlier history of feeling that commercial pursuits were the natural pursuits for them – that is, an earlier history in commercial endeavours (in this case, in petty trade). I will return at the end of the chapter to the issue of whether this propensity to enter trade should be interpreted as a 'cultural' attribute. For the moment I simply want to stress that this propensity is the only distinctive ethnic characteristic I discuss in this chapter; for my purposes here, all other arguments about Jewish cultural continuities between Jews in Russia and Russian Jewish immigrants in the United States can be ignored.[6]

As I mentioned, I am sceptical about two of the three interlocking arguments about Jewish economic mobility: first, that the Jews who left eastern Europe for the United States were much more likely to have worked in industrial (especially handicraft) occupations rather than in commercial occupations and second, that this background of industrial skills in fact largely accounts for unusually rapid Jewish mobility in the American industrial economy. I will consider each claim in turn.

The claim for the occupational selectivity of the Jewish migration has a long and distinguished lineage, dating back at least to the 1906 work of Isaac Rubinow that I have already mentioned. Rubinow juxtaposed the figures on Jewish occupations reported in the first Census of the Russian Empire (in 1897) and the figures on the prior occupations reported by Jewish immigrant arrivals during the years 1899–1905, that were tabulated in the *Annual Reports* of the United States Commissioner of Immigration. The immigrant arrivals were much more likely to report prior work in manufacturing and much less likely to report prior work in trade than was the case among the Jews of Russia. Later, Kuznets used the same figures, and elaborated on them somewhat. Nevertheless, the work of Rubinow, Kuznets and all other such comparisons, were limited to a fairly crude comparison: namely, the occupations of all Russian Jews compared to the occupations of all Jews arriving in the United States – with no controls for age, sex, region or even country of origin. Since I have been working extensively with very detailed published tabulations in the Russian Census (much more detailed than the summary tables cited by Rubinow and Kuznets) and since at the same time I have gone back to the manuscript passenger lists that report the characteristic of each arriving immigrant to the United

States, I could make a much more precise comparison between the most important group of East-European Jewish arrivals, those from Russia, and the groups of gainfully employed Jews in specific regions of Russia.[7] Now not all the Jews were coming from Russia, of course, but by this time three-quarters were. And in any case in order to test for a occupational selectivity of migration, a comparison of groups precisely matched up is best. Indeed, because the data is especially strong on the Russian Jews and because so many of the East-European Jews came from there, I will limit my discussion in the rest of this article to the Jews of Russia and the Russian Jewish immigrants to the United States.

I coded the occupations of the immigrant sample members drawn from the passenger lists in the same classification scheme that the Russian Census used for occupations. As a result, it is possible to compare with some precision the occupations of the Russian-Jewish immigrant arrivals and the occupations of the Jews in the Russian Pale of Settlement at about the same time. Table 6.2 presents the figures on the Jewish occupations in Russia; note the great involvement in trade. Indeed in the '7 core provinces' from which most of the immigration was coming (see Figure 6.1),[8] Jews accounted for nine-tenths of everyone involved in trade and a third of all Jews worked in the trade sector.

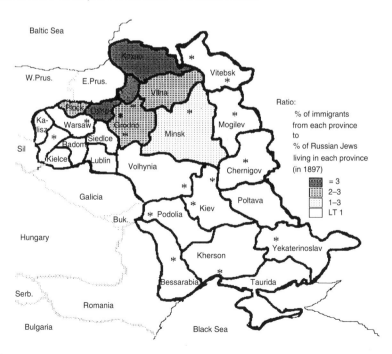

Figure 6.1   Provincial origins of Russian-Jewish immigrant arrivals to the US, 1900

Table 6.2   Jewish occupations in the Pale of Settlement, 1897

Industrial Sector	Pale: Men and Women		7 Core Provinces: Men and Women	
	% of All Jews with Occupations	% that Jews Comprise of All in this Sector	% of All Jews with Occupations	% That Jews Comprise of All in this Sector
trade – in agriculture	15	78	12	92
trade – other	19	69	14	85
mfg. – clothing	18	51	19	68
mfg. – other	20	25	24	46
labour/personal service	13	13	12	16
transport*	3	21	4	33
agriculture	3	1	4	1
military	3	6	3	6
all other**	7	19	8	27
Total (000s):	100	30	100	41
non-agricultural, civilian workforce***	[1264]	[4196]	[323]	[778]

* Nearly all carters and draymen
** Includes (in about equal proportions) (a) 'clergy, non-Christian', 'persons serving about churches, etc.', 'teachers and educators' and (b) miscellaneous groups of other workers (included among whom were all other professionals).
*** For the sake of meaningful comparisons with the non-Jewish population, the total row is limited to the non-agricultural civilian workforce.
Source: From Source a, note 2. Nearly all Jews in the Russian Empire were confined to the 25 western provinces of the Pale of Settlement, including principally Russian Poland, and parts of Lithuania, White Russia and western Ukraine. The 7 core provinces refer to provinces in the Northeast of the Pale from which most Russian Jewish immigrants originated.

On the other hand, Jewish immigrants arriving in the United States were much more likely to say they were in manufacturing occupations than were the Jews in the Russian Pale (Table 6.3). When we adjust for the age, sex, and region of origin of the emigrants, the contrast between the relevant Jews in Russia and the Russian Jewish immigrant arrivals was somewhat muted, and the proportion in trade slightly less under represented. Nevertheless most of the under-representation in trade and over-representation in manufacturing is not adjusted away; there was a big difference of the sort that Rubinow and Kuznets had discussed. In Kuznets' comparison (1975), the contrast was between 7 per cent in trade among the immigrants and 31 per cent in trade in the Pale; after all my adjustments the contrast is still a noteworthy 11 versus 28 per cent. And the manufacturing workers are still over represented among the immigrants 66 versus 43 per cent.

Table 6.3 The occupations of Jews in the Pale (1897) and of Jewish immigrant arrivals from Russia (1899/1900)

Sector	% Jews in the Pale				% Jewish Immigrant Arrivals from Russia, 1900 – Sample Data	
	Female	Male			Male	Female
		No Adjustment	Adjusting for Region**			
			Only	And for Age		
trade	24	36	31	28	11	1
clothing mfg.	17	18	18	18	32	78
– garment mfg.	na	11	11	11	23	na
– shoe mfg.	na	7	7	7	9	na
other mfg.\ labourers	11	22	24	25	34	7
personal service	41	6	5	5	20	13
transport	0	5	5	5	**	0
agriculture	2	3	4	3	2	0
military	0	3	4	9	0	0
other	5	8	8	7	1	1
total	100	100	100	100	100	100
total N	na	na	na	na	1091	108

* The occupational distribution when workers in the various provinces of the Pale are included in the same proportions as are found in the sample of immigrants (in column 4); the estimated age distribution for workers 20–39 years of age.
** Less than half of 1%; included with agriculture.
Sources: Russian figures from Source a, note 2, US figures from Source b, note 2.

However, there is more to say about the occupational reports of these immigrant arrivals and specifically about the reliability of the occupational reports. It is possible that some Jews may indeed have lied about prior occupation, because they, like Rubinow, knew that Jews were viewed as an unproductive commercial class, instinctively drawn to trade. Nontrivial proportions who had worked in trade may have said they had been involved in something else to avoid the stigma. Alternatively, even if they did not lie, many may still have given a misleading report; they may have answered in terms of the sort of work they expected to get in the United States, not in terms of the sort of work they had actually had done in Europe. A peddler might have said he was a labourer for example and someone without skills may have said 'tailor'.

Some evidence is available to support the hypothesis that a notable minority of Jewish immigrants reported themselves out of trade as they entered the United States. In 1909, a well-known United States Senate commission, known as the Dillingham Commission, took up the issue of immigration. They undertook a remarkable amount of survey research, interviewing many thousands of immigrants. In one of these surveys, they asked immigrants in industry a host of questions, including the nature of their occupations prior to arrival in the United States. Fortunately, thousands of 'Russian Hebrews' and 'Other Hebrews' (as they were designated) were canvassed. The percentage indicating a background in trade was much closer to what we would expect in the Russian Jewish population than to what the Russian Jewish immigrant arrivals were reporting at the gate. For example, among 1057 Russian Hebrew male clothing workers in New York City, 19 per cent claimed a background in trade; among 480 such workers in Chicago, 25 per cent claimed a background in trade, and so on (see Table 6.4).[9]

Now these surveys were undertaken independently in several different cities so it is unlikely that any local city biases determined the outcomes. Second, the workers surveyed were found in industrial work, not in commerce. Presumably had the survey covered immigrants in the trade sector of these cities, the reports of a background in trade back in Europe would have been greater still, given a degree of occupational continuity. Third, these immigrants, many of whom had been resident in the United States for several years, were unlikely to regard these government interviews as especially threatening when the latter asked about prior occupation in Europe. By contrast, immigrant hopefuls, when they filled out the passenger lists at the point of seeking entry to the United States, might well have felt threatened by the government inquiry into their European background. At the time of immigration, then, the incentive to lie may have been great. We cannot rule out, of course, a possible tendency, in the city surveys, to exaggerate one's earlier experience; but if so, and if the exaggeration was in the direction of claiming experience in trade, that in itself is revealing of a wider connection to trade as a plausible higher status.

Table 6.4 The occupations of Jewish immigrant men prior to their immigration to the United States: 1909 (from the US Immigration Commission Reports)

Type of Employment 1909	Prior Occupation of the 'Hebrew–Russian'					Prior Occupation of the 'Hebrew–Other'				
	%Trade	% Mfg clthg	% Mfg other	% Other	N	% Trade	% Mfg Clthg	% Mfg Other	% Other	N
Clothing workers										
NYC	19	63	13	95	1 057	29	59	5	7	509
Chicago	25	53	13	91	480	27	48	9	16	147
Baltimore	30	50	13	7	267			na		
Other workers – US										
Shoe	21	52	18	9	272			na		
Silk	5	91	1	3	185					
Textile	24	34	29	87	100					
Meat	18	27	31	24	153					

na – not applicable: less than 100 respondents.
Source: Note 2, source c.

In a word, then, the evidence that those in trade were so very unlikely to come to the United States is at best problematic, and a good deal less certain than has been claimed across the nine decades since Rubinow. A modest amount of the supposed occupational self selection away from trade was no doubt due to the nature of the immigration stream (age, sex, regional origin); more important, surveys of immigrants in the United States contradict the reports at the gates on this point. This evidence for bias in the passenger list data is not conclusive; however, the evidence does show that the argument in favour of selectivity is far more problematic than had been appreciated. I suspect there was indeed some occupational selectivity of the sort Rubinow and Kuznets claimed, but considerably less than they claimed.

Moreover, there is also another consideration relevant to evaluating the significance of the occupational selectivity in favour of industrial workers. Recall that the great majority of the European Jews in 'industrial occupations' were in fact artisans; artisans working in a more or less traditional setting, a setting of small shops with high proportions of self-employed individuals. Even those who were not themselves self-employed observed self-employment in the context of the small shop, that is to say observed it at close range. Therefore, many of those classified as 'manufacturing workers' in their employment prior to emigration would also have had some considerable background with the world of buying and selling, the world of running a kind of small business. And of course, from a social point of view, these East-European Jewish artisans lived in close proximity with the rest of Jews in the same town or city and a third of that community of Jews were in trade.

So for numerous reasons, the lines between those who had been 'skilled industrial workers' and those who had worked as 'merchants and dealers' was far less clear cut than some of the social scientific discussion would lead one to think. In order to appreciate the size of this trade sector, recall (see Table 6.2) not only the proportions of Jews engaged in trade in the Russian Jewish Pale of Settlement, but also the predominance of Jews among all engaged in trade there. Given that predominance, it is difficult to see how many more Jews could possibly have been engaged in trade in the Pale. All this relates directly to my larger argument, namely that more attention must be paid to the issue of Jewish trade and not to expect too much explanatory power to flow from the Jewish advantage in 'skilled industrial work'. And these considerations about the blurred line between artisanry and trade in Europe also bear on the issue of occupational selectivity in the migration. Thus, if I can show that many more Russian Jewish immigrants had worked in the trade sector in Russia than has been previously supposed, it will be easier for me to make the claim that trade was central to the experience and outlook of these immigrants. However, it is possible for me to stress the role of trade for the immigrants even if I cannot establish that more of these immigrants had worked in trade than has been supposed;

I can do so because even among those who had a background in 'manufacturing' the particular nature of that manufacturing background was typically artisanal and thus close to the experience of petty trade.

I turn now to the evidence of early Russian Jewish immigrant occupational mobility in the United States. Here I draw on the 1910 and 1920 censuses, in particular, on huge national samples of individuals that have been selected from the manuscript schedules of these censuses; these datasets are known as the public use microdata samples and each sample includes data on many hundreds of thousands of individuals. With such large national samples, we can draw out all sorts of substantively interesting subgroups. There is another huge advantage to these datasets. In both 1910 and 1920 the United States Census asked for information on mother tongue. By focusing on the Russian-born, who gave Yiddish as their mother tongue, criterion also eliminates virtually no Jewish immigrant from Russia (Perlmann 1997).

I have limited the analysis to male immigrants who had arrived in the United States during a period of about a dozen years (between 1897 and 1910) and I have limited the analysis also to those who were old enough to have held an adult occupation before they left Europe. That is, I limited the analysis to those who were at least 17 years of age when they arrived in the United States. The two samples were selected independently from the census manuscripts of two different enumerations, 1910 and 1920. Thus they do not include the same individuals; these samples include different people, but people selected to be the same on numerous characteristics, namely nativity, date of arrival, age at arrival, mother tongue and sex. I have classified my subsamples of immigrants into three groups. The first is the Russian-born, Yiddish mother tongue group, on whom I have been focusing. By the time of the 1910 and 1920 censuses, the Russian-born were about four-fifths of all the relevant Yiddish mother tongue immigrant arrivals, so the patterns we will observe would have been about the same if I had included all Yiddish mother tongue immigrants.

Now, what other groups of immigrants should be distinguished? Recall that the theory I am challenging stresses the importance of artisan skills, 'the industrial skills', of the Russian Jewish immigrants. I therefore classify the rest of the immigrants in the 1910 and 1920 samples according to the prevalence of skilled workers among them (see Table 6.5A). Upon arrival, the East-European Jewish immigrants were indeed much more likely than the rest of the immigrants to tell the immigration authorities that they had had a prior occupation in skilled manual work – in fact, whereas 70 per cent of the Jews claimed a background in skilled work, only 22 per cent of immigrants generally indicated such a background.

Nevertheless, even if the Jews were the most likely to claim such experience, there were some other groups that were almost as likely as the Jews to claim experience with skilled manual work, most notably the English and Scottish immigrants. There were many English and Scots, so we can study

Table 6.5   Occupations of immigrants to the United States, 1899–1920
A. Occupations of the immigrant groups at time of entry, 1899–1914

Percentage of the Immigrant Group whose Occupations at Time of Entry to US were classified as 'Skilled'	Hebrew	English and Scottish	All Other
	70%	58%	15%

Note: Skilled here includes also 'professional', 1% of the Hebrew, 8% of the English and Scottish and 1% of all other.

B. Occupations of male immigrants in the 1910 and 1920 United States Censuses – men who had arrived 1897–1910, at adult-work age (17 or older)

Occupations by Industrial Sector	Immigrants by Origin					
	Russian-born, Ymt		English and Scottish		All Other	
	In 1910 Census	In 1920 Census	In 1910 Census	In 1920 Census	In 1910 Census	In 1920 Census
Trade	28	52*	6	12	8	15
Garment mfg	29	13	1	0	2	1
Other mfg	29	24	54	49	45	45
all other	15	10	39	39	45	39
Total	100	100	100	100	100	100
% self employed	36	48	8	14	10	20
N =	463	688	409	610	7453	8558

* Includes 15% in wholesale or retail apparel trade.
Sources: Panel A taken from Hersch (1931: 491). Panel B from Note 2, source d. The Russian-born comprised 79% of all male Yiddish-mother-tongue immigrants with an occupation. Since sampling ratios differ for the two census years, the absolute numbers should not be compared across sample years.

them effectively enough, and the percentage of English and Scottish immigrant arrivals who claimed skilled work as their occupation was 58 per cent. Well, 58 per cent is not as high as the 70 per cent figure among the Jews. But compared to the group of all other immigrants, the English and Scottish percentage skilled seems very close to percentage skilled among the Jews. In the group of all other immigrant arrivals – that is, all immigrant arrivals except Hebrews, English, Scots – only 15 per cent claimed to have had a prior occupation in skilled manual work. This huge residual group includes great numbers of Italians and Slavs.

Now, if what characterizes the distinctiveness of the East-European Jews is that they came with industrial skills, does much the same occupational mobility pattern characterize the English and Scottish immigrants? Do we find, that the Jews had patterns of occupational concentration like those of the English and Scots – or at least that the Jewish pattern of occupational concentration was far more similar to the pattern of English and Scots than to the pattern found among the group of all other immigrants?

I am aware, of course, that the precise sort of skilled occupation in which a group is concentrated makes a big difference; the Jewish immigrant arrivals had a very high concentration in garment manufacturing, the English and Scots did not. I return to that point shortly. But at a minimum, requiring that our explanation of Jewish advantage stress that the Jews were concentrated not merely in skilled manufacturing, but in a particular type of industry, would sharpen our explanation. For example, it would lead us to speculate that it was not merely the experience in skilled work that mattered; rather, the garment trade was especially conducive to moving into self-employment and trade, probably because it did not require a large capital outlay to get started (it is cheaper to buy a sewing machine than to build an automobile plant). However, I also want to stress that we should not make too much of this point; the garment industry may have been distinctive, but it was not unique in allowing for entry with relatively little investment.

Table 6.5B shows us the percentage of each group of immigrants in trade, as shown in the 1910 and 1920 censuses. In 1910 and in 1920, we find that there is no difference whatever between the percentages in trade among English and Scots on the one hand and among the group of all other immigrants on the other. The premigration skill advantage did not lead the English and Scots into trade. On the other hand, the Jews show a much greater concentration in trade already in 1910 and sustained in 1920. The same exercise can be performed, with the same results, by substituting self-employment for trade in the comparisons: the percentage self-employed was not higher among the English and Scottish than among the group of all other immigrants (if anything, the reverse was the case); but the percentage of self-employment was very much higher among the Jews than among either of these groups. These are not the outcomes that a theory appealing strictly to transferable industrial skills would predict.

One reason not to try to explain too much by the Jewish concentration in the garment industry was already noted: this industry was not the only one requiring low capital to start. Another reason not to try to explain too much by the Jewish concentration in the garment industry is that the gravitation to trade was *not* by and large simply a shift from making garments to selling garments. Table 6.5B shows that 52 per cent of the Jews in 1920 worked in trade. But the footnote to the 1920 figure shows that only 15 per cent worked in the retail or wholesale apparel trade. To put it differently,

Table 6.6 Recent immigrants in 1910: those 1910 sample members from Table 6.5B who had arrived 1905–10

Occupation, industry and self-employment	Immigrants by Origin		
	Russian-born, Ymt %	English and Scottish %	All Other %
employees – skilled manual in mfg or construc.	24	30	9
self-employed – skilled manual in mfg or construc.	5	1	1
self-employed – in trade	15	0	2
self-employed – nec	7	4	3
employees – nec	49	65	85
total	100	100	100
N =	241	253	4493

Source: Note 2, source d

Table 6.7 Immigrants by sector in 1920: the 1920 sample members shown in Table 6.5B

Occupation, Industry and self-employment	Immigrants by Origin		
	Russian-born, Ymt %	English and Scottish %	All Other %
employees – skilled manual in mfg or construc.	10	24	13
self-employed – skilled manual in mfg or construc.	3	1	1
self-employed – in trade	35*	4	7
self-employed – nec	9	9	12
employees – nec	42	61	67
total	100	100	100
% employers	10	15	5
N =	688	610	8558

* Includes 6% self-employed in the wholesale or retail apparel trade.
Source: Note 2, source d.

even if the wholesale and retail apparel trade were *excluded* from the 'trade' category, no less than 36 per cent of the Jewish men in this 1920 subsample would still be listed in trade, two to three times the proportion in trade found in either of the other two groups of immigrants. A close look at the Jews in the sample might turn up still others in trade who were connected to clothing in one way or another. Nevertheless, since retail and wholesale apparel is the most obvious way for traders in garments to be listed, and since only 15 per cent of the Jews were found in retail and wholesale apparel, there is plenty of room for a margin of error.

Two other comparisons from the same datasets appear in Tables 6.6 and 6.7. Table 6.6 restricts attention to recent arrivals only – that is, it limits attention to the 1910 census and it shows those who have arrived only during the years since 1905 – so these were men who had been in the United States for a maximum of five years. Among this group, we should be able to observe an early stage in the process of economic adaptation. Was the reliance on artisan skills (especially in apparel) clearer here? Both the English and Scots and the Jews exhibit similar proportions in skilled manual work and higher proportions than among the other immigrants. Nevertheless, more Jewish skilled manual workers were already self-employed and the percentage of proprietors in trade is already much higher among the Jews. Once again, the premigration skill advantage would not predict the distinctive Jewish pattern.

Finally, Table 6.7 gives us, as it were, the other end of the process; it focuses on those who had been in the United States for a long time (10–23 years). The major change is the Jewish shift into self-employment in trade, apparently drawing from all other categories. And while this group includes those in apparel trade, only 6 per cent of the Jews are self-employed traders in apparel; 29 per cent are self-employed traders in other lines.

How then should we explain these patterns of Jewish immigrant occupational concentration? I want to distinguish between three lines of explanation for the patterns we have just seen in the 1910 and 1920 censuses. These are not the only possible explanations, but these three lines of explanation all share a common feature: they all stress the premigration economic position of the Jews. The first line of interpretation is the one I described at the outset as the belief prevailing among many social scientists. In this view, the Jews started in skilled work in small shops, especially in the garment industry and from that basis they were poised for work in trade when they did well through skilled industrial work; the Jews knew (for example) how to use a needle and thread, and that knowledge gave economic advantage that in turn led them into trade. This is the line of argument that I have tried to argue cannot stand alone. If this argument were adequate, the English and Scottish immigrants should not have provided such contrasting patterns to those of the Jews. Nor can we resolve the problem by noting that the Jews were concentrated in the garment industry; there were other low capital industries, and in any case very impressive percentages of the Jews appear to have been engaged in trade outside apparel. A second line of explanation could be regarded as a friendly amendment to the structural fit approach. I would urge that the transferability of specific skills was more complex than has been thought and that skills of buying and selling were also relevant. These buying and selling skills were relevant in the same way that the prior experience in industrial skills was relevant. Jews knew about petty capitalist ventures, about how to buy and sell, just as they knew how to use a needle and thread. Thus they came with two sorts of skills useful in an industrial economy.

Finally, in the third line of argument, the Jews' familiarity with trade also involves another dimension; a dimension that we might say is closer to an argument about premigration cultural values. The Jews may have been, to paraphrase the anti-Semites of that day, drawn to trade, predisposed to it – or more precisely, that they accorded trade a higher status, found it more pleasant, or (quite apart from skills) found it more familiar. More generally: an ethnic preference for certain kinds of work may create patterns that cannot be easily explained without such preference and by definition these preferences are not shared by all immigrant groups who might share the advantage of transferable industrial skills.

Well, then, if there are two forms of 'the propensity to enter trade' argument – one based on transferable commercial skills and the other on a 'cultural' preference for trade – can we, and should we, chose between them? I want to tentatively suggest that this is a case in which the cultural variant of the explanation is so close to a structural variant that it is difficult to imagine a way to test between them, at least not with any data of the sort I have available. A rational choice theorist might protest, saying, that if the cultural variant of the argument means anything, it means that we should expect a behavioural difference in outcome predicted by the second and third lines of explanation I have laid out – between the structural argument about skills in trade and the cultural argument about a preference or taste for trade. And so we should be able to explore whether the Jews entering trade did so to an extent that was economically irrational; that other ethnic groups facing the same economic choices did not enter trade. Perhaps one could in fact test such a formulation (making the additional assumption that income data could be interpreted as a measure of economic rationality).

If the Jews did engage in such irrational economic behaviour, we might then conclude that the cultural dynamic operated. However, even if we adopted this rigorous separation of the two variants of the argument about a propensity to enter commerce, other complications can be expected. Suppose, that the Jews in fact entered commerce in proportions that suggest non-rational behaviour when judged by criteria derived from other groups rate of movement into trade (or from skilled industrial occupations into trade). It might still be the case that among the Jewish immigrants this supposedly irrational rate of entry into trade was advantageous. After all, at a minimum, it is not irrelevant to speculate that those who are especially drawn to a line of work may also be especially likely to succeed in that line of work.

We can conceive of an abstract, subtle distinction between skills and values, and it is I think often useful to keep that distinction in mind. Nevertheless, when the 'values' themselves concern judgements about kinds of work, the distinction between 'skills' and 'values' become tightly intertwined even at the conceptual level, and they are especially unlikely to be differentiated at the empirical level. It is, therefore, sufficient unto the day to argue that an ethnically distinctive pattern of entering commercial occupations can be observed among these Jewish immigrants. In order to explain that pattern, we need one or both variants of the commercial emendation to the manual skills argument – that the Jews exploited experience in trade as well as in industrial work, or that in addition to all this the Jews also had a preference for trade; we need at least one of those arguments if we are going to make sense of the Russian Jewish economic patterns in the new world.

Notes

1. For a review see Perlmann 1988.
2. The sources re-analyzed for this chapter are:
   a) from the published volumes of the *1897 Russian Census*: virtually all the data relevant to Jews published for each of approx. 230 local administrative areas (uezds) and for approx. 250 cities and towns in the Pale of Settlement; and parallel provincial-level data on all peoples of the Empire.
   b) from US Lists of arriving immigrants (the manuscript *Passenger Lists*): A sample of 5300 Jewish immigrants reaching the Port of New York in 1899–1900, and a second sample of 3600 Jewish immigrants reaching the Port of New York in 1907–08. The passenger lists include information on religion, mother tongue, age, country, province, last residence, occupation, prior stay in US, amount of money brought and so on.
   c) from the published *Reports of the United States Immigration Commission* (1911): information on the occupation of 'Hebrew' immigrants prior to immigration.
   d) from the public use microdata samples of the *US Census* of 1910 and 1920: a sample of Yiddish-mother-tongue immigrants.
   Note: Sources a, b and d are large, machine-readable datasets.
3. See also, for example, Steinberg 1981.
4. Kuznets 1975, Rubinow 1907: 498, 500 and 506.
5. See Glenn 1990, Gutman 1977, Howe 1976. There is, of course, also an older genre of labour union histories of the 'Jewish Unions'. See, among many others, Herberg 1952 and Yivo 1961.

6. One other formulation dealing with Jewish cultural continuity that has gone largely unnoticed is worth mentioning in this context. Simon Kuznets concludes his magisterial monograph on the characteristics of Russian Jewish immigrants with a reminder. 'Our account dealt mainly with the measurable. (…) These records do not reflect directly the major features of the historical heritage of Russian Jewry that shaped the human capital transferred to the United States by immigration. It is this transfer of human capital that constitutes the essential content of migration (…) the more fundamental characteristics of capacity for social organization and for adjustment to the challenges of a new environment. Nor do they describe the long-standing scale of priorities inherited from the past and likely to shape the goals of immigrants and their descendants for several generations after their arrival in the country of destination. One may assume that after centuries of coexistence with hostile majorities, after migrations from one country to another in Europe and the Middle East, and after self-selection over time by the loss of some of its members, the Jewish people in Europe and especially in its largest subgroup in Tsarist Russia, must have acquired a distinctive equipment in human capital. (…) But the tools needed for such a study of the historical heritage of Russian or East European Jewry are not those of economics and demography; and the above account, long as it is, must be left incomplete' (1975: 123–4). Thus, the author of the most detailed argument for transfer of concrete manufacturing skills was not willing to rule out other sorts of transfer. Kuznets focuses on the experience of minority status, it appears, as the primary engine in the creation of this 'distinctive equipment in human capital', and he does not claim to say in what specific respects the distinctiveness mattered. Nevertheless, I see no reason to think his choice to close his essay in this deliberate way can be dismissed as a throw-away comment that he took lightly.
7. A fuller description of this comparison of occupations may be found in Perlmann 1996a.
8. See Perlmann 1996a and 1996b.
9. In a footnote to his 'Opportunities and some pilgrims' progress. Jewish immigrants from Eastern Europe in the United States, 1890–1914', Arcadius Kahan recognized that Rubinow (and by extension Kuznets) had overstated the case for selective migration. Kahan wrote 'The various inquiries conducted not at the time of entry into the United States but years later, reveal that the share of those gainfully employed in commerce prior to their arrival varied between 20–30 per cent of the total employed' (1986: 114–15). I assume that the 'various inquiries' Kahan had in mind were in fact these reports of the United States Immigration Commission.

References

Glazer, N., 1960, 'Social characteristics of American Jews, 1654–1954', in: L. Finkelstein (ed.), *The Jews*, 3rd edn (New York: Harper)

Glenn, S., 1990, *Daughters of the Shtetl. Life and Labor in the Immigrant Generation* (Ithaca NY: Cornell University Press)

Goldscheider, C., and A.S. Zuckerman, 1984, *The Transformation of the Jews* (Chicago: University of Chicago Press)

Gutman, H., 1977, *Work, Culture and Society in Industrializing America. Essays in American Working-Class and Social History* (New York: Vintage Books)

Herberg, W., 1952, 'The American Jewish labor movement', *American Jewish Yearbook*

Hersch, L., 1931, 'International migration of the Jews', in: W.F. Wilcox (ed.), *International Migrations* (New York)

Howe, I., 1976, *World of Our Fathers* (New York: Simon & Schuster)

Kahan, A., 1986, *Essays in Jewish Social and Economic History*, edited by R. Weiss (Chicago: University of Chicago Press)

Kuznets, S., 1975, 'Immigration of Russian Jews to the United States. Background and structure', *Perspectives in American History* 9: 35–126

Perlmann, J., 1988, *Ethnic Differences. Schooling and Social Structure among the Irish, Italians, Jews, and blacks in an American City, 1880–1935* (New York: Cambridge University Press)

Perlmann, J, 1996a, *Selective Migration as a Basis for Upward Mobility? The Occupations of Jewish Immigrants to the United States, Ca. 1900*, working paper 172, Jerome Levy Economics Institute, October 1996

Perlmann, J., 1996b, *Geographic Origins of Russian Jews, ca 1900*, paper presented at the European Social Science History Meetings, May 1996

Perlmann, J., 1997, 'Russian-Jewish literacy in 1897. A re-analysis of Russian Census and United States immigration data', *Papers in Jewish Demography 1993 in Memory of U.O. Schemlz, Jewish Population Studies* 27: 123–38

Rubinow, I.M., 1907, *Economic Condition of the Jews in Russia*, Bulletin 15, United States Bureau of Labor (Washington: US Goverment Printing Office) [reprint 1975]

Steinberg, S., 1981, *The Ethnic Myth. Race, Class and Ethnicity in America* (Boston: Beacon Press)

US Bureau of the Census, 1960, *Historical Statistics of the United States* (Washington: US Bureau of the Census)

Yivo, Institute for Jewish Research, 1961, *The Early Jewish Labor Movement in the United States*, translated and revised by A. Antonovsky, and edited by E. Tcherikower (New York: Yivo)

7
Peasantry and Trading Diaspora. Differential Social Mobility of Italians and Greeks in the United States*

Hans Vermeulen and Tijno Venema

Italian and Greek immigration to the United States provide an excellent case for comparison for those interested in differential social mobility patterns. Despite many similarities in background and conditions of immigration, the patterns of social mobility for the two groups have differed markedly with respect to both education and employment. Many Greeks in the US were quick to enter the middle class, while most Italians and their offspring long remained in the working class. The vast literature on the Italian-Americans is devoted mostly to the southern Italians, who constituted about 80 per cent of the Italian immigration. Far less has been written about Greek-Americans and what has been written is not widely known. Explicit comparison between the Italian- and Greek-Americans is entirely lacking, except for a few incidental cross-references in works devoted to one of the two ethnic groups.[1]

Before we seek explanations for these diverging trajectories of Greek and Italian adaptation in America, it will be useful to look at some of the similarities between the two groups. Their processes of migration and remigration contain many analogies. Although the Greeks arrived on average somewhat later than the Italians, both Greek and Italian immigration were mostly concentrated between 1900 and 1920. The volume of emigration in terms of the population of the old country was very high in both cases. Coming from a smaller country, though, the Greeks numbered barely 10 per cent of the total of Italians in the United States.[2] Another important difference was that at least 20 per cent of the Greek migrants originated from the diaspora outside of Greece (Saloutos 1973: 390–1; see Petmezas 1995: 427–8 for a higher estimate).[3] Remigration was high, and reached similar levels for both groups; during the first decades of the 20th century about half of each group returned home (Perlmann 1988: 120, 278; Saloutos 1956: 30, 1973: 390–1). Similarities can also be observed in the social and cultural backgrounds of the immigrants. Like most southern

Italians, the Greek immigrants were largely peasants or children of peasants. Resemblances can be seen in both the social structure (for example centrality of the nuclear household, systems of inheritance, role of spiritual kinship) and the cultural codes (for example honour and shame) prevailing in the regions of origin. In fact, southern Italy is in many ways more culturally similar to Greece than it is to northern or central Italy. This is explainable in part by the historical relations between the two regions.

The settlement process in the USA and the demographic composition of the immigrant population during the first few decades were also very much alike. Both groups settled in cities, often the same ones, such as New York and Chicago. They took up work in similar blue collar occupations like mining and railway construction (see, for example, Moskos 1980: 1–29; Sowell 1996: 163–4). Greek and Italian communities at first consisted almost exclusively of males. When women joined the men, female employment outside the home remained restricted for a long time in both cases, under the influence of similar cultural notions about the proper roles of men and women. Because the mass immigration of Italians and Greeks took place in the same historical time frame and because they established themselves in the same types of cities, the opportunity structures for both groups – understood as the general conditions encountered after immigration – may be assumed to be roughly equivalent. In the analysis to follow we concentrate on the premigration situation and the early phase of settlement in the US, roughly until 1930. We first review some interpretations of Italian and Greek mobility patterns suggested by a limited number of authors. We then present our own interpretation, focusing on several points which we consider crucial for understanding the differences.

Some interpretations of Italian social mobility

For the Italians we will examine the views of Steinberg, Sowell and Perlmann. These authors have all dealt with the Italian case in a comparative, historical perspective, making use of the existing body of literature on the Italians and, in Perlmann's case, new historical evidence. Steinberg weighs the arguments of writers who have reflected on the low regard Italian-Americans supposedly had for education (1989: 141–5). He seeks the explanation in three factors. In the first place he points out that the immigrants came predominantly from southern Italy, where they had been peasants, and he argues that education is of little value to peasants as a means of enhancing one's own social position. Second, he observes that there just weren't many schools in southern Italy. In places where there *were* schools, people did make use of them. And finally he cautions that we should not just presume that 'Italian attitudes toward education were simply a carryover from Europe' (ibid.: 142). These could be attitudes typical of the working class in general, or it could be that Italians didn't have such a low estimation of education after all. What we could be seeing is a correct assessment that 'their chances of reaching college are slim, and consequently their futures are not likely to depend upon their school performance' (ibid.: 143). So Steinberg seems inclined to see the ideas that people harbour about education as a correct appraisal of the possibilities open to them. He furthermore seems to assume that, if values play any role at all, they must be traceable to the *material conditions* prevailing in the people's country of origin. His conclusion is therefore that 'if Italians (...) have not excelled academically, this cannot be blamed on a value system that discouraged education, since these values themselves only reflect the operation of social factors' (ibid.: 144). Values apparently cease to be values if they can be linked to present or former *social* conditions.

Sowell treats the Italian case in more detail than Steinberg and puts more emphasis on culture. He believes the existing literature demonstrates that Italians indeed had a negative attitude towards education and that they also performed badly in school (high dropout rate, poor achievement and so on). Their poor educational accomplishments were so conspicuous that the idea even arose that Italians were genetically inferior in their intellectual capacities (1981: 121). Yet Sowell stresses that Italians were willing to work longer and harder than many others were and that this is how they succeeded in improving their lot:

> The channels through which the Italians advanced over the years were generally not those requiring formal education. Italian-American workers became more skilled over time, and their earnings rose to levels above what might be expected on the basis of their formal schooling alone. Sheer willingness to work remained a potent force in their economic rise.
> (ibid.: 123–4)

How does Sowell account for this pattern? Like Steinberg, he focuses his attention on southern Italy and observes that most immigrants were of poor peasant origin. But contrary to Steinberg he seeks the answer primarily in their *premigration culture*. He highlights the poverty, exploitation and colonial status that then prevailed and concludes that their 'attitudes toward life in general reflected the realities of southern Italy' (ibid.: 106). Back in southern Italy, he succeeds in tracing down both an emphasis on hard work and a negative attitude towards education.

> The first compulsory school attendance law was passed in 1877. It met with resistance, noncompliance, and even rioting and the burning of schoolhouses. Education was not seen as an opportunity for upward mobility by the peasants – as in fact it was not in such a castelike society. Rather, it was seen as an intrusion into the sanctity of the family, singling out the child as an individual and teaching values at variance

with those of the home. To desperately poor people, the loss of a child's work or outside earnings was also a painful sacrifice.

(ibid.: 106)

Sowell underlines here the strong family ties and the weak organizational structures outside the family, a well-known theme in the anthropology of southern Italy. Working hard, he maintains, was seen as being in the interest of the family, and the introduction of the school as being hostile to that interest. He thereby links the negative attitude not to long-standing cultural values, but to very *specific and contemporary* circumstances prevailing in southern Italy around the turn of the century. Such an assertion, however, sharply contradicts one of the general conclusions of his book that attitudinal changes require 'generations or centuries' (ibid.: 284). Such a conclusion does not seem justified in the light of the preceding case studies, at least not as far as the Italians are concerned.

Sowell's *Ethnic America* and Steinberg's *The Ethnic Myth* are both well-written polemical texts. Joel Perlmann's book *Ethnic Differences* is very different, in that it is a detailed empirical study of one particular case. Perlmann attempts to determine the relative significance of class, culture and racism in the social mobility patterns of the Irish, Italians, Russian Jews and blacks in the town of Providence, Rhode Island, between 1880 and 1935. He has unique material to work with, including detailed information about the school careers of the groups in question. What does Perlmann have to say about the Italians? In the period of mass immigration from 1880 to 1920, Italians formed the largest immigrant group in the United States. Even more so than other groups, the Italians in Providence found themselves in the lowest reaches of the labour hierarchy, working mainly as unskilled labourers in places like the building industry. Mothers were unlikely to have paid jobs, but children were expected to earn money from an early age – child labour was more widespread among Italians than in other immigrant groups. Italian children performed markedly worse in school than the children of other immigrants: they left school earlier (girls more so than boys), got poorer marks and a far smaller percentage of them ever reached high school (Perlmann 1988: 90–5). The disparities between them and other groups are explained only to some degree by social class and other aspects of social background.[4] Education is especially prominent within the remaining difference.

Italian school achievement differed from that for other groups in Providence, but their occupational attainments did not differ much (once schooling and family background factors are taken into account). The striking and distinctive feature in Italian behavior, then, is the pattern of schooling.

(ibid.: 100)[5]

Perlmann also looks for effects from still other factors, such as a high degree of remigration and what he calls contextual effects (the nature of the ethnic community as a whole), but none of these can explain much of the remaining difference either.[6] He subsequently concludes that nothing else remains but to seek the differences in 'the heritage the Italians brought with them'. He does not have in mind *skills* – since they have already figured in his analysis – but *values, attitudes and orientations* (ibid.: 112).[7] The material Perlmann has available does not enable him to draw direct conclusions, so like Sowell and Steinberg he bases his analysis of this question on the literature. He too asserts that the southern Italian culture cannot be viewed in isolation from the economic and social relations prevailing there and he likewise refers to facts such as the predominantly peasant roots of the southern Italian immigrants. He believes this also explains why the Italian pattern resembled that of the Slavic immigrants to the United States.

Some interpretations of Greek social mobility

Contrary to the Italian case, no literature in a comparative and historical perspective is available for the Greeks. However, Moskos's general view of Greek-American life in his book *Greek Americans* and the work of the Greek sociologist Tsoukalas do offer some interpretations of the Greek case. The Greek-American trajectory of upward social mobility appears to contrast with the Italian experience on two points in particular. Greeks were quick to secure positions as small businessmen, notably in the catering industry. They also showed a keenly positive attitude towards education and many children of simple Greek peasant immigrants did very well in school.

Moskos (1980) has documented the rapid social mobility of many Greek immigrants. By the US censuses of 1960 and 1970, second generation Greeks could boast the highest educational levels of all ethnic groups and were surpassed only by the Jews in average income (ibid.: 111).[8] He traces this process in some Greek communities. Most children of workers left the working class and entered white collar and even professional occupations. Many children of businessmen became professionals. Moskos (1980: 111) refers to a comparative study by Bernard C. Rosen (1959) which found Greek-Americans to have a higher achievement motivation than white Protestants and a whole series of other ethnic groups in America. Although Moskos realizes this subject is controversial and formulates his views carefully, he is still convinced that 'the utility of such a cultural predisposition toward success' is demonstrated by the facts of Greek life in America.[9]

Moskos not only examines contemporary cultural predispositions in trying to understand the Greek case. In his concluding chapter he also goes back to the situation in Greece at the turn of the century. Referring to the work of Mouzelis – and especially to the latter's comparisons of Greek and Bulgarian peasants (Mouzelis 1978: 93–104) – Moskos (1980: 140) argues that the Greek peasantry was far more involved in the market than the peasants in other eastern European countries, who lived mostly in subsistence economies. This greater degree of market penetration into the countryside, together with the cultural hegemony of the urban merchant class – both within the Greek state and in the Greek diaspora – had fostered an individualistic outlook on economic activities. Though Moskos does not refer here to the work of Tsoukalas, it was Tsoukalas who developed this point of view more than any other.

Tsoukalas (1977) deals only indirectly with the migration of Greeks to the United States and their socioeconomic position there. His topic is the role that the *educational system* in Greece played between 1830 and 1920 in reproducing Greece's dependence on Europe. In his neo-Marxist analysis, he shows that in the period in question large numbers of Greeks were living outside Greece, in areas such as Romania, southern Russia, Asia Minor and Egypt, where they were active primarily in trade and the liberal professions. The Greek communities in some of these areas had been present since time immemorial, but there was also a sizeable stream of contemporary emigration to them from the small, emergent Greek nation-state.[10] It was chiefly a migration of men from rural regions characterized by small land holdings and their ties with their regions of origin remained vitally important.[11] Return migration was very high.

Another way in which these ties manifested themselves was in monetary remittances that helped to sustain the extensive Greek state machinery. Emigrants also financed education in Greece in large measure, founding schools in their native villages and providing most of the state budget for education. This furthered the rapid development of primary and secondary education, even in many rural areas. As early as 1860 more than a quarter of all peasant children were attending school, and almost half of the boys (Tsoukalas 1977: 395). After 1860 primary school attendance increased substantially, also for girls. The expansion of secondary education was even more remarkable, at least for boys. Tsoukalas reports that in 1870 there was one pupil in secondary school for every 138 inhabitants of Greece, compared to only one in 229 in France and one in 500 in the United States (ibid.: 398) – remarkable figures even considering the young and fast growing population. Greek university education also made great strides in the 19th century and it was relatively accessible to the poor, even those from rural areas. Tsoukalas records that in 1885 the proportion of Greeks at university was higher than in any other Western European nation (ibid.: 432).[12] He speaks of 'overeducation' in Greece (see also Tsoukalas 1976), because the educational system there had developed far beyond what one would expect given the stage of development of the productive sectors of the economy.

In rural areas, no hostility towards education was in evidence, nor even an attitude of indifference. Quite the contrary, people maintained links with relatives, friends or fellow villagers in the diaspora – some of whom had perhaps founded or financed the local school. Tsoukalas argues that such contacts, along with the relations of patronage that villagers had with people in the enormous state bureaucracy, explain the emergence of a petit bourgeois ideology in large areas of the Greek countryside. In the world view of the Greek peasants in these regions, the primary – and even more so the secondary – education made available to them could be a stepping stone to a job in the state bureaucracy or to a career in the diaspora. And it was precisely from the regions characterized by a petit bourgeois ideology – with the Peloponnesus as the most outstanding example – that so many Greeks were to depart for the United States.

According to Tsoukalas, the nature of the Greek emigration areas explains why the Greeks in America – despite their class background as peasants and despite their 'objective position as proletarians' upon arrival – plunged en masse into petit bourgeois trades so soon after their arrival. Tsoukalas (1977: 157) speaks in this context of a 'national cultural element' which helped them to fit profitably into the American capitalist system.

Like Steinberg, Sowell and Perlmann for the Italian case, Tsoukalas analyses the situation in the country of origin before and during the period of mass migration to understand the immigrant experience in the United States. The comparison between Greeks and Italians that is implicit in the above account raises new questions and creates a need for more precise data. In the remainder of this article, we will examine in more detail some individual characteristics of the immigrants from both groups in terms of their education and social class, the condition of the peasantry in the regions of origin, the relationship between the peasantry and the state there, and the first period after settlement in the United States.

Class background and the peasant condition

Certain individual characteristics of immigrants may be taken as indicators of their class background, namely their occupation before migration, the amount of money they brought with them, and their level of education upon arrival. Table 7.1 shows occupational distribution in four categories – unskilled labourers/peasants, skilled workers, professionals and 'other' – for northern and southern Italians, Greeks (including immigrants from Greece and Greeks by 'race', that is ethnic Greeks from other countries) and three other ethnic groups. The majority of both Italian and Greek immigrants were from peasant backgrounds. In southern Italy, skilled workers (*artigiani*) constituted a more or less separate class with a distinctly higher status than the peasants (Lopreato 1970: 31). Both northern and southern Italians included higher percentages of skilled workers (20 and 14.6 respectively) than the Greeks (7.7). Comparison of the Greeks to the Jews and the Armenians – three peoples with histories in trading diasporas – reveals that skilled workers were far more strongly represented in the latter two groups.

Table 7.1 Occupational backgrounds of some 'new' immigrant groups, 1899–1910 (percentages)

	Labourers	Skilled workers	Profes- sionals	Other
Romanians	94	3	0	3
Greeks	86	8	0	6
Southern Italians	77	15	0	8
Northern Italians	67	20	1	12
Armenians	41	39	2	17
Eastern European Jews	14	67	1	18

Note: the category of (farm) labourers apparently includes peasant smallholders as well as tenants/sharecroppers.
Sources: Klein 1983: 316 (Northern Italians) and Mirak 1983: 73 (all other groups).

In terms of monetary assets brought to the United States, Greeks and southern Italians appear similar. In 1910, for example, 7 per cent of each group had more than 50 dollars with them (Lieberson 1963: 72). Though this may seem a low percentage, it is higher than that in most other 'new' immigrant groups. The figure for northern Italians, however, is much higher (16 per cent). The greater relative affluence of the northern Italians is also reflected in the average sums they brought along in the period 1899 to 1910: $30.76 compared to $17.14 for southern Italians (Klein 1983: 316).[13]

The data so far would suggest that the Greeks had a more difficult start than the southern Italians. However, the relatively minor occupational advantage of the southern Italians stands in sharp contrast to the major differences in illiteracy. Illiteracy was still high among the so-called 'new' immigrants in the early 20th century, that is those from southern and eastern Europe. Between 1900 and 1914, illiteracy among immigrants from southern Italy (52 per cent) was conspicuously high by comparison with the new immigrants as a whole (36 per cent) or with any of the other larger groups (see Table 7.2). Illiteracy among Greek immigrants in the same period was not even half as high (25 per cent) and it was substantially below the average of the new immigrants. The low level of education among southern Italians is also reflected in their median years of schooling, a figure lower than that for the Russians and Poles, the largest immigrant groups after the Italians (see Table 7.3).[14] We have no comparable data on the Greeks, but it seems likely that the level was substantially higher.

Looking at the overall illiteracy rates of the countries of origin and comparing them with those of the immigrants gives us some further insights (see Table 7.2). In contrast to the very high relative level of illiteracy

Table 7.2 Illiterates among 'new' immigrants over 10 years of age, arriving in the period 1900–14, and illiteracy in some regions of origin (percentages)

	Illiteracy in USA	Illiteracy in Regions of Origin
Portuguese	65	73 (1900)
Lithuanians	54	
Southern Italians	52	68 (1901)
Italians(All)	44	48 (1901)
Bulgaris, Serbs and Montenegrins (1899–1910)	42	
Serbia		79 (1900)
Bulgaria		66 (1905)
Poles	36	
All new immigrants (1899–1910)	36	
Slovenes and Croatians	33	
East European Jews (1899–1910)	26	
Greeks	25	57 (1907)
Armenians(1899–1910)	24	
Slovaks	23	
Spaniards	17	59 (1900)
Magyars	11	41 (1900)
Northern Italians	11	34 (1901)

Source: Cipolla 1969: 97 (immigrants 1900–14), Klein 1983: 312 (Southern and Northern Italy), Mirak 1983: 74 (immigrants 1899–1910), Waters and Lieberson 1992: 174–5 (other areas of origin).

Table 7.3   Median years of schooling of immigrants and their sons

	1st-Generation Born Before 1905		2nd-Generation Men, by Age Cohort		
	Men	Women	Born 1906–15	Born 1916–25	Born 1926–35
Italians	4.8	3.8	9.0	11.4	12.2
Poles	5.5	4.3	9.2	11.5	12.4
Czechs	7.4	7.1	9.2	11.9	12.4
Russians	8.0	6.1	12.3	12.7	13.6
Yugoslavs (including Bulgarians)	–	–	9.5	12.0	12.4

Sources: Perlmann 1988: 120 (second-generation men, based on 1960 census), Waters and Lieberson 1992: 183 (first-generation, based on 1950 census).

among the southern Italian migrants (52 per cent), illiteracy in southern Italy as a whole (68 per cent in 1901) was not much higher than that in many of the other source countries of the 'new' migrants (Klein 1983: 312). This indicates that a larger share of the illiterates in southern Italy took part in emigration than in most other areas. We can even say that, if we control for sex and age, the immigrants were on average more illiterate than the comparable demographic categories of the southern Italian population as a whole.[15] This is a very different conclusion from what has been argued in the literature, for example by Klein (1983: 311):

> ... as many commentators have stressed, there was a tendency for selectivity of immigrant groups in all zones. It was obviously not the poorest and least prepared groups that migrated from either the *nord* or the *mezzogiorno*. (...) All recent studies stress that the immigrant groups usually came from the better situated and more mobile upper elements of the working classes in all regions, thus tending toward a homogenization of immigrants, despite the regional variations that did exist.

Klein's homogenization hypothesis is contradicted not only by the negative literacy selection in the south, but also by a positive selection in the north. Over 1899–1910, illiteracy among north Italian immigrants was 12 per cent, compared to 30 per cent in northern Italy itself. It should be emphasized that the negative literacy selection in the south does not exclude the possibility that the middle stratum of the peasantry was more strongly represented in the emigration than the lowest stratum consisting of landless day labourers: both groups were highly illiterate.

If southern Italian immigrants constituted a below average selection of the population in terms of literacy, it can be argued that the Greek immigrants were above average in the same respect. On this point Greece resembles northern Italy. That Greek immigrants were more literate than the Greek population as a whole is clear from the available figures on literacy among Greek immigrants and within Greece itself (see also Tsoukalas 1977: 154).[16] The higher level of literacy is at least partly a result of regional selection. According to Moskos (1980: 33), at least four out of seven Greek immigrants to the US came from the Peloponnesus, a region that compared rather favourably in terms of literacy. Data on literacy say little, of course, about the education levels of the literate. Tsoukalas (1977: 414–23) has shown that regional differences in Greece were more pronounced at the higher levels of education and that in this respect the Peloponnesus was even further ahead of other regions. One cannot but agree with Tsoukalas: taken as a whole, Greek immigrants to the United States were 'overeducated' poor peasants.

Several authors have followed the example of MacDonald (1963) by investigating what type of rural areas peasants tended to emigrate from, especially since it was apparent that most emigrants did not come from the poorest regions.[17] The general picture that has emerged is that, while poverty is not irrelevant, there is no simple linear relation between poverty and emigration. Although regional variations should not be overlooked, emigration seems most characteristic of regions with mixed property – that is, with large as well as small property or with smallholders as well as tenants, sharecroppers and landless labourers (Barton 1975: 27–47, Bodnar 1985: 1–56). Emigration regions also tend to be more subject to market penetration and erosion of the old status system. Individualism and a low degree of collective organization and class struggle are associated with a conception of social mobility in terms of individual and family strategies.

Both southern Italy and the Peloponnesus seem to fit this pattern rather well, but there are some key differences between the two. The Peloponnesus had a better developed infrastructure, including electric railways, so that the countryside had more connections to the outside world. Probably more important are the differences in class structure and class relations. In contrast to the above general description of emigration regions, Greece did not have a native class of landless labourers. Landless labourers in Greece were predominantly Albanian and Bulgarian migrants. Many peasants, and even more emigrants, were smallholders.[18] In southern Italy, by contrast, landless labourers (*giornalieri*) constituted about half of the peasant population.[19] In all likelihood their daily wages were far below those of the labourers in Greece (Cinel 1982: 85; Covello 1967: 60; Saloutos 1973: 394). Although there is some disagreement in the literature about whether the landless labourers constituted a representative part of the migration flow to the US, it is clear that their share in it was substantial, especially in the later phases.[20] Besides these differences in class composition, there were also significant differences in class relations. Social distance and class antagonisms were far more pronounced in the Italian than in the Greek case. To understand this we also need to look at relations with the state.

There were great contrasts between the two regions in the relationship between the peasantry and the state and these reflected a different historical development. In Greece, the rural population had taken an active part in the War of Independence (1821–29), for which the diaspora had delivered most of the ideas and the money. Though the situation of the peasants in the Peloponnesus after the war was not at all favourable, it was improving in several respects. First of all, like most Greek peasants, they profited from a slow but ultimately successful land reform campaign. Second, the expanding state bureaucracy drew most of its personnel at all levels from this region, including from the peasantry. Third, the Greek diaspora in the eastern Mediterranean was experiencing a new period of growth and this opened opportunities for migration to peasants in the

Peloponnesus and some other regions. In southern Italy, on the other hand, a deep cleavage existed between the social classes, especially between the peasantry and the (partly foreign) gentry. Italian unification, basically a conquest from the north, had brought no improvement. As the political and economic situation deteriorated, southern Italy was turned into an internal colony and one effect of this was deindustrialization. The land reform promised by Garibaldi never really materialized and any remaining peasant hopes were finally crushed at the failed Fasci insurrection in Sicily in 1893. The status of the peasants in southern Italy was 'lower than a dog' (Lopreato 1970: 28). The peasants, for their part, were deeply distrustful of any person or institution beyond the level of the family or the village community. Given the 'individualism', the lack of cohesion between the classes, the relatively weak organizational structure and the chronic poverty, one wonders to what extent Banfield's controversial notion of 'amoral familism' – coined to characterize southern Italy in the 1950s – might be applied to the situation prevailing there 50 years earlier. The basic rule of amoral familism, according to Banfield, is 'Maximize the material, short-run advantage of the nuclear family; assume that all others do likewise.' (1967: 83) Whatever the descriptive validity of this maxim may have been for the 1950s (cf. Silverman 1968), its utility for the earlier period seems limited. While it is true that most peasants lived in nuclear households at the time, more extended family ties were still very important – even if conflict-ridden – and so was the village community (*campanilismo*). In the New World, such networks proved very strong and also functional, resulting in phenomena such as massive chain migration and highly concentrated settlement, even to a greater extent than was the case among other 'new' migrants (see, for example, Barton 1975: 52 ff). And even if these networks had become reinforced in the situation during and after migration (Bodnar 1985: 57–84; Yans-McLaughlin 1977: 25–54), some base must have existed to expand on in the first place. Nor should one exaggerate organizational weakness. Many multifunctional associations of mutual aid existed, many of them village-based and these, too, survived for a long time after emigration.[21]

Regarding education, we have already seen that the Greek state, and especially the diaspora, invested heavily in schools in Greek rural areas, often in co-operation with local emigrants, and that schooling often led to concrete job and business opportunities in the state bureaucracy and the diaspora. In southern Italy the situation was entirely different. Most government spending went to northern Italy and that applied to education too. Briggs (1978: 60) has identified a very strong correlation between expenditure on education and the literacy rates in southern regions. What schools did exist were in no way attuned to peasant needs, either in terms of curriculum or in terms of their daily and yearly time schedules. As a result, even poor peasants sometimes turned to private schools or tutors.

Local elites were vehemently opposed to peasant schooling, for one thing because a certain level of schooling was a precondition for voting rights, which they preferred to keep for themselves (ibid.: 46). They could, and did, use their political power to restrict local educational budgets and, indirectly, state budgets as well. The Roman Catholic Church did not show much commitment to education either, in stark contrast to the Greek Orthodox Church. Finally, some peasant resistance against state-imposed (and bad) schools certainly did exist, though not to the degree that Sowell rather one-sidedly suggests (see above). The actual situation was more ambiguous, for there are also indications of peasant commitment to education.[22]

The early period in the States

Those Greek and Italian immigrants who entered the *general* labour market in the United States were dependent in both cases on low-paid occupations – the Greeks perhaps even more than the Italians, since there were fewer skilled workers among them. This is reflected in the low wages obtained by Greeks compared to new migrants as a whole. Around 1904 Greek workers were earning $300 a year on average, while the mean for 15 groups of new immigrants was $391.[23] Despite this, Greek per capita remittances to the old country between 1903 and 1908 were $50 a year, the highest of all immigrants. Italians came second with $30.[24] If we assume these data are correct, this suggests that Greek incomes were higher than Italian ones, rather than lower. Italians certainly did not save less than Greeks. The explanation for this paradox of low wages and high remittances may lie in the existence of a much larger and more successful Greek ethnic economy alongside the mainstream labour market. In 1907 the Greek consul general in New York City, Botassi, estimated that only about one quarter of the Greeks in the US were employed in the general labour market. The other three quarters were either entrepreneurs themselves or were working for Greek entrepreneurs (Saloutos 1964: 47). Although this may well have been based on patriotic exaggeration, it is clear that Greek ethnic employment was quite substantial from an early date, and far greater than Italian ethnic employment. Corroboration of this can be found in Table 7.4, which gives some indications about the social position in 1920 of immigrants who arrived between 1897 and 1912. Although still strongly present in the working class, it is striking how many Greeks are classified as proprietors (shopkeepers) and to a lesser extent as salesmen. The proportions working as self-employed and in trade and finance are also remarkably high. Italians, on the other hand, are still heavily overrepresented in the working class. How did this situation come about?

Greek immigration was always partly a phenomenon with links to the Greek trading diaspora, notwithstanding the peasant background of the majority of the immigrants. The initially limited Greek presence in the

Table 7.4 Some occupational data from the US Census of 1920 on Greek, Italian and other immigrants who arrived between 1897 and 1912

	Greeks	Italians	Other
unskilled	24	36	24
semi-skilled	30	30	28
skilled	9	18	23
subtotal	*63*	*84*	*75*
salesmen	6	2	3
proprietors*	28	9	9
professionals, technicians, managers and officials	1	2	4
other	1	4	10
total	*99*	*101*	*101*
self-employed	35	20	22
trade and finance	43	16	17

*That is, mostly proprietors. This category includes also some managers and officials, but most of them have been included in the next category.
Source: US Census of 1920, public use microdata samples.

United States had already increased after 1850 with the arrival of several large Greek trading houses. This small trading bourgeoisie was to play some role in the adaptation of Greek peasant immigrants who came later. Its attitude towards the peasant immigrants was clearly more positive than that of the Italian elite in the US. Nonetheless, its role remained limited.[25] The primary narrative was written by the poor but enterprising peasants themselves. The first known peasant immigrant was Tsakonas, the 'Columbus of Sparta', who arrived in the US in 1873 by way of Alexandria, presumably as a migrant worker. Although it is not clear whether he ever started his own business, many migrant labourers certainly did. Wage labour was viewed mainly as a necessary step towards self-employment, just as it was in the eastern Mediterranean Greek diaspora (Tsoukalas 1977: 345).[26]

An equally important date in this respect is 1869, when a trading duo from Sparta and Smyrna started the first confectionary (*lukum* shop), which soon multiplied into several branch outlets. These 'furnished employment for many of the first immigrants from Sparta, providing an opportunity to learn the skills of the trade' (Saloutos 1964: 262). Chicago soon became the centre of a Greek confectionery industry. In many towns and villages, modern candy stores were founded using capital, training and supplies from Chicago. An impressive case – in which peasant initiative, mutual support and chain migration come together – is that of Tsintsinon, a village close to Sparta. In 1877 about a dozen people left their native village with a small sum of capital. This eventually resulted in an organization of over two hundred candy store owners in 1926 (Saloutos 1964: 24, 264).

Immigrants from the neighbouring (and poorer) Arcadia region began arriving after 1890, and they developed a network of shoeshine parlours that was at least as impressive. 'It was the wholesale invasion of this business that attracted a flood of new youth into the country and took the Greeks from the cotton mills of New England to the shoeshine parlors of America' (Saloutos 1964: 49). Mutual aid and credit networks again played an important role. Starting entrepreneurs often needed only to rent a shop, and they were furnished with most materials and equipment on credit. The shoeshine entrepreneurs developed a Greek version of the Italian *padrone* system of labour recruitment: profitability depended heavily on the exploitation of young Greek boys, soon to be recruited from all over Greece and the Greek diaspora.

Notwithstanding their pronounced individualism, Greeks were quick to organize themselves according to good diaspora tradition. This tradition provided the model for the early phases of Greek life in America. Wherever Greeks settled in sufficient numbers, they established a *kinotis*, a financially self-supporting community of Greek Orthodox believers, whose first aim was to found a church and a Greek language school. This *kinotis* then provided the basis for numerous other associations. Kopan (1984: 135–6) has observed that

> in the Greek community, formal organizations appeared as early as did the informal ones like the coffeehouses. Despite their factionalism, the Greeks were quicker than most other immigrants, with the possible exception of the Jews, to develop enterprising community organizations to meet utilitarian needs. The long period of persecution by the Turks had forced them to gain expertise with self-help organizations in the absence of a civil government. The formation of voluntary associations was as much a part of community life as the establishment of churches and Greek-language schools.

As Kopan indicates, this diaspora model was backed up by the Greek Orthodox church, which also functioned as a Panhellenic cohesive force. We shall see that this diaspora tradition proved flexible enough to adapt to American circumstances.

In Chicago, even the Greek peddlers, as 'pariah entrepreneurs', did not hesitate to organize for a legal and political battle when they were threatened by the Grocers' Association in 1904, or later when the municipal authorities tried to ban the sale of food on city streets (Saloutos 1964: 260–1, 266). In the end, they collectively decided to establish shops and restaurants. To raise the necessary funds they often had to form partnerships. 'Squabbles between business partners became part of the Greek-American scene, but somehow most of the restaurant owners made a go of it' (Moskos 1980: 123). Although many peddlers had no previous business experience, they clearly profited from the subtle entrepreneurial skills of their more experienced colleagues and from the diaspora tradition in general.

From 1900 onwards, Greeks began moving into the restaurant business. This represented a new phase in the adaptation of Greek business – more capital, more safety and more commitment to servicing the US general public.[27] In 1910 Greek restaurant owners formed an association, Hermes, which failed because of regional antagonism between Laconians (Sparta area) and Arcadians (Tripolis area). This rivalry had apparently been over- come by the time the American Association of Greek Restaurant Keepers was founded in 1919. This organization strongly promoted Americanization, including naturalization, partly as a reaction to nativistic hostility. In many ways it reflected a fundamental shift in orientation, and as such it was a precursor to AHEPA, in which this new trend reached full maturation. The AHEPA (the American Hellenic Educational Progressive Association), the most important Greek-American organization, was founded in 1922. AHEPA clearly targeted the middle class. By 1928 it had 17 500 members. Only English was spoken and members were expected to obtain American citizen- ship. AHEPA later declared itself 'apolitical' (implying an exclusion of Greek national politics) and 'non-sectarian' (implying exclusion of Church politics). It devoted much energy to publicity campaigns promoting the Greek cause and to establishing connections with prominent Americans. Altogether, such steps amounted to a decisive move towards integration and a radical break with the old diaspora model (Saloutos 1964: 246–57).[28] At a later stage, AHEPA would again devote more attention to its Greek roots.

In contrast to the Greeks, the Italian immigrants and their children remained predominantly in the working class, slowly moving up from unskilled to more skilled occupational levels (see also Table 7.4). Their story is much better known, and we will not deal with it in detail here. Whereas the key to Greek success can be formulated as 'first generation in business, second generation into the professions', such a pattern was far less common among Italians. Even so, a good number of Italians of the first generation did start their own business – more, in fact, than immigrants in many other groups (Lopreato 1970: 144–5). In Boston, for example, 22 per cent of the Italians were in business by 1909 and in Monroe County, New York, 14 per cent around the same time (Briggs 1978: 114; Sowell 1981: 123).

The second-generation Italians, however, seem to have profited less from the entrepreneurial experience of the first generation than in the Greek case. Many children of entrepreneurs evidently did not stay in business, nor did they move into the professions. Writing on Cleveland, Barton (1975: 172) has observed that 'Italian fathers who gained middle-class status consistently failed to pass on their status to their children' (see also Briggs 1978: 114–15). Inadequate entrepreneurial skills, poor education and a weaker co-operative spirit all seem to have played a role. For example, Barton (1975: 128 and 137) found that only 5 per cent of the sons of Italian entrepreneurs in Cleveland finished high school and that their educational attainment did not even equal that of the sons of unskilled workers. Most of the two-thirds of Italian sons who did not follow in their fathers' footsteps lapsed into lower blue collar jobs.[29] With regard to co-operation, Italians were apparently more reluctant than Greeks to enter partnerships (Cinel 1982: 234). Social cohesion in Italian communities was generally low compared to the Greeks. Family and village networks were strong, as we have seen, as were village-based mutual aid societies. So much the Italians shared with the Greeks. However, Italians had no organization comparable to the Greek *kinotis*, and they had far less effective utilitarian and national organizations than the Greeks. Co-operation above the village or regional level or between different social classes proved difficult to achieve.

Greek social mobility patterns in the second generation were, as noted, characterized by rapid upward mobility via education, which is partly explainable by the higher level of education their parents had upon entry, including the mothers, which might be of special relevance here (see Lindo in this volume). As early as the 1930s there were many Greek academics and professionals. In comparison with most groups, Italian school achievement lagged behind. A number of authors believe this to be the prime cause of the slow upward mobility among Italians. Some have put it down to an anti-school culture or to some other kind of cultural legacy (Perlmann 1988: 116). For the girls, such a cultural legacy seems undeniable, as is the case with most 'new' immigrants. As for the boys, however, the picture is more complex. Not only do we see parents pressing their sons to quit school at 'working paper age', but we also see sons dropping out against their parents wishes, often under peer-group influence, and parents losing control over their sons' behaviour (cf. Briggs 1978: 237; ff. Gans 1982: 133).

Whatever the case, the Italian pattern of educational mobility was similar to that of many other new immigrants, Slavic groups in particular (Perlmann 1988: 118–21). Certainly if one takes the low starting point of the first-generation Italians into consideration, they did not fare badly at all. Table 7.3 reveals a strong parallelism over time, especially between Italians and Poles. The Russians, who were overwhelmingly Jews, scored much higher, both the immigrants and the second generation. The Greek pattern, for which we have no data, can be assumed to be closer to that of the Russians than to that of the Italians and Poles, even though, unlike most of the Russian Jews, the Greeks did not enter the States as skilled workers.

To what degree might differential discrimination explain the differences between Italian and Greek social mobility? Both Greeks and Italians suffered discrimination, and differences between them in this respect seem relatively small. Italians, especially southern Italians, had a much more criminal image and were, probably more than the Greeks, often considered to constitute a separate racial category between whites and blacks (Foerster 1924: 361, 408). Northern Italians, in their wish to dissociate themselves from southern Italians, had succeeded in convincing US immigration authorities of the need for separate registration of southern Italians. On the other hand, Greek entrepreneurial activity was sometimes seen as a threat to local interests, and Greek workers were subject to discrimination just like Italian workers. Especially among the political elite, however, the Hellenic cause enjoyed strong support. Noteworthy is Theodore Roosevelt's remark in 1911 at Jane Addams's renowned Hull House in Chicago that the Greeks, 'unlike other ethnic groups who were expected to abandon old-world loyalties and look toward a new life in America, were exempt because of their own illustrious history' (Kopan 1984: 144). On the whole, the image of the Greeks was probably slightly better than that of the southern Italians, but this may merely reflect differences in their social position.

Conclusion

Although there were many similarities between Italian and Greek immigrants to the United States around the turn of the century, they were markedly different in their occupational and educational histories. Whereas Italian presence in the States manifested itself strongly in a working-class status and outlook, Greeks were soon engaging in entrepreneurial activities and moved into the middle class in great numbers. Education played a crucial role in these diverging patterns of upward social mobility. Better educated from the outset and profiting from their entrepreneurial good fortunes, many Greeks were able to realize their educational aspirations for their children. We have restricted our analysis in this article to the period up to the 1930s. In the period that has ensued, the differences have become less pronounced, though they still retain their relevance.[30]

We have come to the conclusion that differential treatment by the majority had no more than a marginal influence on the diverging social mobility of Italians and Greeks. At the beginning of this article, we argued that the divergence is also not explained by differential opportunity structures available to the two groups in the urban centres where they tended to settle. This last point now needs some qualification. It is valid only at the group level and then only in a very broad sense. From the standpoint of an individual migrant, the Italian and Greek communities must have been dissimilar environments, offering different opportunities and role models.

Since the opportunities provided or withheld by the American cities could not explain the differential mobility patterns, we have focused on the groups themselves and on their histories before their arrival to the

United States. Here again we encountered similarities, of a structural as well as a cultural nature. Both Italians and Greeks were, for example, over-whelmingly from peasant backgrounds. Following Perlmann, we concluded that the Italian pattern of upward mobility was similar to that of eastern European groups of predominantly peasant background. This is important to note, because much attention has been focused on the internal colonial status of the south within Italy and the cultural effects this had. We have found no evidence at all for a specific, southern Italian pattern of low per-formance resulting from amoral familism – a kind of variant on a culture of poverty – as one perhaps might expect.[31] Amoral familism is probably not an adequate notion to describe the cultural condition of southern Italy at the time of mass emigration. Emigration could just as well be interpreted as a break-out from exploitative and disabling power relations, a way of removing major external and internal obstacles to school achievement and upward mobility (cf. Ogbu and Matute-Bianchi 1986: 75–99).

If the southern Italian case may best be viewed as a variant of peasant migrations from 'underdeveloped' areas, the Greek case is best interpreted as a variant of a trading diaspora model, in spite of the peasant back-grounds of the overwhelming majority of the immigrants. The villages and regions from which many Greek migrants came, such as Laconia and Arcadia, had more connections to the outside world, and more of their inhabitants were smallholding peasant entrepreneurs, than was the case for the Italians. Probably more important, since the early 19th century the regions had already experienced a high degree of emigration towards the capital and towards Greek trading communities in the eastern Mediterranean, before migration to America got underway. As a conse-quence, villagers had not only built up 'cultural capital' in the sense of wide-ranging experience with trade and with geographic and social mobil-ity, but they also now had vital social connections with covillagers else-where, both inside and outside Greece. These networks could aid potential emigrants in finding work, even self-employment or white collar jobs for which a basic education was required – an education largely funded by the diaspora. Those who did leave the village for the United States were willing to accept waged labour inside or outside the ethnic economy, but they tended to see it – quite realistically it seems – as a necessary step towards self-employment. Such an attitude appears rather typical of trading minori-ties (cf. Light and Rosenstein 1995: 207, note 34; Vermeulen 1991).

One important feature of this trading diaspora model is the practice of intraclass and interclass integration, expressing itself in a strong tendency towards co-operation and organization. Especially between the middle classes and the workers/peasants we find strong ties and fluid boundaries. Organizations, both formal and informal, are very important, if necessary, even functioning as a substitute for civil government. Another key aspect of the trading diaspora model is its flexibility, its potential for adaptation to new or changing circumstances. Accumulated, diverse collective experience plays a vital role in this, as does the characteristic educational focus of diasporic culture. This is a crucial point of distinction between Italians and Greeks in the United States. Italian communities were much more divided along class lines. First there was the division between northern and southern Italians, which was both a regional and a class division. Second, there were internal divisions within Italian communities on the basis of local origin and class. In the Greek diaspora, the local community or *kinotis* played a central role. It consisted of the church, the school and the associations which united Greeks from different social classes. It was compatible with the economic organizational structure in which poor Greeks worked as wage earners for their compatriots while aspiring to become entrepreneurs themselves in due time. This trading diaspora model also characterized the Greek communities in the United States, particularly in the early phase, but it is typical not only of the Greek communities there. Other groups like the Jews, the Armenians, and probably the Syrians, the Lebanese and the Chinese fit this pattern as well.[32] The Greek case differs from that of the Armenians and Jews, and resembles that of the Chinese, in that most Greek immigrants, particularly during the phase of mass immigration, were peasants. But they were peasants who were in close contact with cities and markets, as well as with covillagers in the diaspora.

Notes

* This article elaborates on a case study included in Vermeulen (1992). We thank Joel Perlmann for his help in analyzing the 1920 data presented in Table 7.3.
1. Lopreato (1970: 161–5) remarks, for example, that the Italians are not underachievers, as some have argued, but that other groups like the Greeks, to whom they have been unfavourably compared, are overachievers.
2. Lieberson (1980: 279–82) has suggested that smaller groups have more opportunities to exploit economic niches, for example through various forms of self-employment. Light and Rosenstein (1995: 189, 195), however, found no statistical connection between group size and self-employment rate.
3. Until 1922 more Greeks were living outside the Greek state than within. According to the 1907 census Greece numbered some 2.6 million people, whereas various estimates put the total number of Greeks somewhere between 7 and 11 million (Saloutos 1964: 16). Moreover, the Greeks in the diaspora were much more concentrated in urban areas.
4. Perlmann holds 'social background factors' constant. In his analysis these include father's occupational score, estimated value of family possessions, number of siblings and presence or absence of one of the parents. The social background factors thus include more than just class and they are therefore not 'free of culture'.
5. The remarkable thing about Italian-American social mobility, we should point out, is that people managed to work their way up *in spite of* their relative educational deficiencies. Americans of Italian descent had higher incomes over the period 1972–80 than those of Dutch descent. It is noticeable that 'Northern

144 Immigrants, Schooling and Social Mobility

Europeans are for the most part worse off than Southern or Eastern Europeans' and that Americans of English descent also lag behind many of the later immigrants (Jencks 1983). This is partly because most new immigrants, including Greeks and Italians, settled in urban areas, which developed higher levels of prosperity (for example Moskos 1980: 111).

6. Perlmann argues that discrimination in the transition from school to work, though certainly existent, was not an important factor in the case of the Italians. Labour market differentials between Italians and others vanish as soon as education is taken into account. For blacks, discrimination is of overriding importance.

7. He does not control for the level of parental education, however, which he sees as a marker of premigration cultural attributes (Perlmann 1988: 114, 280, note 47).

8. This picture is somewhat distorted by age distribution. The Greek second generation is 'younger' than most others, including the Jewish. As a consequence, the younger – better educated – age cohorts are more strongly represented. Comparison by age cohort would probably yield a different ranking (Moskos 1980: 112; Perlmann 1988: 120; see also Lieberson 1980: 281–2, Lieberson and Waters 1988: 304).

9. Saloutos expresses a similar view: 'A natural-born competitor with a determination to succeed, he reconciled himself quite early to hard work; he accepted the cult of success without ever having heard of capitalism and the Protestant ethic' (1964: 258). 'He soon discovered that there was a "God named Business" which was to cast its spell over him and many of his compatriots. For the Greek, work, to be in business, to succeed were moral duties' (ibid.: 46).

10. This migration stream was a concomitant of the privileged intermediary position of the Greeks in the growing trade between the West and the Middle East. Their trading privilege was based on the system of the so-called 'Capitulations', 'historically rooted in the economic logic of eastward capitalist penetration' (Kitroeff 1989: 2), which was imposed upon the Ottoman Empire by the Western powers.

11. Tsoukalas (1977: 112–23) distinguishes between regions of large-scale land ownership and areas with small independent peasants and he shows that the emigration in the 19th and early-20th centuries stemmed from the latter type of regions.

12. These figures say nothing, of course, about the nature and quality of the education being provided. Although Tsoukalas does discuss this, we will not go into it here.

13. The average for all immigrants, including the 'old' immigrants, was $28.95.

14. Data from Lieberson (1980: 213) on 'indexes of difference between educational levels of foreign-born and native white of native parentage men' also indicate that Italians had the lowest educational level as compared to groups from central and eastern Europe, with the exception of the rather specific case of Lithuanians born before 1885.

15. Let us look first at the gender difference. In the period from 1899 to 1910, 54 per cent of the southern Italian immigrants were illiterate – as against 12 per cent of the northern Italians – and 78.6 per cent were male, as against 21.4 per cent female (Klein 1983: 316). Illiteracy in southern Italy averaged about 55 per cent for men and 70 per cent for women in the same period (estimate on the basis of Klein (1983: 312) and Cipolla (1969: 19)). If we control

only for gender, the expected illiteracy among immigrants would have been 58–9 per cent. If we control for age, too, we can be virtually certain that illiteracy was higher among the immigrants than among comparable segments of the southern Italian population – considering that 93 per cent of the immigrant population above 14 years of age was younger than age 45 (Klein 1983: 316) and that illiteracy among the younger age cohorts in southern Italy was far lower than among the older ones (Cipolla 1969: 94).

16. If we look at the Greek data in the same way as we did at the Italian (see the previous note), we find the following. The illiteracy rate in Greece in 1907 stood at 57.2 per cent, 40 per cent for men and 72.8 per cent for women (Waters and Lieberson 1992: 174–5). If we control for sex only, the expected immigrant illiteracy rate would have been 42 per cent, given that about 95 per cent of the immigrants were male (Saloutos 1964: 45). The ratio between actual (25 per cent) and 'expected' (42 per cent) illiteracy among the immigrants is much lower than in the Italian case (25/42 or 0.60 versus 54/59 or 0.92). We do not have comparable data on age cohorts for the Greeks, but we do know that the age distribution was quite similar to that of the Italians.

17. See Barton 1975, Bodnar 1985, Briggs 1978, Cinel 1982.

18. This point is stressed particularly by Tsoukalas (see note 8). According to Petmezas (1995: 455–7), there were also sharecroppers among the migrants.

19. Lopreato (1970: 31) gives a not very well founded estimate of the class composition of rural southern Italy around 1900: elite (gentry/professionals) 1 to 2 per cent; artisans/shopkeepers/minor officials less than 10 per cent; and the remaining peasantry (100 per cent) is divided into landowners 15 per cent, tenants/sharecroppers 45 per cent, and landless day labourers 40 per cent. Covello (1967: 49), however, citing the Italian census of 1921 (two decades later), gives quite different figures for the major agricultural classes in the south: landowners 29.8 per cent, tenants 4.3 per cent, sharecroppers 7.1 per cent, farm day labourers 50.4 per cent, and shepherds 5.3 per cent. By 1921 a good many returning 'Americani', some of them former landless labourers, had bought land in Italy.

20. MacDonald argued in 1963 that from the beginning of the 20th century there were few financial obstacles to emigration. Klein disagreed, as mentioned earlier (see also Briggs 1978: 1–14). Cinel (1982: 46), following MacDonald, has estimated 'that over a fourth of Italian emigrants had tickets prepaid by relatives and friends already overseas'. In addition, shipping companies, agents and US-based *padrones* actively recruited potential migrants, even using 'lists of families in great poverty' (ibid.: 42; see also Dore 1974: 19 ff; Martellone 1984: 407). Foerster (1924: 104) stressed the prominent place of day labourers in the Sicilian emigration, which accounted for 24 per cent of the total Italian immigration to the US (Lopreato 1970: 35).

21. These were less common than in the north, however. Judging from their membership in proportion to the population, they were one-third less strong in the south than in the north in 1885, and only half as strong in 1894 (calculated from Briggs 1978: 21).

22. In addition to the private schools already mentioned, most of the numerous mutual aid associations obliged their members to learn how to read and write within one year after subscription and to send their children to school; many organized their own educational programmes for children and adults. More than 80 per cent of adult evening school activities (measured in terms of the

number of participants, exams and certificates) were concentrated in southern Italy (see Briggs 1978: 37–64 for other examples).

23. These figures are based on a survey by the Immigration Commission in random industries across the country (Mirak 1983: 83–7). We can therefore assume that wages earned in the nonindustrial ethnic economy are not included. These annual figures also took into account 'voluntary lost time', or temporary unemployment. Like most immigrants, many Greeks were not employed on a year-round basis. But more than others they had opportunities to secure additional incomes in their ethnic economy. Hence, the real annual incomes of these Greek wage earners were probably higher than the figures of this survey indicate and that differential was probably greater than it was in most other new immigrant groups.

24. These data are taken from Kopan (1984: 133, 571), who refers to Fairchild (1911: 191–2) quoting US consular officials in Greece. The Slavs came third at $28.10, but that is much lower than the estimates given by Morawska (1985: 69).

25. Whereas the 'old' diaspora capital does not seem to have been strongly linked to the Greek mass migration, at least not in any direct way, one wonders what the possible significance was of 'young', especially Peloponnesian, capital accumulated during the later 19th century. For instance, what kind of financing was behind the remarkable confectionery chains of the Tsintsiniotes, to be mentioned shortly? Who exactly sponsored the Greek takeover of the wholesale banana and fruit business in Chicago around 1895 (when barely a thousand Greeks were living there), as the Italians were pushed out in a kind of commercial feud (Kopan 1984: 130)? And what about the marked increases in southern Peloponnesian food exports around the turn of the century? '... Many Greek merchants, especially those in New York City, were energetic in pressing these articles on immigrants from other countries, especially those of Italy' (Saloutos 1973: 399). Obviously they could only do so through the many Greek retailers.

26. Not all succeeded, of course. As Moskos (1980: 143) reminds us, 'A sizable number of the immigrants (in the US), probably a majority, never escaped from the working class.'

27. The candy stores and especially the shoeshine business were confronted with a severe crisis in the 1920s. In spite of ingenious attempts to survive, most of them folded. The Greeks had begun moving out in time.

28. A counterpart of AHEPA was GAPA (Greek American Progressive Association), founded in 1923 (Moskos 1980: 42). This organization was smaller, more working-class and more traditionally Greek-oriented.

29. On the other hand, the sons of skilled workers from an *artigiani* background seem to have been more successful (Barton 1975: 93 ff).

30. Portes and Rumbaut (1996: 89), for example, have characterized Italians as working-class and Greeks as entrepreneurial/professional on the basis of the 1990 census (see also Thernstrom and Thernstrom 1997: 542).

31. Though Banfield did not relate his notion of the ethos of amoral familism to the internal colonial status of the south – as we implicitly do here – others have done so. Silverman (1968), for example, criticized Banfield strongly for attributing the underdevelopment of the south to such an ethos, although she did believe the notion had some descriptive validity. She did not regard it as some inherent cultural quality, however, but as a product of the south's internal colonial status after 1870 and its resulting underdevelopment.

Ideas like Banfield's about a somehow dysfunctional culture continue to pop up in the context of southern Italy (and beyond). For example, Putnam (1993) has argued that economic development in southern Italy is thwarted by the absence of mutual assistance, which is linked to 'the ancient culture of mistrust' (see the discussion in Schneider 1998: 6–7).

32. For the Armenians, see Mirak 1983: 286. In a selection of 20 ancestry groups with over 30 per cent foreign-born members, the Russian Jews, Lebanese, Greeks and Syrians, in that order, have been found to have the highest self-employment rates, ranging from 11.7 to 9.3 per cent; all other groups were below 7 per cent (Portes and Rumbaut 1990: 73–5). In this selection the Chinese occupied a meagre eighth position with 6 per cent, but their firms were relatively large. Besides, they had a strong position in the professions (Sowell 1981: 145). The Chinese, who were the object of heavy discrimination and adverse policies, needed more time for their upward mobility than the other groups mentioned here (cf. Lieberson 1980: 381).

References

Banfield, E.C., 1967, *The Moral Basis of a Backward Society* (New York: The Free Press) [1958]

Barton, J.J., 1975, *Peasants and Strangers. Italians, Rumanians and Slovaks in an American City, 1890–1950* (Cambridge: Harvard University Press)

Bodnar, J., 1985, *The Transplanted. A History of Immigrants in Urban America* (Bloomington: Indiana University Press)

Briggs, J.W., 1978, *An Italian Passage. Immigrants to Three American Cities, 1890–1930* (New Haven and London: Yale University Press)

Cinel, D., 1982, *From Italy to San Francisco. The Immigrant Experience* (Palo Alto: Stanford University Press)

Cipolla, C.M., 1969, *Literacy and Development in the West* (Harmondsworth, Middlesex: Penguin)

Covello, L., 1967, *The Social Background of the Italo-American School Child. A Study of the Southern Italian Family Mores and Their Effect on the School Situation in Italy and America* (Leiden: Brill)

Dore, G., 1974, 'Some social and historical aspects of Italian emigration to America', in: F. Cordasco and E. Bucchioni (eds), *The Italians. Social Backgrounds of an American Group* (Clifton: Kelley)

Fairchild, H.P., 1911, *Greek Immigration to the United States* (New Haven etc)

Foerster, R.F., 1924, *The Italian Emigration of Our Times* (Cambridge: Harvard University Press)

Gans, H.J., 1982, *The Urban Villagers. Group and Class in the Life of Italian-Americans*, updated and expanded edition (New York: The Free Press) [1962]

Jencks, C., 1983, 'Discrimination and Thomas Sowell', *New York Review of Books* 30(3): 33–8

Kitroeff, A., 1989, *The Greeks in Egypt, 1919–1937. Ethnicity and Class* (London: Ithaca Press)

Klein, H.S., 1983, 'The integration of Italian immigrants into the United States and Argentina: a comparative analysis', *American Historical Review* 88: 306–29

Kopan, A.T., 1984, 'Greek survival in Chicago. The role of ethnic education', in: M.G. Holli and P.D. Jones (eds), *Ethnic Chicago*, revised and expanded edition (Grand Rapids: Eerdmans) [1981]

Lieberson, S., 1963, *Ethnic Patterns in American Cities* (New York: Free Press of Glencoe)

Lieberson, S., 1980, *A Piece of the Pie. Blacks and White Immigrants Since 1880* (Berkeley: University of California Press)

Lieberson, S., and M.C. Waters, 1988, *From Many Strands. Ethnic and Racial Groups in Contemporary America* (New York: Russell Sage Foundation)

Light, I., and C. Rosenstein, 1995, 'Expanding the interaction theory of entrepreneurship', in: A. Portes (ed.), *The Economic Sociology of Immigration. Essays on Networks, Ethnicity and Entrepreneurship* (New York: Russell Sage Foundation)

Lopreato, J., 1970, *Italian Americans* (New York: Random House)

MacDonald, J.S., 1963, 'Agricultural organization, migration and labour militancy in rural Italy', *Economic History Review*, 2nd ser., 16: 61–75

Martellone, A.M., 1984, 'Italian mass emigration to the United States, 1876–1930. A historical survey', *Perspectives in American History*, New Series, I: 378–423

Mirak, R., 1983, *Torn Between Two Lands. Armenians in America, 1890 to World War I* (Cambridge: Harvard University Press)

Morawska, E., 1985, *For Bread With Butter. The Life-Worlds of East Central Europeans in Johnstown, Pennsylvania, 1890–1940* (Cambridge: Cambridge University Press)

Moskos, C.C., 1980, *Greek Americans. Struggle and Success* (Englewood Cliffs: Prentice-Hall)

Mouzelis, N.P., 1978, 'Greek and Bulgarian peasants. Aspects of their socio-political situation during the inter-war period', in: N.P. Mouzelis, *Modern Greece. Facets of Underdevelopment* (London: Macmillan)

Ogbu, J.U., and M.E. Matute-Bianchi, 1986, 'Understanding sociocultural factors. Knowledge, identity, and school adjustment', in: Bilingual Education Office, *Beyond Language. Social and Cultural Factors in Schooling Language Minority Students* (Los Angeles: Evaluation, Dissemination and Assessment Center, California State University)

Perlmann, J., 1988, *Ethnic Differences. Schooling and Social Structure among the Irish, Italians, Jews and Blacks in an American City, 1880–1935* (Cambridge: Cambridge University Press)

Petmezas, S.D., 1995, 'Diverse responses to agricultural income crisis in a South-Eastern European economy. Transatlantic emigration from Greece' (1894–1924), in: I. Zilli (ed.), *Fra Spazio e Tempo: Studi in Onore di Luigi de Rosa*, Volume 3 (Napoli)

Portes, A., and R.G. Rumbaut, 1990, *Immigrant America. A Portrait* (Berkeley: University of California Press)

Portes, A., and R.G. Rumbaut, 1996, *Immigrant America. A Portrait*, 2nd ed. (Berkeley: University of California Press)

Putnam, R.D., 1993, *Making Democracy Work. Civic Traditions in Modern Italy* (Princeton, NJ: Princeton University Press)

Rosen, B.C., 1959, 'Race, ethnicity and the achievement syndrome', *American Sociological Review* 24(1): 47–60

Saloutos, T., 1956, *They Remember America. The Story of the Repatriated Greek-Americans* (Berkeley and Los Angeles: University of California Press)

Saloutos, T., 1964, *The Greeks in the United States* (Cambridge: Harvard University Press)

Saloutos, T., 1973, 'Causes and patterns of Greek emigration to the United States', *Perspectives in American History* VII: 379–437

Schneider, J., 1998, 'Introduction. The dynamics of neo-orientalism, in Italy (1848–1995)', in: J. Schneider (ed.), *Italy's 'Southern Question'. Orientalism in One Country* (Oxford: Berg)

Silverman, S.F., 1968, 'Agricultural organization, social structure, and values in Italy. Amoral familism reconsidered', *American Anthropologist* 70: 1–20

Sowell, T., 1981, *Ethnic America. A History* (New York: Basic Books)

Sowell, T., 1996, *Migrations and Cultures. A World View* (New York: Basic Books)

Steinberg, S., 1989, *The Ethnic Myth. Race, Ethnicity and Class in America*, updated and expanded edition (Boston: Beacon Press) [1981]

Thernstrom, S., and A. Thernstrom, 1997, *Americans in Black and White. One Nation, Indivisible* (New York: Simon and Schuster)

Tsoukalas, K., 1976, 'Some aspects of "over-education" in Greece', in: M. Dimen and E. Friedl (eds), 'Regional variation in modern Greece and Cyprus: Toward a perspective on the ethnography of Greece', *Annals of the New York Academy of Sciences* 268: 419–42

Tsoukalas, K., 1977, *Eksartisi ke Anaparagoji. O Kinonikos Rolos ton Ekpedeftikon Michanismon stin Ellada, 1830–1922* (Dependency and reproduction: The social role of the educational mechanism in Greece, 1830–1922) (Athens: Themelio)

Vermeulen, H., 1991, 'Handelsminderheden, een inleiding', *Focaal* 15: 7–28

Vermeulen, H., 1992, 'De cultura. Een verhandeling over het cultuurbegrip in de studie van allochtone etnische groepen', *Migrantenstudies* 8(2): 14–30

Waters, M.C., and S. Lieberson, 1992, 'Ethnic differences in education. Current patterns and historical roots', *International Perspectives on Education and Society* 2: 171–87

Yans-McLaughlin, V., 1977, *Family and Community. Italian Immigrants in Buffalo, 1880–1930* (Ithaca and London: Cornell University Press)

8

The Internationalization of Black Culture. A Comparison of Lower-class Youth in Brazil and the Netherlands

Livio Sansone

In trying to determine whether culture makes a difference, researchers usually compare different ethnic groups in the same society. In that way they try to keep external conditions constant by choosing groups that have similar class backgrounds and that entered the society at roughly the same time. This approach has been taken by several contributors to this volume. In my contribution, however, I look at the 'same' group – or rather, two groups that can be considered similar in many respects – in two different countries and try to understand their similarities and differences. A key question is how similarities should be explained and to what degree culture is a viable indicator for interpreting them. The two groups I have chosen to compare are the 'black' populations of two countries, Brazil and the Netherlands. Obviously what is 'black' in one context or country may be 'brown' or even 'white' in another. By 'black' I understand here the people who, in some specific context, see themselves and are seen by outsiders as being of African or partly African descent. Hence, I am not exactly comparing the same ethnic group in two situations. I am comparing people that either identify themselves as 'black' or have been constructed as such in two societies.

To gauge the ongoing importance of local contexts in explaining variance in black culture and race relations, without losing sight of the developing global black culture, I examine here two very different cities, Salvador and Amsterdam. They have been chosen for two reasons: my own research experience in these cities, and the fact that they differ in terms of ethnic history, size and demographic trends in the black population, as well as in the place that ethnicity or colour occupies in the labour market.[1]

The central question here is whether similarities exist in the ways in which young, lower-class black people in the Netherlands and Brazil try to improve their position and status in society. We shall indeed see some striking resemblances, but also some key differences. Should the common features be interpreted as a response to similar local conditions or as the consequence of cultural elements embedded in the black condition worldwide?

The black population is often regarded as one transnational ethnic group formed through the common history of slavery, the experience of racial discrimination and, according to Afro-centric scholars and many black leaders, a grounding of all variants of the black experience in 'African culture'.[2] Are the cultural similarities that are manifest in the black populations of different countries the result of roughly equivalent class positions (after all, we are dealing with populations at or near the bottom of the social ladder)? Or do they result from a common ethnic background – a condition deriving from the African and/or the slave past? Is the ethnic black background very ancient, or could it also be a by-product of contemporary globalizing processes? What role does the black community in the USA play in the development of a global black culture?

In studying the relationships between ethnic culture, ethnicity and social position, one feels intrigued by the economic success, or lack of it, within certain minority groups. As I address this question for the black populations of the two cities, I suggest that the ethnic habitus in which black people construct survival strategies, particularly in the sphere of economic activity, results from the combination of 'hard' and 'soft' factors. An example of the former is the demographic structure of the population; examples of the latter are the traditional black presence/absence in certain sections and niches of the labour market, and the accompanying discourses that naturalize racial difference.

I begin by sketching the situation of the black population in the two cities and by summarizing the findings of my research among young lower-class blacks in Salvador and Amsterdam. The particular focus is on (a) the system of opportunities and the ethnic stratification of the labour market; (b) the role of the state in the system of race relations; and (c) the black self-image and the construction of survival strategies. I analyse similarities and differences, and while I do touch on some key differences in the histories of the two populations, in this paper I have chosen for a synchronic comparison. The article is meant to generate ideas rather than to test them. Any generalizations and snapshots found throughout the article may be due to a lack of empirical data suitable for systematic comparison.

Salvador versus Amsterdam

Black presence in the two cities is very different. Since the first half of the 16th century, Salvador and its surroundings (Recôncavo) have been one of the main urban concentrations of blacks and dark-skinned mestizos in the New World – perhaps even the largest one of its kind. Inspired by the pursuit of 'Africanisms' in the New World or the 'origin' of black culture, many anthropologists have held Recôncavo to be an area where African traits have been strongly maintained.[3]

However it might be viewed, Salvador can be called the 'Roma Negra', the black cultural capital of the country, with by far the largest black population outside Africa. Totalling 2.5 million inhabitants, it is the principal city of northeastern Brazil, a region that has been described as 'the south edge of the Caribbean'. Salvador has a long tradition of miscegenation, and that has sometimes led to problems. Bahian black culture (*cultura afro-baiana*) enjoys considerable recognition, even from official institutions, but Afro-Brazilians act very little as a cohesive ethnic community (for instance, in terms of forming electoral blocks or distinct political platforms). Nonetheless, over the past two decades Afro-Bahian culture has been experiencing what some have called a process of 're-Africanization' (Agier 1990, 1992; Bacelar 1989; Sansone 1993, 1997). This includes a conspicuous display of symbols associated with African 'roots' in certain aspects of social life, particularly in the leisure sphere and in local mass media.

The census of 1991 reported that blacks and mestizos (*pretos* and *pardos*) make up 80 per cent of the inhabitants of the Salvador metropolitan area, making the percentage of whites much lower than in the country as a whole. The three main colour groups in the region were *brancos* (17.2 per cent), *pardos* (67.4 per cent) and *pretos* (15.0 per cent) (IBGE 1995).[4] Nonwhites are rare in the upper class and are underrepresented in the middle class. In spite of the concentration of the black-brown population in the lower classes, it has numerous subgroups, and it exhibits a diversity of lifestyles and ways of relating to black ethnicity and Afro-Bahian culture.

Although blacks and mestizos are represented in all economic sectors and positions in Salvador, the higher a job rank is, the smaller numbers of blacks that will be found there, and the lighter their skin is likely to be. Historically, heavy or dirty work is usually associated with the darkest skin and with negroid features, and light skin with management and white collar positions. In the city, dark skin also tends to be associated with farm work, as dark people constitute up to 90 per cent of the population in the rural areas immediately surrounding Salvador. However, since *pretos* are historically concentrated in the coastal area, while mestizos are the overwhelming majority in the interior of Bahia, the figures for the state of Bahia as a whole do not show any overrepresentation of *pretos* in agriculture. *Pretos*, especially women, are heavily represented as cleaners, waiters and housemaids. To a lesser extent, they are also overrepresented in all sections of the manufacturing industry. Even after making significant gains in the last two decades, *pretos* remain underrepresented in the civil service, in teaching and nursing, and in the oil and chemical industries. In the civil service, however, the PNAD survey (PNAD 1997) listed *pretos* in 1996 as making up 11.1 per cent of the civil service, up from 9.6 per cent in 1988 – especially noteworthy considering that this sector of the labour market lost about a third of its jobs over the past decade.

In Brazil, the poor have very few options. The army of working poor has developed in the absence of a welfare state. The regular labour market – the 'regularity' of which would often make it 'informal' by Dutch stanards – has never managed to harbour more than 50 per cent of the total labour force.[5] In Brazil, informal economic activities are called *biscate*. In the official statistics, those who do *biscate*, or operate within the informal economy, are not counted as unemployed. The term *biscate* has no ethnic connotations and carries little or no stigma. It is simply the acknowledged survival activity of the huge unemployed and underemployed masses. Nor is there any specifically black term for these kind of activities.[6] For many poorly educated young people in urban areas – most of whom are blacks or mestizos – petty crime and even organized crime form a real 'alternative' to doing nothing or performing low-paid work. The cocaine rackets recruit a small but growing number of young men as street peddlers and 'soldiers'. Petty (though violent) robberies and burglaries are another alternative to the outright exclusion from consumerism (or worse still, starvation). Street crime and other types of crime, which are traditionally high, have risen further in the past two decades. Afro-Brazilians are heavily overrepresented in urban prisons, even if class origin is taken into consideration. (see Tables 8.1 and 8.2)

Traditionally, *pretos* participate in the labour market more than *pardos* and far more than *brancos*. *Pretos* enter the labour market at a younger age and leave it at an older age. This applies to both men and women. Racist stereotypes on the supposed laziness of black men are seldom heard in Brazil. Instead, racist remarks and jokes in popular cultural expressions such as folk theatre, musical lyrics and *literatura de cordel*[7] tend to depict blacks as violent, aggressive, passionate and *preseperos* (behaving like nouveaux riches). It is the *Índio* that tends to be portrayed as lazy.

Although colour, usually in combination with class, status and lifestyle, is an important determining factor for one's position in the Brazilian labour market, the highest barrier to surmount in the eyes of most Afro-Brazilians is that of education or, more broadly, lower-class origin. While they think colour can be manipulated to a large degree, they see class as much more rigid. There are a number of explanations why even dark-skinned Brazilians put so much emphasis on class. The high labour participation rate of dark-skinned Brazilians, together with their massive presence in class-based protest movements (labour unions and the landless movement) and sometimes even in the leadership of these movements, is something

Table 8.1   Unemployment rates in Salvador and in Brazil as a whole in 1991

	Men	White *Branco*	Brown *Pardo*	Black *Preto*	Total	Women	White *Branca*	Brown *Parda*	Black *Preta*	Total
Salvador		6.6	9.1	12.8	9.1		4.7	8.7	11	8.2
Brazil		3.5	4.1	4.8	3.8		3.3	3.6	4.4	3.4

(*Source:* PNAD 1997)

Table 8.2 Extent of differential educational attainment per colour/ethnic group: percentage of persons above the age of ten who have not completed the first grade in the State of Bahia and in Brazil overall in 1996

	White	Brown	Black	Native American	East Asian
Bahia	74.9	82.8	86.5	93.3	75.4
Brazil	62.9	79.4	80.3	80.7	42.9

(*Source*: PNAD 1997)

that deserves further research. It might help us understand why in Brazil, much more than in the USA or the Netherlands, a constant osmosis takes place between the social lives, the survival strategies and the mores of the lower classes and of the majority of the black population.[8] In fact, participation in black culture, for example as an active member of an Afro-Brazilian temple or as a samba percussionist, is often seen by insiders and outsiders alike as something only fit for black people of 'poor condition'. It is only recently that middle-class blacks, usually people under 40 and highly educated, are claiming that participation in black culture need not be associated with lower-class status. The commercial success of a string of new glossy magazines such as *Raça Brasil*, which are aimed at the black population and especially the segment with buying power, indicates that growing numbers of black people feel uncomfortable with traditional definitions of blackness and its association with poverty, bad manners, kitsch consumption and premodern attitudes.

The salience of class and the relative downplaying of colour differences is linked to a system of racial classification that allows considerable individual manipulation of the colour line. Brazil is well known for the 'lexical proclivity' (Harris 1970) and the relational character of its racial classification. The same black person can be referred to by a range of racial terms, such as *negro* (black), *preto* (negro), *escuro* (dark), *moreno* (light brown), *escurinho* (dark boy) and *neguinho* (black/negro boy). This depends on the context, the position of who is speaking, their gender, the time of day and the life domain (leisure, work or family life) (Sansone 1996).

Amsterdam is the principal city and cultural capital of a wealthy country where the black population is just one of the many small and recently arrived minorities. In 1994, Afro-Surinamese, Dutch Antillean and black African people made up 9 or 10 per cent of Amsterdam's 720 000 inhabitants. Compared to Salvador – where relations between blacks and non-blacks are centuries old and are constitutive of the city's structure and segmentation, and where foreign immigration has been of little relevance in recent decades – Amsterdam is an open society in ethnic terms. Interethnic relations are, as it were, still in the making, and the black population constitutes a more clear-cut ethnic minority than the Afro-Brazilian population in Bahia.

I focus here on the largest black group in the city, the Surinamese Creoles,[9] and in particular on lower-class youth and young adults. Class differences are sharp among both Creoles and Antilleans (Martens and Verweij 1997: 37). On the labour market and in society in general, the Creoles are situated in many ways between the white Dutch and the relatively large groups of former Turkish and Moroccan guest workers and their offspring (van Niekerk 1994). This favourable position vis-à-vis other large immigrant groups is due mainly to the relative success of the large minority of Creoles that are relatively well integrated into certain areas of the labour market, in particular the public sector. Their success is tempered by the marginality of the large lower class and poorly educated group. The vast majority of the young Creoles that I observed from 1981 to 1991, and whom I will describe in more detail below, belong to the latter category.

For two decades, from the mass immigration from Surinam in the mid 1970s to the early 1990s, unemployment among the Surinamese was alarmingly high.[10] In 1992, for young Surinamese aged 18 to 30, it was as high as 50 per cent, rising to 60 per cent in neighbourhoods like the high-rise district of Zuidoost that were home to large concentrations of lower-class Creoles. In recent years, however, the Dutch economy has staged a relative recovery and unemployment has declined in all groups, including the Surinamese. Whereas in 1994 registered unemployment among the Surinamese was still 19 per cent, nationally, it went down to 10 per cent in 1998 (compared to 6 and 4 per cent among the autochthonous Dutch, respectively). Youth unemployment as well fell from 27 per cent to less than 15 per cent (Martens 1995 and 1999). However, these figures should be seen in the light of an extremely favourable labour market situation, in which even some 'hard-core unemployed' can find a (temporary?) job. Besides that, part of this new employment is generated through government-subsidized jobs, from which the Surinamese profited somewhat more than most others, but which generally are not being converted into regular jobs, in spite of good intentions. With these qualifications in mind, we tend to agree with Martens and Verweij (1997), who argue that the Surinamese population still finds itself in the section of society hardest hit by unemployment and least able to benefit from the general economic recovery.

Many of the unemployed Creoles, as well as some of the officially employed ones, operate in the informal economy. In Amsterdam, most 'alternatives' to wage work deployed by lower-class Creoles in the informal and criminal economy are still associated with one specific ethnic group, although the ethnic connotation is more strongly present in the rational- izations and discourse surrounding the informal activities than in their actual practice (Sansone 1992: 135–41). Creoles refer to such practices by the Surinamese-Dutch word *hossels*.

Since mass immigration, the Creoles, and especially the lower-class young men, have acquired a certain reputation in the urban labour market. They are seen by outsiders, as well as by job centre officers, as belonging to the hard-to-place category, due to a lack of technical skills combined with a 'different' work ethic and a 'choosy' attitude about prospective jobs. Sometimes they are even regarded as undisciplined, aggressive and haughty – getting to work late in a country were punctuality is expected, balking at orders from superiors, holding unrealistic expectations as to work alto- gether and exhibiting consumption patterns that are not just conspicuous but far beyond their means as well.

In many ways, Creoles are inclined to agree with these outsiders' opin- ions. Most of them present themselves as being profoundly different from the Surinamese Hindustanis – the descendants of indentured labourers who arrived in Surinam over a century ago. Creoles say they love fun and partying, live from day to day and adore spending. They say Hindustanis are stingy, love to save money, can't dance groovy and have no sex appeal. In Lafontaine's tales, the Creole would be the cicada and the Hindustani the ant. The Creoles not only compare themselves to the Hindustanis, but also to the ethnic Dutch and to other large immigrant groups they arrived with, who were mostly Turkish and Moroccan. They tend to rank them- selves between the Dutch and the other groups. They feel Western in their life orientation, but not in the same way as the Dutch. They also feel ethni- cally different, but not as much as the Turks or the Moroccans. Interestingly, this self-perception is very similar to the way the white Dutch see the Creoles (Leeman and Saharso 1989) – as a sort of intimate strangers.

Lower-class black youth in Salvador and Amsterdam

I will focus here on two particular areas in the greater Salvador region: a lower- and lower-middle-class neighbourhood in the city of Salvador, Caminho de Areia, and the poorer and more industrial satellite town of Camaçari. Both areas bear testimony to a modern Third World plight. Absolute poverty goes hand in hand with a feeling of *relative* deprivation. Elements of so-called 'modern poverty' are combined with the 'traditional' poverty of this country whose distribution of wealth is considered one of the worst in the world. I carried out field work in these areas from 1992 to 1994 (Sansone 1994b, 1997).[11] The employment situation was similar to that of most Brazilian urban lower-class areas. A minority of adults in the age bracket 30 to 60 held steady jobs (though many of these were in the informal sector), and they were supporting, at least to some degree, a majority consisting of unemployed, underemployed, idle or disabled people, old age pensioners and children. The educational level of young people in the 15-to-25 age bracket was substantially higher than that of their parents. As in many other Third World countries and similar to most colonial minorities in Western countries, the educational revolution of recent decades had been more effective for females than males. Many lower-class women were now finding it hard to meet the right partner within their narrow social environment and the pool of marriageable men was further reduced by the high rate of crime and violent deaths that mostly affected young men with poor educational backgrounds. Many such young people saw themselves as *formados*, properly educated, a perception reinforced by parental pride about their children's diplomas.

However, this education level, which was indeed formidable when compared to that of their parents, had not resulted in a better position on the labour market. Several factors were responsible for this. One key issue was that their higher level of schooling was not being matched by higher job requirements. Informants complained that they, like many of their friends and relatives with school diplomas, wound up having to take unskilled, badly paid jobs. To find employment as a rubbish collector, a security officer or a worker in the oil industry you now needed a primary school certificate (8 years); to work in a bank or as a civil servant you needed a higher education diploma. One generation before, entry into such occupations had been far easier. This had led to a situation in which parents were convinced their children had enough education to find a proper job while the children felt deeply frustrated in their expectations. In addition to sparking conflicts at home, this discouraged young people in the long run from studying longer and harder. For those still in school, another factor negatively affected their motivation. The quality of teaching in state schools, especially for the first four forms, was very poor – most pupils with a primary school certificate were still half illiterate – and the situation had been worsened by drastic public spending cuts in recent years. In the neighbourhoods I studied, large numbers of children and adolescents hung about on the streets all day: they only went to school from time to time and stayed there no longer than one or two hours a day. Regular school attendance up to the age of 14 was rapidly ceasing to be a 'natural' part of their socialization. Attending school was neither an event around which the week was organized nor was it essential to prepare them for adulthood and working life (cf. Willis 1977).

The peer group (*turma*), the neighbourhood age group (*galera*) and the more impersonal factor of television were becoming more important agents of socialization than school – and the youngsters obviously had other priorities. Conversations in peer groups in the many 'hours off school' revolved around consumption, courting and fun. School tests, homework and teachers were no longer a major focus of concern. The crisis of Brazilian public education which had begun about 20 years previously had led to a situation that was best summed up by the popular saying 'Teachers pretend they teach and pupils pretend they learn.' It will come as no surprise that the school dropout rate was extremely high. The reason why many parents had dropped out of school were obvious: they had needed to find work to support the family income. For these young people, though, the causes were more complex. In both Salvador and Camaçari, only half of those who had already dropped out of school had done so to find work. The other half had no explanation for why and how they had left school. But it was mainly a lack of confidence in education that pushed them out of school, rather than a need to work.

The percentage who said they were unemployed was stunning: in 1993 it was 44.2 per cent in Salvador and 62 per cent in Camaçari. These high figures need closer inspection. Young people in general, including those with higher levels of education, tended to make a clear distinction between unemployment and employment, and between a formal job and a *biscate* (an informal job, a hustle). They were more inclined to say they were unemployed, even if they were engaged in some informal economic activity. The term 'unemployed' seemed to carry less of a stigma for them than it did for their parents and grandparents. To them, hustling was something you did while you could not find a proper job. Their parents, who were accustomed to designating any number of informal economic activities as 'my occupation', were much less likely to call themselves unemployed and were generally more content with their work situation. In the neighbourhood they were more inclined than their offspring to identify each other by their 'occupation': Zé the bricklayer, João the plumber, Maria the laundry woman. Many girls that earned their living as cleaners or laundry women defined themselves as unemployed, feeling ashamed to be associated with such work – to them that was no 'occupation'.

The parents felt they were better off in comparison with their own parents: they ate better, had more comfortable housing and lived longer. The younger generation was less satisfied with its living standards and was disenchanted by its poor chances in the labour market. Young people had learned to believe in social mobility, in 'progress', but felt excluded from it. One important reason for the frustration was that the under-25s measured success more in relation to the middle classes, which they were more familiar with than their parents, and compared to which they were poor. They did not see their present higher standard of living, and the more modern work standards that had spread rapidly into the lower classes since the mid-1970s, as an outcome of the relative success of their parents.

In both Camaçari and Salvador the rate of labour market participation increased with age. The fact that most parents were employed, even holding more than one job, whereas most children were better educated but still unemployed, led to the absurdity that the former had a bit of money but little time to relax, while the latter had little money but plenty of time on their hands. The under-25s had a different attitude towards work. Most were basically idle. They were waiting for a 'proper job' that did not really exist for them (they had neither the manual skills of their parents nor the more advanced diplomas required to obtain the 'modern jobs'). They were expecting the right *concurso* (a public contest for one or more government jobs) to pop up one day, and meanwhile they refused to accept the poorly paid and generally 'dirty' jobs available in the region for the poorly skilled or altogether unskilled. Even though parents complained about the supposed laziness and fussiness of their children, most under-25s who were out of work seemed less bothered about relying on their parents' meagre earnings than about doing a job 'below their level' – one that did not correspond to the expectations created by the school, the mass media and their peer group.

Generational differences could also be seen in survival strategies in the labour market. Neither the parents nor the children were inclined to seek work in regions of the labour market they presumed inaccessible to people with little education or to blacks, such as in 'posh' places like expensive restaurants and shopping centres. However, the big difference between parents and children was in how they dealt with 'respect'. The parents showed considerable 'respect' for wealthy and/or white people. The children regarded such 'respect' as a loss of face, and they often did not know how to cope with the 'respect' that employers, managers, or even crew chiefs and foremen still expected from menial workers (or from workers in general). If they had a job, the under-25s were less inclined to humbly accept orders from superiors and were more easily offended. In other words, the self-exclusion of the younger generation was less reticent and less deferential than that of the parents.

Another interesting generational difference was the type of escape valve used. Traditionally the older generation had vented its frustration with the labour market in a religious practice. *Candomblé*, the Bahian variant of the Afro-Brazilian religious system, is replete with practices and techniques that magically invert low job status. Those who are servants in the daytime can be kings and queens in *candomblé* ceremonies. They can even be those who heal their masters, so it is still not uncommon for a middle-class housewife to draw upon her housemaid for magical practices. The younger generation is much more secularized than that (Sansone 1993). The under-25s in my research might have used *candomblé* symbols to reformulate their black identity, but they used the practices much less systematically than their parents to negotiate status or favours or to get better jobs. Rather than elbowing their way through poverty by negotiating with the masters or with spirits, the under-25s would simply pretend they were not poor. They might attempt to hide their lower-class position from outsiders by conspicuously consuming the status symbols they associated with the middle-class and/or with youth culture. (In Brazil, conspicuous participation in the incipient local version of *global* youth culture is by and large a privilege of middle-class youth (Sansone 1998).)

A growing minority of young people were looking for alternatives to steady paid work. Those with better educations turned to the street peddling of cheap electronic goods or beauty products smuggled in from Paraguay or to the growing Bahian folklore market for the tourists (performing as dancers, *capoeira* players or musicians). A small group chose emigration to Europe or North America. For young men with little or no education, one 'alternative' could be petty crime – bag snatching, unplanned burglary, dealing marijuana. For girls the main 'alternative' was a conspicuous use of the body, charm and beauty (or knowledge of how to create beauty), either by working as seamstresses, manicurists or hairdressers (beauty parlours were springing up everywhere in Brazil) or by 'catching the man' – one who showed he liked her by giving her presents and who would pay for her on a night out. They hoped for a man who would show 'respect' and was not a womanizer. That was an ideal. Although no figures were available, there was evidence that prostitution was on the increase. As in most Third World countries, prostitution is practised in Brazil as a last-ditch survival strategy rather than as a profession. It is worth stressing that most of these 'alternatives' relate in one way or another to the use of the (black) body and beauty.

As the parents' main source of status, their labour market position, became an increasingly precarious basis for that status, the under-25s in particular were putting more emphasis on spending power – on a new, more aggressive consumption pattern that would have been impossible to satisfy with any of the conventional jobs these lower-class young people could ever hope to get. Their peers asked 'How much do you earn?' and much less 'How do you earn money?' and a boy who tried to continue in the same trade as his father would be called an *otário* (a sucker). The status created by conspicuous consumption was shown off especially during the leisure time spent in public. This gave public leisure time special relevance even for the unemployed or underemployed. Compared to the older generation, then, the younger generation was investing less in the family and was believing more strongly in a vertical, individual improvement of the social condition, by 'moving on' from the lower to the middle class. This was to be done without the hassle of first establishing a good working-class position, as most of their parents had tried to do in the very different context of one or two decades ago, when the heavy industrialization of the Salvador area was in progress.

In the neighbourhoods I studied, the number of under-25s who were prepared to take any job whatsoever was on the decrease. So was the number of girls who preferred to find a partner with a proper job, even a poorly paid one. Most unemployed youngsters were doing some *biscate* – a grow-ing number even preferred this type of activity in the informal economy to a steady but underpaid job. Only a minority of young men ever ventured into criminal activities as an alternative to a job or a simple *biscate*. A larger-than-ever number of young people seemed dissatisfied with their job prospects and were seeking alternatives to what they saw as the drudgery of low-status jobs or the poor housewife's existence. Job-hopping (from one bad job to another bad job) and spending long periods out of work were the ways most of them expressed their discontentment. As we shall see below, this is similar to what happens among lower-class young Creoles in Amsterdam, even though Brazil provides no social security.

Let us turn now to the situation of black young people of lower-class origin in Amsterdam. The data in this section of the article are derived from qual-itative research in 1981–91 among lower-class young Creoles in the Amsterdam districts of West and Zuidoost. Most informants had been liv-ing in the Netherlands at the time for 15 years or more. In Surinam most of their parents had belonged to the urban lower classes.[12]

Of the core group of 75 informants that were interviewed throughout the entire study, only 16 had a job during the final phase; 49 were jobless, most of them for more than two years and some even up to seven years. Two were in prison and eight were involved in education, though none in day courses. Only two of the young women had jobs and of the 14 who had children, 10 lived on social security benefit. Over the ten-year period of my research, this core group of informants maintained a pattern in which a small minority were in steady employment and another minority were engaged full-time in informal economic activities called *hossels*. The majority were living from social security, some with occasional income on the side. The few informants with steady jobs tended to isolate themselves from unemployed relatives and friends for fear of being 'pulled under', as they put it. For most informants, though, full-time work and passive unemployment were two ends of a scale of possibilities along which some mobility occurred.

Besides being acquainted with unemployment, these Creole young peo-ple, especially those who had grown up in the Netherlands, were increas-ingly familiar with Dutch society. That meant they had also attuned their consumer expectations to the pattern of the young white Amsterdammers, especially the 'fashionable' ones they were sharing the dance floor with. By way of the media, they also indirectly experienced the social achievements and the lifestyles of blacks abroad, particularly in the USA. This, too, had influenced their expectations as to consumption, ideal careers, 'respect' (the status they felt they deserved, but did not usually get) and how to achieve it. Such expectations, which were high in relation to their low level of education, existed side by side with the 'normality' of unemployment in their own surroundings. This, in turn, influenced their commitment to education, their attitudes to work, their behaviour at work and the type of jobs they ended up in. For some it might be a driving force behind a desperate, continuous pursuit of alternatives to steady paid work. These could be in show business, but also in the informal or the criminal economy.

The survival strategies these young Creoles deployed to achieve social mobility or 'respect' were underpinned by a specific ideology. Informants said their marginalization was above all historically rooted in the Surinam-Creole past and in their Creole nature, or sometimes in the black character in general. *Hossels* were typically Surinamese; the importance of having a good time, being a mother and holding certain types of jobs was rooted in the Creole 'mentality'. The aversion to the status of manual worker was also historical in origin. Just as in the past, blacks were still being forced today to do work they did not want or enjoy. They saw this aversion as a rejection of monotonous work in particular, a product of the historical resistance of slaves to plantation work. This ideology was strongest among the street *hosselaars*, who were in the minority. What was important was the amount of money, not where it came from. Spending power was more important to the *hosselaar* than job status or education. He did not distinguish between worker and unemployed, but between active people and inactive 'do-nothings'. It was the scruffy, loud-mouthed junkie who was not respectable, not the dealer; it was not the pimp but the whore who was 'dirty'. The pimp said he did what he did because blacks had no other route to success. His under-the-table earnings were to be spent for a good cause someday – helping to build Surinam, a house for his mother or a respectable business. His *hossel* was also a form of protest against the Dutch exploitation of Surinam and the deprivation of blacks in Dutch society. He was not 'working', but living life to the full.

Despite all these attempts to explain their own survival strategy as typically Creole, the *hosselaars'* attitude to work, their methods and their ideology derived from a number of different sources. Certainly their approach was partly rooted in the social and cultural traditions and background of lower-class Creoles in Surinam and in centuries of experience in living with social instability. The very low status assigned to monotonous manual work is part of this tradition (Brana-Shute 1978, Sansone 1992). Creole traditions also include a number of *hossels* brought over from Surinam, such as the savings clubs or the organizing of commercial parties. But the survival strategies of the informants were also a product of their life in the Netherlands. Many *hossels* had been originated by the white Dutch themselves: under-the-table jobs for benefit claimants, *snorren* (driving a pirate taxi) and the street drugs scene on Amsterdam's Zeedijk had all existed before mass immigration from Surinam got underway. Generally speaking, then, the *hosselaars* were not innovators and they opened no new 'market opportunities', but just took over methods already existing in Amsterdam and repackaged them in Surinamese fashion. My informants' methods appeared to be influenced in part by the survival strategies of the white Dutch long-term unemployed, as with benefit abuse. Some ways of dealing with stolen goods were influenced by the methods of Dutch marginal youth they met on the streets, in youth institutions or sometimes in prison; and their activities with sex lines and escort services were influenced by the *penose*, the existing Amsterdam underworld. Still another influence was the anti-work ethic of white 'alternative' youth such as punks and squatters whom the Creoles met in places like youth centres. In the early 1970s, Biervliet (1975: 200) had already pointed out the similarities between the Creole *hosselaar* subculture in Amsterdam and the highly visible subcultures of white long-term unemployed and 'alternative' youth.

The low social position of my informants was determined by a combination of exclusion and self-exclusion. Prospects in the labour market and attitude to work influenced each other. Most informants were long-term unemployed. The few among them who did have a job derived no great status from it. All informants responded to the selectivity of the labour market by creating their own survival strategies. These attempts to evade selectivity often ended in self-exclusion – though it was sometimes unconscious and painless. The combination of the marginal position in the labour market with failure in the informal economy led many of them to concentrate more on leisure time (Sansone 1992: 186–92), motherhood and in some cases criminal *hossels*. Status, self-esteem and excitement were then sought mainly in these 'alternatives'. Leisure time, motherhood and criminal *hossels* were connected to one another and to school and the formal labour market like communicating vessels. Success at a steady job could lead to less interest in street-wise alternatives and success as a *hosselaar* could diminish one's interest in school. As longitudinal research has also demonstrated, the popularity of the two extremes on this continuum, steady jobs and criminal *hossels*, could fluctuate in accordance with employment trends and individual factors. The duration of unemployment was also a factor, since years of living on benefit had forced many informants to adopt lower, or more ethereal, expectations. It also made them less alert to new opportunities. Creole traditions continued to play a key role in the ways informants expressed their discontentment about their low social position and created 'alternative solutions'. The longer these Creole youths had lived in the Netherlands, though, the more their poor employment status and their work ethic was governed by factors intrinsic to Dutch society (cf. Cross and Entzinger 1988: 11). The obstacles associated with migration had become less relevant. It was now the process of exclusion from the Dutch labour market, the evolution of the informal sector, and the effects of the social security system that tended to make steady work less attractive and informal *hossels* more so. Their self-exclusion – an inability to profit from existing routes of advancement, such as student grants – had come more and more to resemble the subtle hindrances that frustrate individual social mobility for those white Dutch youth referred to as marginal youth.

There were nonetheless two important differences between the lower-class Creole and white Dutch youth. First, the black youth *felt* different. They attributed that to Creole culture and to their sense of a common past of slavery, colonialism and social deprivation. Second, they often felt discriminated against by the white majority on the grounds of their physical appearance. This racism not only played an important part in their self-image and in the process of creating a new black ethnicity, but it also influenced how they perceived the available routes to advancement. In the informants' daily lives, the skilful display of blackness was a central theme, but so was the fear of racial discrimination and their constant efforts to avoid it. Their fixation on sectors and occupations where, in their eyes, blackness was not treated so negatively had become part of their survival strategy, but at the same time it was instrumental in their self-exclusion. Although racial discrimination was not the only cause of their persistently low position in society, it did form a major impediment to their social advancement – from outside by the exclusion of black youth, and from inside by fostering disillusionment and escapism.

Similarities and differences

Obviously the local systems of opportunities in Amsterdam and Salvador are very different. Although the Netherlands has gained quite some reputation for the flexibility of its labour market, the process of flexibilization occurred in a context of a relatively stable and rigid labour force, limited informality and a well-articulated welfare system. The option for the unskilled can be assisted unemployment. In Salvador, the poor and the unemployed have fewer options. Thus, whereas the question for many Dutch Surinamese is whether you get a job that pays acceptably better than your social security benefit, the key question in Brazil is whether you get a decent job at all and manage to keep it. Official figures on unemployment and labour participation in the two countries are hard to compare, because they are not collected according to the same standards and because the official Brazilian figures heavily underreport the actual unemployment rate.[13] Even if we bear this in mind, converging structural conditions have led to one interesting set of similarities between Amsterdam and Salvador: the collapse of the status system based on the labour market position of one's parents. This is due in large part to the decline in purchasing power in the types of unskilled jobs that the informants might be able to get. Such a trend occurs in societies that are attaching more value than a generation ago to lifestyles that entail conspicuous consumption. In addition, there is now a growing number of people for whom a steady job has become a strange activity indeed.

In both Brazil and the Netherlands, the increasing specialization and a resegmentation of the labour market have gone hand in hand with a narrowing of the symbolic distance between the expectations of different social classes in terms of quality of life, purchasing power and quality of work. One consequence of this demand for ascending mobility is that, in the consciousness of the lower classes, a growing number of jobs are regarded as undesirable or 'dirty'. Similar strategies are also being deployed in the two countries for achieving social mobility. The significance of the civil service, the army and state-owned companies as avenues of social mobility for black populations is a phenomenon common all over the Black Atlantic – and state-owned companies are especially important in Brazil (Figueiredo 1998; da Silva 1997). In all probability that is because colour is of relatively little consequence in the hiring criteria and the career prospects in the public sector. Another relative similarity between the two countries is an overrepresentation of blacks in certain spectacular professions in the leisure sphere (primarily sports, singing, dancing and pop music), although the size and importance of these professions in the two countries diverges considerably.

One major difference between the two groups under comparison lies in the degree of state intervention in the daily lives of the urban poor. In both Salvador and Amsterdam, the relative marginality of black people to large sections of the labour market is a long-standing fact. In many respects, today's lower-class Creoles, together with other groups of 'problem' immigrants, are viewed in ways reminiscent of how the 'anti-socials', a problematic group of deviant white 'undeserving poor', were portrayed in Dutch popular and scholarly literature before the Second World War (de Regt 1984; de Swaan 1988). In Brazil, too, old cultural constructions relating to the pathologies of the 'undeserving poor' – most of which originally applied to the wave of new urban poor that preceded and followed the abolition of slavery in 1888 – still appear to codetermine present-day constructions applying to the largely mestizo and black urban poor.

In the years of the First Republic, immediately following the abolition of slavery, the preoccupation with the poor was limited to the implementation of 'social hygiene' measures and the combating of contagious diseases (Stepan 1991). Until the corporatist dictatorship of Vargas in the 1930s, quality of life, family life and interethnic relations and admixture in the Brazilian masses developed largely outside, if not counter to, the operations of the state. From the 1940s to the 1970s, attempts by the state to improve the living conditions and, in the process, to 'organize' the lives of the urban poor have been spasmodic and have not resulted in a powerful and care-providing welfare state. Over the past 20 years, moreover, with the general withdrawal of the state and the cuts in public spending, urban living conditions have yet again been developing with a relative degree of autonomy from the state. Starting from the (very late) abolition of slavery, this nonchalance on the part of the state has gone together with the absence of any strategy to associate blackness with the (undeserving) poor – at least not explicitly in writing or official pronouncements. In public policies, issues like poverty, social maladies and public hygiene have rarely been given an explicit black tint, though that has always occurred in the practice of policing (Chalub 1990).

With a sweeping statement, one could say that in Brazil the social exclusion of dark people, and their overrepresentation among the poor, have largely resulted from the absence of the state, whereas in the Netherlands these phenomena occur *in spite of* the measures taken by the state and in spite of the presence of one of the world's most fully developed welfare states. Rather different social contracts apply in the two countries. In the Netherlands, the state guarantees individual rights and the satisfaction of a number of basic necessities, even to the poor. Generally speaking, the law is adhered to. In Brazil, the persona determines in a dramatic fashion the application of the law. The rule of the law is not as efficient and democratic as in the Netherlands. The state is a machine that people tend to 'neutralize' through individual actions. This individualized relationship to the law and the state has produced major disparities in race relations and in an inequitable negotiation process between the black population and power and the state (Damatta 1987; Fry 1997; Viotti da Costa 1989).

In recent years, the role of the state in racial formation has receded in both countries, while that of the mass media and advertising is growing. Nonwhite people in the Netherlands, despite their proportionally small numbers, are increasingly present in both commercial and public constructions of Dutchness, whether as a part of advanced marketing strategies or because advertising has chosen to paint a picture of society based on an emergent multiculturality. In Brazil, in contrast, black people are grossly underrepresented in advertising and in the mass media, especially in highly popular television serials, although more black people are being seen in recent years in advertisements from public and semi-public companies and services. The underrepresentation of blacks may perhaps be accounted for by the relative absence of a multicultural discourse on how Brazil is to be portrayed by the market, or perhaps by the fact that popular consumerism is rather limited. Marketing strategies, especially for goods considered sophisticated by local standards (these include commodities that would seem ordinary in the Netherlands, such as processed food, economy cars or portable telephones) are still basically aimed at the upper echelons of the white half of the Brazilian population. Aggressive strategies to seduce new consumer groups are only scantly deployed, and even though the number of middle-class Afro-Brazilians is growing steadily (Figueiredo 1998), ethnicity is still definitely not one of the lines along which consumer groups are constituted.

Let us turn now to the construction of black identity. In both Brazil and the Netherlands, black culture is increasingly aestheticized through the use of symbols associated with the black body and a purported black sensibility. For people who can use them skilfully, these symbols enhance their chances to gain access to youth culture and to what is apparently a new sensual niche in the division of labour in modern Western urban society. From being the bearer of a stigma, the black body is turned into the show window of a new, 'natural', often hedonistic, way of relating to modernity. This aestheticization of black culture is especially evident in the domain of popular music – the interplay between what is perceived as black music and mainstream or 'white' music.

This hedonistic emphasis adds a degree of 'naturality' to the construction of the difference of the 'black race'. In both Salvador and Amsterdam, this is a process that operates both from without, through the outsider's perspective on black people, and from within, through the self-image of many black people, especially certain spokespeople, who maintain that black people are indeed biologically different from the rest – closer to nature, more sensual and sentimental. The emphasis on consumption is a double-edged sword. Consumerism can be seen as a means to achieve citizenship and to participate in society, but it is also a contested field in which not only success is felt, but also exclusion and frustration, since it is only a minority that manages to acquire the status symbols of modern consumerism. Among young lower-class blacks, glamorous images of black global success, mostly in show business and professional sports, can both stimulate superachievement in certain limited sections of the labour market as well as spread frustration about what is perceived as worldwide underachievement (Cashmore 1997).

In both cities there are many groups of black people who look to US blacks for cultural inspiration as well as for a frame of reference – in general the USA is a country with which comparisons are likely to be made. The way in which black culture is constructed in the US is a necessary point of comparison for the study of black culture in other contexts. A whole string of highly naturalizing ethnic 'truths' (or truisms?) on the personality of the black male or female, on the lower-class black population, on black job preference, on the black family, and on the sensuality and sentimentality of black people has become part and parcel of the ethnocultural division of labour in the US. Such constructions are often reflected in advertising, in the media and in movies. Because of the power of US black (and white) imagery within the global cultural flows – for example in the way black people are portrayed in advertising campaigns for popular status symbols like sport shoes – many such images are now well known worldwide. They permeate the imagery of black people, as well as black people's self-image, even in faraway places.[14] Hence, it seems appropriate to draw some conclusions here about the specificity or universality of certain traits of the US race relations system and about the 'Americanization' of local variants of black culture.

In the US, as in other countries of the Black Atlantic, blacks are overrepresented among the poor, the modern poor and non-work generation. Yet the distribution of the black population in the labour force is specific and so are the strategies deployed by black people in the labour market, from the middle class down to the 'underclass'. In the US, black people in the margin of society tend to be far more antagonistic towards the mainstream than do black Bahians and, to some extent, black Amsterdammers. Over the past few decades, the US blacks have developed survival strategies based on keeping their distance from the white middle class. In Brazil practically the opposite is the case: black people have historically tried to seduce and court the white middle class. Afro-Brazilian cultural expressions, such as religious rituals and musicmaking, are in principle open to whites. The Creoles in the Netherlands, and the younger generation in particular, are now undergoing a process through which they are, as it were, 'becoming black' (Sansone 1994a). As has already occurred in Great Britain and in France, the Creoles are redefining their ethnic identity through their experience of migration. US-based black culture is an important source of inspiration for this process of redefinition. After all, the US has been part of the cultural horizon of the Surinamese for decades, first in Surinam, where the US stood for modernity without colonialism, and now in the Netherlands, where the US-based black culture offers plenty of evidence that modernity, conspicuous consumption and blackness can go hand in hand. In other words, being ethnic need not mean being marginal.

When young blacks in Amsterdam and Salvador 'shop for culture' – choose among the ethnic symbols that are presented by the new global cultural flows – that is informed by class, age, gender and local circumstances. Global black symbols are drawn mostly from English-speaking regions of the Black Atlantic. Through the worldwide success of reggae music and the popularity of the Rastafari style, the small nation of Jamaica is an important source of inspiration, along with the USA and the UK (Sansone 1994a, 1997; Savishinsky 1994). Such global black symbols are selectively reinterpreted within national contexts and what cannot be combined with one's own situation is discarded. Even though the icons associated with music and youth styles tend to converge (as has happened with the paraphernalia of reggae music and hip hop), musical tastes and concrete reinterpretations of such icons are tenaciously local. Among young blacks in Brazil, English words like *black*, *funk* and *brother* have gained very specific local meanings that elicit associations with conspicuous consumption, speed and hyper-modernity rather than polarized race relations (Midlej e Silva 1998; Sansone 1998; Viana 1988). Amsterdam and Salvador relate to the networks of the English-speaking black *oecumenia* from rather different positions. The extent to which Amsterdam blacks can consume cultural goods and symbols originating in the English-speaking world is much greater than is the case in Salvador, where the vast majority of the black population cannot even satisfy their primary means, let alone buy cd's or hip hop-inspired fashion. Amsterdam is also far more central to Western cultural flows. On the other hand, Afro-Bahian symbols and artefacts have been fundamental to the construction of the image of Brazil abroad, and Afro-Bahian music (primarily the Afro-pop *axé* music and drum bands) and other cultural forms (such as the swift mixture of dance and martial arts called *capoeira*) hold a conspicuous place in world music and are increasingly finding echoes in the US and Europe. If Amsterdam is a transponder city for international black culture, a place where that culture is processed and even 'canned', then Salvador is a source city – a site where 'Africanisms' are produced and reproduced. So much for this digression onto the 'Americanization' of local variants of black culture.

The modes through which black culture is aestheticized are different in the two cities. In the first place this is because they have different traditions in the embodiment of blackness and whiteness and different histories of sexual morality. There is a close connection between the way black male and female bodies are looked upon in a society and the way these bodies are used there in the construction of black ethnicity and 'difference'. Salvador is a tropical city with a lively, street-oriented social life in the lower classes and even in large parts of the middle classes. Beach life and the sea are central in manifestations of popular culture such as massive folk festivals, carnival, and dancing and musicmaking on streets and beaches. Whiteness, not blackness, is exotic. Blue eyes spark off a frenzy in the opposite sex that compares to the arrival of dreadlocks in lower-class Dutch schools in the 1970s. (One could argue that blue eyes have a very different sexual appeal from dreadlocks, but it would go beyond the scope of this article to discuss that here.) In Salvador, courting is done in public much more than in Amsterdam. Being a good dancer is seen as something characteristic of all Bahians, rather than as a quality specific to the intimate stranger, the Creole.[15]

The second reason for the differing aesthetic modes is the differential 'visibility' of young blacks in the two cities. In Amsterdam, the simple fact of gathering on a street corner, speaking loudly in a group, drinking beer with your peers on the street, or commenting audibly on the girls that pass by can help to turn a group of young black men into an 'ethnic' phenomenon in the eyes of non-blacks. In such cases, their blackness is associated with behaviour that is considered highly sexualized, impolite by mainstream standards and even threatening. In Salvador, the stigma of blackness – where being black means low status – is not so much associated with young black men hanging around in the streets (there would be too many of them) as with certain ways of showing off your black body. This is either because your black body carries the stigmas associated with poverty and heavy work (unhealthy appearance, ill manners, missing teeth, scars, calluses, varicose veins, skin diseases and wounds) or because you present yourself as an indecent or nonworking person. In the past, the *malandro*, the Brazilian streetwise hustler,[16] showed off proudly all attributes that demonstrated he was not performing any heavy work: long nails, perfumed skin, immaculately white shirts. Today's young *malandro* differentiates himself from the *otários* (suckers) by his funkified reinterpretation of California beachwear (made more accessible by the forged first-class labels smuggled in from Paraguay). The police, who at least at the street level are overwhelmingly black or mestizo,[17] reinforce the importance of these lower-class and black signs of distinction. Until 30 years ago, in their frequent night raids, they would have arrested a young man without calloused hands; today they arrest the ones wearing 'too expensive' funky beachwear.

Central to the present chapter is the issue of whether exclusion and self-exclusion are ethnicized. Both Afro-Brazilians and the Creoles in Amsterdam can be regarded as colonial minorities. As many others before him, Ogbu (1978), writing on US schools, showed how lower-class young people, especially males, from colonial minorities tend to adopt an attitude of resistance towards school education and unskilled work. The main reason for this antagonism towards mainstream values, Ogbu argued, is that their forced incorporation into the labour market goes hand in hand with their keen awareness of the job ceiling. 'At the level of individual efforts, blacks traditionally avoid direct competition with whites for fear of reprisals' (1978: 180). Their fear of the job ceiling, instead of stimulating them to study harder, often discourages any education at all. Similar attitudes could be found among my informants in both cities. In Salvador, however, the self-perception of exclusion is not in terms of black and white, nor of ethnicity. Victimization is perceived there in terms of *fracos* (the weakest) rather than colour or race, even though negroid phenotypes are part of the construction of 'weakness'. Most lower-class black Brazilians firmly believe that any upward mobility results from the capacity and the opportunity to integrate, to join the mainstream of society, which they see as 'Brazilian' and not 'white'. The same young black Brazilians who shun certain jobs because they feel these are not 'ideal' for them reason in ways that might puzzle many of us: while insisting that such avoidance is not a consequence of racism, they know they would benefit by making white friends and establishing 'connections' with relevant white people. In other words, in the group I studied in Salvador, their exposure to racial discrimination and social exclusion, and their self-excluding reactions to these, were not accompanied by an ethnically based attitude of resistance (cf. Warren 1997), although they did resist school and humdrum work. As writers like Waldinger and Perlmann (1997) have emphasized, much of this countercultural attitude, rather than being ethnically based, is typical of the lower classes in general, which historically have tended to stress group solidarity and to scorn individual attempts at upward mobility. Thus, self-exclusion can be linked to what is commonly seen as an antagonistic stance towards white majority society, but it can also go together with an integrationist attitude towards life, as we see in Brazil.

Why is black ethnicity less central when Brazilians explain their own social positions? Tentatively I would suggest four interrelated reasons. First, the history of race relations in Brazil differs considerably from that in Surinam and the Netherlands. Brazil is a champion of the Iberian variant of colonialism and race relations (Hoetink 1967), which is characterized by relatively fluid ethnic borders and allegiances, a universalist emphasis on law and the state, the institutionalization of a mulatto group, and the presence of Roman Catholicism as the de facto state religion. The Catholic church 'embraced' both white and black souls, but offered, in its popular manifestations, space for a sectional interpretation of the word of God and of liturgy. Slaves were forcibly converted to Catholicism upon their arrival on the Brazilian shores. In Surinam, by contrast, conversion to Christianity was discouraged if not prohibited. After the abolition of slavery, religious experience remained different in the two countries, because pluralism was accepted in Surinam. I would argue, together with Hoetink (1967), that the religious tradition was particularly important. The universalism of Afro-Latin society (one country, one law, one people/race, one religion) had its origin in the Catholic tradition. The Protestant tradition, if only because it was accustomed to different churches for different people, coincided with, or even strengthened, a liberal attitude towards ethnic diversity in society.

Today Brazil is a federal republic with strong central state power. It operates in a context of strict universalistic dogmas, a history of racial mixture, a non-polar system of racial classification, a long syncretic tradition in the fields of popular culture and religion, a tradition of intolerance towards ethnic otherness in political life, a general aversion to ethnicity and, more recently, considerable difficulty in allowing any multiculturalism in education (see Sansone 1999; Souza 1996). In 'heterophobic' Brazil,[18] the right to cultural diversity is effectively denied in both the highbrow and lowbrow variants of the racial democracy discourse. Both not only abhor racism, but also celebrate biological and cultural intermingling in public rituals of miscegenation in leisure activities (for instance, the making and consumption of traditional and popular music) and in popular religion.

The Netherlands, on the other hand, is a country where black people are a relatively small, recently immigrated minority whose ethnic borders are sharper than those in Brazil. The country also has a tradition known as pillarization, which formerly prescribed far-reaching segregation along political and religious lines. Although this tradition has considerably weakened in the past few decades, it laid the groundwork for the emergence, on a larger scale than in most other European immigration countries (Vermeulen 1997), of many new religious schools that cater to the offspring of immigrants. Most but not all such schools are Muslim. Ethnicity and the right to cultural and religious diversity are celebrated as assets in the Netherlands – as some of the nation's finest characteristics.[19] Along with this celebration of diversity, however, the Netherlands has also experienced a very high rate of miscegenation in the past four decades, resulting in particular from unions of indigenous Dutch people with Dutch citizens of Indonesian, Creole, Antillean and Moluccan origin. Although the development of a 'mixed' ethnic identity is still limited, this ethnic admixture is already bringing into disarray the established system of ethnic classification, which is based on the polarity *allochtoon/autochtoon* (foreign/indigenous), or sometimes white/nonwhite (van Heelsum 1997).[20]

The second reason for the differential emphasis on black ethnicity is that the ethnocultural divisions of labour have historically been quite different in the two countries. In Brazil the discourse on heavy work is by and large associated with the black body (violated and ill-fed). In the Netherlands an ethnic division of labour did not emerge until in the 1960s and then it was mostly the labour immigrants from Mediterranean countries rather than the Creoles who became associated with heavy and dirty work. The position of the Creoles in the Dutch labour market is a product of two factors: the ethnocultural segmentation of the labour market in Surinam (see for example van Lier 1971, and the contribution of van Niekerk in this volume) and the problematic incorporation of Surinamese immigrants who arrived in the Netherlands after the mid 1960s. In Brazil, the ethnocultural division of labour is based on the legacy of slavery, the low position historically assigned to manual labour, and the distribution of work and work status according to a combination of colour, class, status and demeanour. It works as a mosaic rather than as a polarity.

Third, most black Brazilians see themselves as part of the lower class, even though they know that racism exists among the lower classes too, for example when it comes to marriage partners (Poli Teixera 1988). They behave accordingly in lower-class neighbourhood associations, in trade unions and in their voting patterns – there is no distinctly black vote or black viewpoint in opinion polls (Datafolha 1995). The majority of the Creoles in the Netherlands are in a lower-class position, and they feel deprived and disadvantaged. They have traditionally been social democratic voters, but they do not seem inclined to identify with the native lower class. My informants actually tended to see lower-class whites as boorish and ugly (Sansone 1992: 42–4).

Fourth, in Brazil black people are an integral part of the national image-building and the public representation of Brazilianness. Mass media do not tend to interpret social or cultural tensions in terms of black and white, although a certain racialization of difference is present, especially in the media embodiment of poverty. As a consequence, attachment to the 'nation' is stronger among the black population in Brazil than it is in the Netherlands. This is reflected for one thing in the fact that record sales of national music hits are not colour-bound – the celebration of Brazilianness often expresses itself through popular music. Dutch national symbols are still predominantly white – which need not mean that the Creoles cannot recognize them as being their own, as with the monarchy. In the Netherlands, blackness still symbolizes the alien, though that may now be changing. In Brazil blackness is a symbol for poverty. Many white Dutch people perceive the Creoles as transplanted colonial subjects, while most white Brazilians see Afro-Brazilians as the descendants of slaves.

Conclusions

Considerable differences have emerged between the Netherlands and Brazil when it comes to the distribution, position and participation rate of the black population in the labour market. The two populations also differ in terms of work ethic, entrepreneurship, urban–rural population distribution, rate of employment in government jobs, degree of dependency on social security, and the 'alternatives' available to them in the informal and criminal economies. We have identified techniques used in the two groups as people strive to achieve social mobility and we have seen mechanisms by which they exclude themselves from those positions in the labour market and society which they deem less suited to black people. Such techniques and mechanisms are patterned by the local systems of opportunities. Survival strategies may include such contrasting tactics as trying to charm white people or keeping at a distance from them. They can emphasize miscegenation and the contributions black people make to popular culture or even the nation, or they can aim at building black community capital by stressing black ethnicity. Other ethnocultural constructions that are influenced by specific national or regional situations, and not only by international stereotypes or imagery, involve the black body and black sensuality, the 'black male' and his 'threat' to the white mainstream, black femininity as a natural, uterine and magic force, and the notion that black people are better at dancing or sport – notions identifiable in both negrophobic and negrophile variants (Gendron 1990). The cases of Amsterdam and Salvador show that there is no such thing as 'typically black' survival strategies.

While we should bear all these differences in mind, we still need to reflect on a remarkable series of similarities between young blacks in the two cities. Cross-national similarities may be traditional, or they may be products of a new phase of internationalization. A mix of class and ethnic factors, often at some odds with one another, can be seen in both periods. This raises the question of whether there is a universal black culture – a specific culture that differs from general lower-class cultures and subcultures. Should this be the case, what is its origin and significance?

In the first place, similarities in black culture and ethnicity across national boundaries may have resulted from the history of international exchanges throughout the Black Atlantic. The term 'black culture' in itself is a result of domination and of dramatic international encounters. Enslavement, deportation and the plantation society laid the foundations for the internationalization of the black condition in the New World. As a consequence, black people tend to be found at the bottom of the social ladders in both Surinam and Brazil. Racism, whether perpetrated by the non-black population in Brazil or by colonial government practices in Surinam, has codetermined black people's opportunities. In the historical past, actual international contacts were few, and they were carried out mostly by scientists (Bastide 1967; Herskovits 1941; Verger 1957), travellers or missionaries.

Such traditional international similarities have been dictated by history and by the diasporic experience. In recent decades, however, a boost to the internationalization of black culture has been provided by the converging structural conditions and the new technical infrastructure of the post-Fordist era, as well as by the new opportunities for cultural creation which the process of globalization is bringing about. The worldwide crisis in employment conditions that accompanies the present stage of society has triggered a general decline in the importance of job status for individual self-definition and for the construction of personality, while at the same time promoting the centrality of consumerism. These global phenomena have appeared in many different countries in recent decades, almost independently of the economic stage in which a country finds itself, whether or not it has an articulated welfare state, whether or not it has a black population. The situations of the informants in the two cities compared here recall those of other lower-class people, for example in certain communities of immigrants in the USA (Gans 1992), in black communities in US regions hard hit by recession (Wilson 1987, 1996) and in traditional mining communities in the north of Britain following pit closures (Wight 1987).

The neighbourhoods I studied in Amsterdam and Salvador bore several resemblances to such areas. Although the majority of the fathers and many of the mothers worked, they remained relatively distant from middle-class values and culture and from other values of the 'white' mainstream. The majority of their children, in contrast, were much closer to middle-class values and culture, but were massively unemployed or fairly marginal to the labour market, as a consequence of a growing lack of jobs for the unskilled and the unattractive nature of the available jobs. The resulting combination of insight into the mechanisms of social exclusion with an ideology and actions which lead to self-exclusion has often been observed in youth of low social status, such as lower-class US blacks (Freeman and Holzer 1986; Ogbu 1978), working-class English boys (Willis 1977) and adolescent Latino drug dealers in the USA (Bourgois 1995; Williams 1989). All such cases involve self-exclusion from many of those jobs that are available, combined with fear of failure, fatalism and an overly keen perception of the obstacles facing their own group. Such traits go hand in hand with individual resistance, passive discontent, a pursuit of 'alternatives' to ordinary work and a misjudgement of one's own capacities. The wide gulf between expectations and career prospects is a problem for virtually all poorly qualified youth in Western cities (see for example Anderson 1990: 110; Willis 1990: 14–15). The displacement of the source of status from work to consumption has likewise been previously observed in other situations, such as among white working-class youth in England in the 1970s (Hall and Jefferson 1976; Hebdige 1979) and lower-class youth in contemporary urban Mexico (Canclini 1995). The language of government, social work and education, with its emphasis on equality, combined with the effects of advertising and the media, have inflated these young people's expectations of consumption and personal advancement (cf. Gottfredson 1981). The reality of scarce, unattractive jobs with few career prospects forms a stark contrast to these high hopes. Although this does not entirely prevent poorly qualified youths from finding work, it does lead to chronic job dissatisfaction and frequent lapses in employment.

Historically, the black populations of both Brazil and the Netherlands are highly overrepresented in the ranks of the poor, and of the 'undeserving poor' in particular (such as prisoners, prostitutes and problem youths). In Brazil, black people are also disproportionately present in the working class. This explains why, in all its local variants, black culture has much in common with lower-class culture and sometimes with a 'culture of poverty', and why in Brazil it is also closely linked to working-class culture. However, if we were to simply equate black culture with lower-class culture or some variant of it, we would be making two mistakes. Too often black culture is perceived as antagonistic to mainstream values – one forgets that many black people just want to belong. On the other hand, forms of black identity have frequently emerged among middle-class and better-educated blacks, even those who did not normally practise traditional black culture.

There is yet another factor that produces common features in local variants of black culture – the experience of racism and the racialization of the black body. The latter is the origin of the emphasis put by many young blacks on their supposedly inborn musicality and sensuality or on their physical strength, in the conviction that this will be the best route for the poorly qualified to gain status – not just in the leisure sphere, but in the labour market too. Many informants in both Amsterdam and Salvador suggested at some point that it would be through one of these 'black qualities' that they could make it in the 'world of the white' at last. Black organizations and leaders in both cities have argued on numerous occasions that black people ought to be given a special, 'cultural' place in the labour market. Little research has been done yet on the size and feasibility of such cultural space or on the economic potential of a black culture industry in Western society[21] (although Brazil qualifies for the catch-all term 'Western' only in part). Research in the US and Great Britain has tended to be highly polemical about the potentiality of a black culture industry (see especially Cashmore 1997; Frazier 1942). What is generally accepted, however, is that intellectual and technical skills are a far greater source of status in a technological society than musicality, sensuality and physical strength.

The globalization of Western urban culture has created new opportunities for the worldwide distribution of a number of symbols associated with black culture, most of which have originated in English-speaking countries. Globalization implies not only a new set of more rapid and powerful technical media, but it also connotes a stage in modern society with a new passion for the exotic, the pure, the natural. This is helping to create a new (commercial and noncommercial) space for those forms of black culture that are more closely related to youth culture and the aestheticization of the black body, as well as for forms that stress 'purity' and 'African tradition'. In essence, by updating old images of the supposed naturality of black people, the globalized streams of symbols are linking young black people to leisure, physicality, sexual prowess, musicality and naturality, while contraposing them to work, rationality and modern technology. This has generated a kind of modern global black hedonism which is both a cause and a consequence of racialization. Such hedonism penetrates into faraway local variants of black cultures through the music and leisure industry, youth culture and advertising. Among these young blacks, generational differences and the job crisis are sparking discontentment with the parental generation, with its traditional black culture and ethnicity, and boosting the popularity of this black hedonism as a modern interpretation of a lower-class black way of life.

Though the popularity of this hedonism may vary, it is certainly a factor of increasing importance both in the making of job careers and in the process of self-exclusion from certain zones of the labour market and society. For a growing number of young blacks in both cities, colour is the lens through which they interpret and experience their own class position. The extent to which colour is seen as explaining success or failure depends on the popularity of 'class' as an alternative explanation. It also depends on local circumstances, which are more favourable to 'colour' in Amsterdam than in Salvador. There is no black culture and ethnicity without racism – the memory of past brutal oppression and the awareness of today's subtler practices. Through old and new processes of internationalization, symbols and discourses connected to this causal relationship between black culture and ethnicity and racism are coming to resemble each other more and more throughout the world, although political articulations and local outcomes still vary widely.

One can agree with Gilroy (1993) that black culture, in its traditional forms, was an offshoot of modernity – a process geared to colonialism and later decolonization. Black culture as we know it today – with its youth culture and its aesthetic dimensions, its mixture of protest and conformism – is tied to globalization and the deterritorialization of ethnicities. This is despite the claims made in many of its cultural forms, such as Rastafarianism or the Afro-Brazilian religious system, that they are the preservers of premodern values.

Notes

1. For their suggestions I owe much to Hans Vermeulen, Joel Perlmann, Fernando Rosa Ribeiro, Antony Spanakos, Tijno Venema, Edward Telles and Carlos Hasenbalg. Of course, I myself am responsible for all the contents of the chapter.
2. A definition of black culture that may be valid in the context of different race relations systems is as follows: black culture is a specific subculture of people of African-American origin within a social system that stresses colour as an important criterion for differentiating or segregating people. The main binding force of black culture is the sense of a common past as slaves and underprivileged people. Africa is used as a 'symbol bank' from which symbols are creatively drawn. Another specific feature of black culture is its high degree of interdependence with Western urban culture. Specific in some ways to black culture, especially in its contemporary forms, is an emphasis on the management of physical appearance. In the terminology as used here, black culture in the singular is a basic taxonomic concept referring to common traits in the cultural production of black populations in different contexts. 'Black cultures' refers to the local or subgroup variants of black culture.
3. See Bastide 1967, Frazier 1942, Herskovits 1941, 1943, Pierson 1942, Verger 1957.
4. The Brazilian national census applies five ethno-racial categories: *branca* (white), *preta* (black), *parda* (brown/mestizo), *amarela* (yellow/East Asian) and *indígena* (native American). The last (1991) census found, among the 146.5 million Brazilians, 51.5 per cent white, 42.5 per cent brown, 5 per cent black, 0.4 per cent yellow and 0.2 per cent indigenous people (IBGE 1995). Many observers have argued that these categories are not clear-cut and are defined differently from region to region. For example, in northern Brazil many '*brancos*' are in fact mestizos.
5. For an excellent and up-to-date overview of the segmentation along colour lines on the Brazilian labour market, see Hasenbalg *et al.* 1998.
6. In modern Brazil, though a few remote rural black communities still mantain a Bantu-based lexicon, black people have not produced anything approaching a 'black way of speaking Portuguese', a style that both linguists and laypeople would accept as characteristic black speech. The existence of numerous regional and class-based variants of Brazilian Portuguese is commonly acknowledged. It might be

argued that such a viewpoint is linked to an approach – dominant in Brazil, also among sociolinguists – which avoids emphasizing ethnic differences among Brazilians, and which instead attributes segmentation and different lifestyles basically either to class or to differential exposure to modernity and globalization.

7. Folk literature sold in food markets and fairs.

8. Edward Telles (1994) has depicted the following relationship between the social pyramid and the labour market in Brazil. The bottom of the pyramid is very wide and contains most blacks and mestizos, but also the majority of white workers. The middle is narrow and mostly white and the top is narrower still and almost exclusively white. He shows that this stratification is practically the opposite to that in the USA and this can help us to understand the salience of class solidarity and the relative absence of ethnic animosity in the Brazilian lower classes. Interracial solidarity is strong in the lower levels of the pyramid, while racism is more acute in the higher echelons. With a sweeping statement, one might say that in Brazil (as in most of Latin America) the *tendency* by both insiders and outsiders to interpret social conflicts as class-based, together with the strong influence of neo-Marxism in the social sciences, may have impeded the development of a politics of identity as we know it in the USA and many European countries. Even if ethnicity has been *eclipsed* by class from the native point of view, however, this need not mean that racism and ethnicity are not significant forces in a society from the *researcher's* point of view.

9. A *Creool* (plural *Creolen*) is a Surinamese person of African or mixed-African descent.

10. Although exact comparisons between years cannot be made on the basis of the available statistics, some studies have given an indication of trends in the period 1972–90. In 1977, unemployment was 22 per cent among the Surinamese and 5 per cent among the native white population (Gooskens *et al.* 1979: 112). In 1990, it had climbed to 40.5 per cent for the Surinamese and 16 per cent for the ethnic Dutch (Amsterdam Bureau for Statistics 1991: 30). Official statistics do not usually distinguish Creoles from the other Surinamese.

11. This chapter is based on a study entitled 'Colour, class and modernity in the daily life of two areas of Bahia', which was part of the Ford Foundation Research Programme 'The Colour of Bahia' at the Federal University of Bahia. Financial support was also provided by WOTRO (Dutch Research Council for the Tropics) and CNPq (Brazilian Research Council).

12. The research was carried out in three phases: 1981–82 (Vermeulen 1984), 1983–84 (Sansone 1986) and 1988–90 (Sansone 1990). A total of 157 informants aged 14 to 37 were interviewed, 46 of them female. I had superficial contacts with many more young people. A core group of 75 informants were interviewed in all three phases. I met most of them at a youth centre in the western part of the Amsterdam inner city, where I was working as a volunteer. I met others at a training centre for Surinamese youth with low levels of education, all of whose 22 participants I interviewed in 1982. In 1983–84 and 1988–90 I carried out field work in the Amsterdam districts of West and also Zuidoost, where some of the core informants had meanwhile moved. This enabled me to record the life histories of 75 core informants, of whom 15 were female. In choosing the informants I did not aim at statistical representativeness, but at obtaining a cross section of lower-class Creole young people in Amsterdam. For example, I tried to limit the number who exhibited overt marginal behaviour – although some others proceeded to develop such behaviour in the course of the research.

13. For example, the national Brazilian bureau for statistics (IBGE) registers as a working person anyone over the age of 10 who undertakes some sort of informal economic activity for at least 20 hours a week.
14. Bourdieu and Wacquant (1998) suggest that globalization as well as a number of US foundations also spread worldwide, specially to Latin America, theoretical approaches to race relations and possible 'policy solutions' to racism that are being generated within the US. The authors argue that the coloniality of Latin American intellectuals facilitates this form of 'academic imperialism'.
15. Interestingly, in some neighbourhoods frequented by European tourists, blackness is 'acted out' in ways that reminded me of Amsterdam. Attractive young blacks, mainly women, who have devised a survival strategy of accompanying white tourists throughout their holiday in Bahia, are called gringo-eater or *negro de carteirinha* (professional blacks) by other young blacks.
16. Among lower-class Creoles in Surinam (Brana-Shute 1978), and later in the Netherlands, one can encounter the popular character of the *wakaman* (literally, the man who walks). His ability to avoid humdrum work makes him very similar to the *malandro*. *Malandro* and *wakaman*, with their hedonistic lifestyle and their ability to shun dull work, were key figures in the construction of the attitude towards work among the informants in both cities. In Brazil, even though most *malandros* were black, they are not celebrated as black figures in samba lyrics and popular novels, but rather as prototypes of a national character and of popular 'Brazilianness'. Research on the *malandro* has led to numerous publications (see, for instance, Damatta 1979).
17. Exact figures on colour within the Bahian police are not available. By way of reference, in the state of Rio de Janeiro, according to the official statistics of the Military Police Statistics Department in 1998, only about 30 per cent of this 28 000-strong police corps self-identifies as white. About a third of these report having kinky hair, meaning that they are actually 'home-grown whites' (*brancos da terra*), light-skinned mestizos.
18. From the mid-18th century until the 1930s, Brazil absorbed massive numbers of immigrants, mainly from Italy, Portugal, Spain, Japan, the Ottoman Empire and Germany. Integration and miscegenation was encouraged by law, while ethnic minority formation was discouraged if not proscribed – in the 1930s the Vargas regime even banned the teaching of languages other than Portuguese.
19. Fernando Rosa Ribeiro (1998) has pointed out that a similar pattern emphasizing separation and ethnic identity has prevailed in most countries that were part of the Dutch empire or that experienced long-term Dutch colonization, such as Indonesia, South Africa and Surinam. For example, from about 1900 to 1930, some important ethnic groups in Surinam, such as the Hindustanis and the Javanese, had special courts in which most minor and some major offences were tried under their own sets of ethnic rights. For the urban Creoles, on the other hand, a politics of assimilation to Dutch mores was enforced (van Lier 1971). In fact, from the mid-18th century onwards, Surinam was the prototype of a pluralist society, where urban Creoles (*stadscreolen*) coexisted with several other ethnic groups.
20. Although less so than the Brazilian one, the Dutch system of racial classification is ambiguous and permits a degree of manipulation of ethnic identity. There is also a lag between official statistics and daily usage. A Creole could be an *allochtoon* for the official statistics and *zwart, Surinamer, donker, Creool* or even the pejorative *neger* in daily life.

21. A step is this direction is the book edited by Livio Sansone and Jocélio Teles dos Santos (1998), which contains several articles on aspects of the black culture industry in Bahia.

References

Agier, M., 1990, 'Espaço urbano, família e status social. O novo operaiado baiano nos seus bairros', *Cadernos* CRH (Salvador) 13: 39–62

Agier, M., 1992, 'Ethnopolitique – Racisme, statuts et mouvement noir à Bahia', *Cahiers d'Études Africaines* EHESS, XXXII(1): 1–24

Amsterdam Bureau for Statistics, 1991, *Arbeidskrachtentelling* (Amsterdam: Gemeente Amsterdam)

Anderson, E., 1990, *Streetwise. Race, Class and Change in an Urban Community*, (Chicago: University of Chicago Press)

Bacelar, J., 1989, *Etnicidade. Ser Negro em Salvador* (Salvador: Yanamá)

Bastide, R., 1967, *Les Ameriques Noires* (Paris: Payot)

Biervliet, W., 1975, 'Werkloosheid van jonge Surinamers in de grote steden van Nederland', *Jeugd en Samenleving* 5(12): 911–24

Bourdieu, P., and L. Wacquant, 1998, 'Sur les ruses de la raison impérialiste', *Actes de la Recherche en Sciences Sociales* 121–2: 109–18

Bourgois, P., 1995, *In Search of Respect. Selling Crack in El Barrio* (Cambridge, Mass.: Cambridge University Press)

Brana-Shute, G., 1978, *On the Corner. Male Social Life in a Paramaribo Creole Neighbourhood* (Assen: Van Gorcum)

Canclini, N.G., 1995, *Consumidores e Cidadãos* (Rio de Janeiro: Ed. UFRJ)

Cashmore, E., 1997, *Black Culture Industry* (London: Routledge)

Chalub, S., 1990, *A Guerra contra os Cortiços. A Cidade do Rio, 1850–1906* (Campinas: Ed. Unicamp)

Cross, M., and H. Entzinger, 1988, 'Caribbean minorities in Britain and the Netherlands. Comparative questions', in: M. Cross and H. Entzinger (eds), *Lost Illusions. Caribbeans in Britain and the Netherlands* (London: Routledge)

Damatta, R., 1979, *Carnavais, Malandros e Herois* (Rio de Janeiro: Zahar)

Damatta, R., 1987, *Relativizando. Uma Introdução à Antropologia Brasileira* (Rio de Janeiro: Rocco)

Datafolha, 1995, *Racismo Cordial* (S. Paolo: Editora Datafolha)

Figueiredo, A., 1998, *Novas Elites de Cor*, MA Thesis (Bahia: Dept. of Sociology, Federal University of Bahia)

Frazier, F., 1942, 'The negro family in Bahia, Brazil', *American Sociological Review* 4(7): 465–78

Freeman, R., and H. Holzer, 1986, *The Black Youth Eemployment Crisis* (Chicago: University of Chicago Press)

Fry, P., 1997, 'O que a Cinderela Negra tem a dizer sobre a "política racial" no Brasil', *Revista da USP* 28: 122–35

Gans, H., 1992, 'Second generation decline. Scenarios for the economic and ethnic futures of the post-1965 American immigrants', *Ethnic and Racial Studies* 15(2): 173–92

Gendron, B., 1990, 'Fetishes and motorcars. Negrophilia in French Modernism', *Cultural Studies* 4(4): 141–55

Gilroy, P., 1993, *The Black Atlantic. Modernity and Double Consciousness* (London: Verso)

Gooskens, I., J. Hoolt and M. Freeman, 1979, *Surinamers en Antillianen in Amsterdam. Part I & II.* (Amsterdam: Gemeente Amsterdam, Afdeling Bestuurinformatie)

Gottfredson, L., 1981, 'Circumscription and compromise. A developmental theory of occupational aspirations', *Journal of Counseling Psychology Monograph* 28(6): 545–79

Hall, S., and T. Jefferson, 1976, *Resistence Through Rituals* (London: Hutchinson)

Harris, M., 1970, 'Referential ambiguity in the calculus of Brazilian racial identity', in: N. Whitten and J. Szwed (eds), *African-American Anthropology* (New York: The Free Press)

Hasenbalg, C., M. Lima, and N. del Valle Silva, 1998, *Cor e Segmentação* (Rio de Janeiro: Contracapa)

Hebdige, D., 1979, *Subculture. The Meaning of Style* (London: Methuen)

Heelsum, A. van, 1997, *De Etnisch-Culturele Positie van de Tweede Generatie Surinamers* (Amsterdam: Het Spinhuis)

Herskovits, M., 1941, *The Myth of the Negro Past* (New York: Harper & Bros)

Herskovits, M., 1943, 'The negro in Bahia, Brazil. A problem in method', *American Sociological Review* VII(8): 394–404

Hoetink, H., 1967, *Caribbean Race Relations. A Study of Two Variants* (New York: Oxford University Press)

IBGE, 1995, *Censo Demográfico 1991* (Rio de Janeiro: Editora IBGE)

Leeman, Y., and S. Saharso, 1989, *Je Kunt Er Niet Omheen. Hoe Marokkaanse, Molukse en Surinaamse Jongeren Reageren op Discriminatie* (Lisse: Swets en Zeitlinger)

Lier, R. van, 1971, *Frontier Society. A Social Analysis of the History of Surinam* (The Hague: Martinus Nijhoff) [1949]

Martens, E.P., 1995, *Minderheden in Beeld. Kerncijfers uit de Survey Sociale Positie en Voorzieningengebruik Allochtonen 1994 (SPVA-94)* (Rotterdam: ISEO)

Martens, E.P., 1999, *Minderheden in Beeld: SPVA-98* (Rotterdam: ISEO)

Martens, E.P., and A.O. Verweij, 1997, *Surinamers in Nederland. Kerncijfers 1996* (Rotterdam: ISEO)

Mascarenhas, D., 1997, 'Um dia eu vou abrir a porta da frente. Mulheres negras, educação e mercado de trabalho', in: A.L. Portela (ed.), *Educação e os Afro-Brasileiros* (Salvador: Novos Toques)

Midlej e Silva, S., 1998, 'O lúdico e o étnico no funk do "Black Bahia"', in: L. Sansone and J. Teles dos Santos (eds), *Ritmos em Transito. Socio-Antropologia da Música da Bahia* (São Paulo: Dynamis)

Niekerk, M. van, 1994, 'Zorg en hoop. Surinamers in Nederland nu', in: H. Vermeulen and R. Penninx (eds), *Het Democratisch Ongeduld. De Emancipatie en Integratie van Zes Doelgroepen van het Minderhedenbeleid* (Amsterdam: Het Spinhuis)

Ogbu, J., 1978, *Minority Education and Caste* (New York: Academic Press)

PNAD-Pesquisa Nacional Amostra Domiciliar, 1997, *Survey 1996* (Rio de Janeiro: IBGE)

Pierson, D., 1942, *Negroes in Brazil. A Study of Race Contact in Bahia* (Chicago: University of Chicago Press)

Poli Teixera, M., 1988, 'A questão da cor nas relações de um grupo de baixa renda', *Estudos Afro-Asiáticos* 14: 85–97

Regt, A. de, 1984, *Arbeidersgezinnen in Nederland* (Amsterdam/Meppel: Boom)

Ribeiro, F.R., 1998, 'The Dutch Diaspora: apartheid, boers and passion', *Itinerario* 1: 87–106

Sansone, L., 1986, *Onder Surinaamse jongeren* (Amsterdam: Stadsdrukkerij)

Sansone, L, 1990, *Lasi Boto. De Boot Gemist. Over Surinaamse Jongeren, Werk en Werkloosheid* (Leuven: Acco)

Sansone, L., 1992, *Schitteren in de Schaduw. Overlevingsstrategieën, Subcultuur en Etniciteit van Creoolse Jongeren uit de Lagere Klasse in Amsterdam 1981–1991* (Amsterdam: Het Spinhuis)

Sansone, L., 1993. 'Pai preto, filho negro. Trabalho, cor e diferenças geracionais', *Estudos Afro-Asiáticos* 25: 73–98

Sansone, L., 1994a, 'The making of black culture. From Creole to black. The new ethnicity of lower-class Surinamese-Creole young people in Amsterdam', *Critique of Anthropology* 14(2): 173–98

Sansone, L., 1994b, 'Couleur, classe et modernité dans deux quartiers de Bahia', *Cahiers des Ameriques Latines* Printemps: 85–106

Sansone, L., 1996, 'Nem somente preto ou negro. O sistema de classificação da cor no Brasil que muda', *Afro-Asia* (Journal of the Centro de Estudos Afro Orientais, Salvador, Bahia, Brazil) 18: 165–88

Sansone, L., 1997, 'The emergence of the politics of black identity in Bahia, Brazil', in: H. Vermeulen and C. Govers (eds), *The Politics of Ethnic Consciousness* (London: Macmillan)

Sansone, L., 1998, 'Funk in Bahia and in Rio. Local versions of a global phenomenon?', *Focaal* 30/31: 139–57

Sansone, L., 1999, 'Racismo sem etnicidade. Políticas públicas e discriminação racial no Brasil e em outros 'países' mestiços na América Latina', *Dados* 41(4): 751-84

Sansone, L., and J. Teles dos Santos (eds), 1998, *Ritmos em Transito. Socio-Antropologia da Música na Bahia* (São Paulo: Dynamis)

Savishinsky, N., 1994, 'Transnational popular culture and the global spread of the Jamaican Rastafarian movement', *New West Indian Guide/Nieuwe West-Indische Gids* 68(3/4): 259–81

Silva, P.C. da, 1997, *Negros à Luz Dos Fornos* (São Paulo: Dynamis)

Souza, J. (ed.), 1996, *Multi-Culturalismo e Racismo. Uma Comparação Brasil-Estados Unidos* (Brásilia: Editoria Paralelo 15)

Stepan, N., 1991, *The Hour of Eugenics. Race, Gender and Nation in Latin America* (Ithaca, NY: Cornell University Press)

Swaan, A. de, 1988, *In Care of the State* (Cambridge: Polity Press)

Telles, E., 1994, 'Industrialização e desigualdade racial no emprego. O exemplo brasileiro', *Estudos Afro-Asiáticos* 26: 21–51

Verger, P., 1957, *Notes sur le Culte des Orisa et Vodun* (Dakar: IFAN)

Vermeulen, H., 1984, *Etnische Groepen en Grenzen* (Weesp: Het Wereldventster)

Vermeulen, H., 1997, 'Conclusions', H. Vemeulen (ed.), *Immigrant Policy for a Multicultural Society* (Brussel/Amsterdam: MPG & IMES)

Viana, H., 1988, *O Mundo Funk Carioca* (Rio de Janeiro: Zahar)

Viotti da Costa, E., 1989, *Da Senzala a Colonia* (São Paulo: Brasiliense)

Waldinger, R., and J. Perlmann, 1997, 'Second generation decline? Children of immigrants, past and present – a reconsideration', *International Migration Review* XXXI(4): 893–922

Warren, J., 1997, 'O fardo de não ser negro. Uma análise comparativa do desempenho escolar de alunos afro-brasileiros e afro-norteamericanos', *Estudos Afro-Asiáticos* 31: 103–24

Wight, D., 1987, *Hard Workers and Big Spenders Facing the Bru. Understanding Men's Employment and Consumption in a De-Industrialized Scottish Village*, PhD Social Sciences, University of Edinburgh

Williams, T., 1989, *The Cocaine Kids. The Inside Story of a Teenage Drug Ring* (Reading, Mass.: Addison-Wesley)

Willis, P., 1977, *Learning to Labour. Why Working-Class Kids Get Working-Class Jobs* (London: Saxon House)

Willis, P., 1990, *Common Culture* (Buckingham: Open University Press)

Wilson, W.J., 1987, *The Truly Disadvantaged. The Inner City, the Underclass and Public Policy* (Chicago: University of Chicago Press)

Wilson, W.J., 1996, *When Work Disappears. The World of the New Urban Poor* (New York: Knopf)

9

Creoles and Hindustanis. Patterns of Social Mobility in Two Surinamese Immigrant Groups in the Netherlands

Mies van Niekerk

In 1992 a Dutch weekly magazine published a cover story on the ostensible success of Hindustani immigrants in the Netherlands.[1] A comparison was readily made between this East Indian group, migrants from the former Dutch colony of Surinam and Asian immigrants to the United States. The Hindustanis themselves have promoted a similar public image now and then, referring to 'the Asian success'. This has in turn been contrasted with the image of the Afro-Surinamese immigrants, the Creoles.[2] The latter have been portrayed as a socially disadvantaged group and, especially in the 1970s and early 1980s, depicted in the media as 'problematic'. Popular thinking on the two groups, both in the Netherlands and in Surinam, strongly assumes a relationship between their ethnic culture and their economic success.

Until recently, ethnic differences in educational and economic attainment were seldom explicitly studied by Dutch researchers. In the vast quantities of social science research on ethnic minorities, much attention has been devoted to their socioeconomic positions in Dutch society, but studies on differential adaptation of immigrant groups are still rare (cf. van Niekerk 1993). One possible reason to object to cultural explanations is that they tend to be one-sided, failing to consider the opportunity structures and processes of exclusion in a society as a whole. Perhaps this is why 'culture' tends to be neglected altogether in social science research on immigrants. However, 'structural' explanations cannot fully account for ethnic differences in the socioeconomic position of immigrant groups, as has been extensively demonstrated elsewhere (for example Modood 1991; Modood and Berthoud 1997; Ogbu 1987; Perlmann 1988).

The Surinamese case is of particular interest because the two Surinamese ethnic groups have some major contextual features in common. First, they originate from the same country in the Caribbean and they came to the Netherlands, at least until 1980, as Dutch nationals.[3] This meant, among other things, that both enjoyed a relatively strong legal status and that

184

both groups were treated alike by government institutions and policies. Secondly, they migrated, largely, during the same time frame. Hence, upon their arrival the structure of opportunities was broadly the same. I will explore here how, given these structural conditions, their respective socioeconomic positions have taken shape, and how this could be related to their premigration heritage. By premigration heritage I mean what Barth has called the distinctive experiential background of immigrants and the fund of knowledge, skills and values they bring with them (1994: 14). I will further consider the ways in which the pre- and postmigration experiences of the first-generation immigrants in these two populations may influence their children's opportunities.

This chapter is based on my research on differences in social mobility between Surinamese Creoles and Surinamese Hindustanis in the Netherlands.[4] The core of this project consisted of anthropological field work in the cities of Amsterdam and The Hague. It studied first-generation immigrants and their offspring aged 18 or older, born in either Surinam or the Netherlands.[5] The focus was on immigrants of lower-class origins, who made up the majority of those arriving in the period of mass migration. My fieldwork data form the basis for the qualitative analysis presented here. The research project additionally included a review of the literature on the premigration histories of the two groups and an analysis of recent survey data on the socioeconomic conditions of Creoles and Hindustanis in the Netherlands. Since a national census is no longer held in the Netherlands, these survey data can be regarded as the primary source for a quantitative analysis.[6] Only since 1994 have data been available for Creoles and Hindustanis separately.

The Surinamese in Dutch society

Creoles and Hindustanis are the two largest ethnic groups in Surinam, alongside smaller groups such as the Javanese and the Chinese. Although the Surinamese tradition of migration to the Netherlands dates back to early colonial times, substantial migration took place from the 1960s onwards. From the period shortly before Surinam's independence in 1975 until the early 1980s, it took on massive proportions. Whereas formerly only select groups of the Surinamese population had emigrated, in the period in question all ethnic groups and social classes took part. Integration into the Dutch labour market and educational system proved far more difficult for the later immigrants than it had been for those arriving before the period of mass migration. There were two reasons for this. First, many of the earlier immigrants were from middle-class or stable working-class backgrounds. They adapted more easily due to their better knowledge of the Dutch language and culture and their higher educational qualifications. Secondly, the restructuring of the Dutch economy in the mid 1970s resulted in growing unemployment. This became most apparent in the years of the so-called oil crisis around 1973 and even more so in 1979. These years coincided with the two major immigration waves, which together brought some 80 000 Surinamese people to the Netherlands.[7] Thus, while in the 1960s the Dutch labour market had been greatly in need of foreign labourers, the situation changed drastically just as the Surinamese were arriving in substantial numbers. Entry into the Dutch labour market was especially difficult for the thousands of unskilled and poorly educated immigrants. By the late 1970s, unemployment among Surinamese immigrants was four to five times higher than that among the native Dutch (Reubsaet *et al.* 1982: 128). As Bovenkerk (1983: 160) noted at the time, the tragedy of the Surinamese immigration was that it took place at the 'wrong' moment.

By the present day, the immigrant population of Surinamese origin has mounted to nearly 290 000, including children of mixed parentage (CBS 1998).[8] Although this constitutes only 2 per cent of the total Dutch population, in the four largest cities the Surinamese share in the population totals up to 8 per cent. The second generation is still relatively young and forms more than one third of the Surinamese population, but it is set to grow substantially in the near future. Although the Surinamese still lag behind the Dutch in many respects, there have been gradual improvements: unemployment has declined, educational qualifications have improved and some occupational diversification has developed. At the same time, long-term unemployment and welfare dependency persist, especially in the cities, where most of the Surinamese have settled. All things considered, however, the Surinamese population is in no way homogeneous in the sense of occupying an undividedly low socioeconomic position in Dutch society (van Niekerk 1994).

If we take a separate look at the two largest Surinamese groups, the Creoles and the Hindustanis, some differences in socioeconomic position do appear. Broadly speaking, the Creoles have higher educational qualifications than the Hindustanis and, probably as a result of this their occupational levels and their incomes are also higher. Unemployment, on the other hand, is equally high in both groups, approximately one-fifth of the labour force (as opposed to 6 per cent for the ethnic Dutch population, Martens and Verweij 1997: 34). Only minor differences are apparent in terms of the economic sectors the two groups work in, their degrees of employment in the private or public sector and the importance of self-employment. Thus, at first sight the differences between the two ethnic groups are not substantial, and when differences do emerge, the Creoles seem to be doing better. This is quite a surprising conclusion, which runs counter to public images of the two populations. In both Surinam and the Netherlands, Hindustanis are regarded as the more successful of the two groups. Surinamese people as a whole seem to have acquired an intermediate status in the 'ethnic hierarchy' in the Netherlands. Former colonial groups like the Surinamese are ascribed a position lower than European groups, but higher than Islamic groups such as Moroccans and Turks (Hagendoorn and Hraba 1989: 449).[9] Whether or not the Dutch distinguish between Creoles and Hindustanis in this respect is unknown.[10] Processes of discrimination and social exclusion may produce differentiation among the Surinamese. Prevailing stereotypes of Creoles, especially with regard to the young men, may cause them to experience more discrimination on the labour market than Hindustanis. Such has been said of the comparable immigrant groups, the Asians and West Indians, in Britain, although others seem more inclined to believe that Asian immigrants, Indians in particular, are successful *in spite of* discrimination (Modood 1991; Modood and Berthoud 1997). Data on this point for the Creoles and Hindustanis in the Netherlands are scant and fragmentary. As far as I can determine, no systematic comparison has ever been made.[11] Thus, evidence for a differential impact of discrimination on the careers of Creoles and Hindustanis is not yet available.

Before considering in more detail the socioeconomic conditions of these two ethnic groups in Dutch society, let us first have a brief look at their premigration history, and in particular at their occupational niches in the ethnic division of labour in Surinam itself.

Ethnic division of labour in Surinam

The ways in which Creoles and Hindustanis are managing to achieve a place in Dutch society derive partly from the occupational specialization that existed back in Surinam, which was rooted in an ethnic division of labour. Historically, that division developed after the emancipation of the slaves in 1863, when Hindustanis were recruited in British India to work as indentured labourers.[12] They served as a cheap supply of labour for the plantations. The ex-slaves did not withdraw suddenly from agriculture (and in fact many of them already lived in town), but it was the Hindustanis who were ultimately to remain in agriculture for a long period of time. As smallholders, they came to play an important part in Surinam's economy, both as local food producers and as cultivators of rice, one of the chief export products. At least up to the Second World War, the Hindustanis largely earned their living in the agricultural sector (van Lier 1971; Speckmann 1965).

Meanwhile, the Creoles were engaged in a long-term process of occupational differentiation, which had already begun before emancipation. The ex-slaves' early participation in education, their involvement in nonagricultural labour (already during slavery as artisans and domestic workers) and their attachment to the only urban centre in the country, Paramaribo, were all significant factors here. Creoles practised a wide range of occupations in the urban economy, working as artisans, waged labourers and employees in the civil service (see, for example, de Bruijne 1976). Occupational differentiation in the Hindustani population gradually developed out of the role of Hindustanis as local food producers. They became involved in commerce and transportation, and developed into a social class of small entrepreneurs, some of whom would later become important businessmen.[13] The economic boom years during the Second World War vastly broadened their opportunities for education and boosted their upward mobility.

Up to that point, the Hindustanis had remained socially and culturally rather isolated out in the country. Their lifestyle was often characterized as sober, thrifty and industrious (de Klerk 1953; Speckmann 1965). The ex-slaves' early contacts with the Creole urban middle class and its lifestyle – and its appreciation of the need for education – generated in them a more Western-style cultural orientation. Obviously the Creole population was heterogeneous in economic, cultural and racial terms, with a light-coloured, European-oriented middle class existing alongside a darker-skinned Afro-Surinamese lower class. However, on the whole the Creoles seized the opportunities that the educational route to upward mobility offered them. Many found employment in the educational system, the growing civil service and other such areas.

Whereas for the Creoles education was the principal route to upward mobility, the Hindustanis initially showed no great interest in education for their children. After their indentured contracts had expired, economic developments and government policies had strongly favoured their settlement as smallholders. Thus, for them agriculture was the first step upwards on the socioeconomic ladder. Since then, though, their attitude towards education has radically changed. Nowadays members of both populations have high educational qualifications, and can be found in the professions and in the higher managerial positions in business and politics. Although the sharp ethnic division of labour no longer prevails, Hindustanis are still engaged predominantly in the private sector of the economy, while the government and the state-run companies remain the chief employers of the Creoles.

The rapid success of the Hindustanis, who have greatly improved their social standing in just a few generations, has often been contrasted with the economic instability common to sections of the urban Creole population. Such instability is due mainly to the Creoles' dependence on wage labour, with its periodic spates of unemployment. The chronic shortage of industrial jobs in Surinam, a country which has primarily been a producer of raw materials, has resulted in an urban labour surplus. Economic boom periods have alternated with periods of crisis, but a good deal of hidden unemployment has always existed. Paramaribo's labour surplus has partly been accommodated in an oversized civil service and a large informal sector (van Gelder 1985).

Economic instability does not, of course, characterize the entire Creole population. Its overall position is strengthened by its elite and middle class. Historically, the economically and politically dominant classes of Surinam were found among the Creoles, while the Hindustani middle class did not arise until more recent times. On the whole, then, the socioeconomic position of the Creole population has long been more favourable than that of the Hindustani population, a difference still discernible in the Netherlands.[14]

The levelling effect of migration

After their migration to the Netherlands in the 1970s and early 1980s, the Surinamese found themselves in circumstances which tended to level out certain differences between the two groups. These circumstances derived mainly from the labour market position of the majority of the immigrants, which was just coming under heavy pressure from rising unemployment. Many immigrants of the first generation experienced a serious loss of status. They were forced to accept work at lower occupational levels than those to which they had been accustomed in their country of origin, or they were forced to switch to entirely different occupations. Especially the low-skilled and unskilled were affected, and the Hindustanis more than the Creoles. The rural backgrounds of many Hindustanis and their more recent urbanization in Surinam had restricted their educational opportunities. Country education had been of inferior quality and the range of choices was limited. For higher education one had to move to town, and parents had to send their children to relatives or to a children's home in Paramaribo. For the Hindustanis this meant that the route to higher education was paved with more obstacles than it was for the Creoles. As a consequence, many Hindustani immigrants had very limited schooling, if any at all.

Irrespective of these limited opportunities, education was not always necessary anyway to earn a living in Surinam, or even to achieve some degree of material well-being. This was especially true for the economic activities that were the traditional mainstays of Hindustani livelihood: agriculture and commerce. For the Hindustanis, then, education and material wellbeing were not necessarily linked. This was the case, for instance, in various self-employed trades, such as peddler, merchant, shopkeeper and artisan. The trade was learned in practice with little or no formal education. For other sectors of the urban economy, however, formal education was a prerequisite. Job-seekers in the civil service, the police or the education system needed at least some educational credentials, and traditionally it was the Creoles who predominated in these urban sectors of employment.

Upon arrival in the Netherlands, many older Hindustanis discovered that their knowledge and skills were irrelevant or inadequate in the Dutch context, or that they lacked the necessary formal qualifications. For many this meant unemployment, and for those who did manage to find jobs it often meant wholly new job settings at very low occupational levels. To give one example: Mr L. (now 73) was a smallholder in Surinam who grew rice and performed an additional task for the Ministry of Agriculture. After arrival in the Netherlands in 1979, he was contracted for a job but soon discovered he was unqualified for it. He was to drive a fork-lift truck, something he had never done before. He then moved on to an unskilled factory job. Other smallholders or otherwise self-employed people wound up as warehouse clerks, lorry drivers, cleaners or packers.

For the largely urbanized Creoles, the transition after migration was less difficult. They were not only better educated on average, but they could also more easily take up jobs and occupations similar to those they had had in Surinam. These were mainly in three occupational sectors: industry, health care and clerical work. In the 1960s, a period of labour shortage in the Netherlands, Creole men often worked as skilled or semi-skilled labourers in the industrial sector (many of them in the metal sector, as in shipbuilding). For later arrivals, though, especially in the late 1970s and 1980s, job opportunities in the industrial sector were severely limited. The same applied, though to a lesser degree, to the clerical sector, where many low-skilled jobs were vanishing. As a consequence, despite their urban background and more relevant work experience, many Creoles still faced unemployment, or ended up working in the same types of low-skilled or unskilled jobs as the Hindustanis. Even so, for the Creoles that was less of a transition than it was for the formerly self-employed Hindustanis, who experienced a process of outright proletarization after migration.

In addition to the employed and the unemployed immigrants, many immigrants opted out of the job market altogether. Among them, in the first place, were many women, both Hindustani and Creole. Many Hindustani women, who had worked both in the household and in the family enterprise in Surinam, now withdrew into the household. Unaccustomed to performing waged labour and often poorly educated, they disappeared from the labour force. The same applied to many of the lesser educated or older Creole women, albeit for different reasons. In Surinam, practically all such Creole women had performed waged labour or worked in the informal economy (for example as domestics). This active economic role had often arisen in the absence of a husband or father who could provide for the family household. Mothers were forced to play a dual role, inside and outside the household, as mothers and as breadwinners (cf. Buschkens 1974).[15] When the necessity to work turned out not to be as great in the Netherlands as it had been in Surinam, many women opted out of waged labour. But this was only one side of the picture. The other side consisted of a complex interplay of three factors: the high Dutch unemployment rate, favourable social security arrangements and the prevailing attitude towards working mothers.

At the time of Surinamese immigration, unemployment was high in the Netherlands and benefit regulations were such that mothers with children under age 12 were not required to seek work. Nor were the attitudes of official labour mediators and employers favourable to working mothers at the time (in fact, until recently female labour participation was generally low in the Netherlands).[16] Further complicating factors were the problem of childcare and the low level of earnings as compared to social benefit, especially for low-skilled single mothers who preferred part-time jobs. Thus, on the one hand Creole women were more or less forced to give up working, while many of them even seized that opportunity because of their sole responsibility for their children (Lenders and Van Vlijmen-van de Rhoer 1983; van Niekerk 1992). Fluctuations in supply and demand on the labour market impinged on the position of Creole men in many of the same ways. While Creole men had had little trouble finding jobs during the 1960s labour shortage, in the later periods of rising unemployment the employers could afford to be more selective in contracting workers. In the 1970s and 1980s, young Surinamese men became labelled as problems by official labour mediators (Gooskens *et al.* 1979: 100; Sansone 1992: 25). While these later immigrants were indeed not as well equipped as their predecessors in the 1960s, it has also been shown that they faced discrimination (Bovenkerk 1978). In a situation of unemployment, these low-skilled Creole men developed survival strategies that were rooted in the lower-class Creole tradition of hustling (Biervliet 1975; cf. Brana Shute 1979; Buiks 1983). They adapted this tradition to city life in a postmodern welfare state, where full employment no longer existed. Even a younger, better-educated Creole generation came to be dependent on long-term welfare assistance. The way such young men survived by illicit economic activities and petty crime has been characterized by Sansone (1992) as a process of interaction between exclusion and self-exclusion.

Long-term welfare dependency was certainly not the monopoly of the Creoles. Formerly self-employed Hindustanis also belonged to the so-called hard core of the unemployed Surinamese in the late 1970s (Reubsaet *et al.* 1982: 154). On the whole, Creoles and Hindustanis still do not differ much in their dependence on social welfare, whether it involves benefits for single mothers, the unemployed or the disabled. In terms of their principal source of income, 42 per cent of the Hindustanis report labour-earnings, compared to 55 per cent of the Creoles, while social security arrangements are reported by 27 per cent of Hindustanis and 23 per cent of Creoles.[17] The proportion of lone mothers is unexpectedly high among Hindustanis. Of all Hindustani households with children, 38 per cent are one-parent families, as against 45 per cent for Creoles.[18]

For Hindustanis, however, lone motherhood is not grounded in a tradition of single parenthood the way it is for the Creoles. Lone mothers among the Hindustanis are for the most part divorced women or widows rather than never-wed mothers. At first sight, the divorce rate among Hindustanis in the Netherlands does appear to have risen substantially, but this may be less dramatic than the statistics suggest. It is a public secret in the Hindustani community that the unexpectedly large number of Hindustani lone mothers is partly due to the incidence of fake divorces, obtained to secure social benefits.[19] In any event, in the older city districts family patterns can now be found among Hindustanis which resemble those of lower-class Creoles. Women sometimes function as heads of family, acting as breadwinners or managing the household budget. This comes close to the latent matrifocal Creole family, in which the woman can count on support from a man, but still fulfils the primary tasks and remains the central family figure.

To conclude, Creoles and Hindustanis come from different historical backgrounds and have different histories of employment and family life. Nevertheless, since migrating to the Netherlands they have converged in a number of ways, resulting in comparable positions near the lower end of the occupational hierarchy and in welfare dependency for many. People in both groups try to survive on today's meagre social security benefits by eking out supplementary incomes in the informal sector. Their shared socioeconomic position in the Netherlands has given rise to similar patterns of economic behaviour. Although, as we shall see below, their informal economic activities are rooted in entirely different traditions, these are reinforced by the economic conditions in which both groups now find themselves.

Ethnic differences

Not all Surinamese immigrants, nor even the majority, are trapped at the bottom of the labour market. Thus far, however, the more successful and socially mobile people in both groups have remained largely out of focus. Notwithstanding the convergences just described, differences between Creoles and Hindustanis have also developed. These are traceable to differences in the knowledge, skills and values the immigrants had brought with them. One of the more notable features of this differential pattern manifests itself in what I will call *resource accumulation*. Whereas the accumulation of *economic resources* appears typical for the Hindustanis, the accumulation of *educational qualifications* is more characteristic of the Creoles. Two brief case studies will exemplify this distinction. The first is the employment history of a Hindustani family, the second the career of a Creole woman.

The Hindustani family D., made up of two parents and two young children, arrived in the Netherlands in 1974, shortly before Surinam's independence. Mr D. had worked in Surinam as a travelling salesman in textiles for a department store. Both he and his wife had enjoyed only a few years of primary education. Until her marriage, Ms D. had worked in the family shop and assisted in agricultural activities on her father's land. In the Netherlands, both worked in a department store. Mr D. rose there from warehouse clerk to stock manager; Ms D. from canteen worker to cashier. In the evenings they ran a small restaurant. When it burned down, they took on jobs as cleaners in the evening hours, alongside their regular jobs. Together they were paid eight hours a day for cleaning a bank building, dividing the work between them and sometimes assisted by their children, who were still in school. In this way they managed to keep the cleaning job within the family. In a reorganization of the department store, both Mr and Ms D. later lost their jobs. Ms D. then performed various temporary jobs until joining the business her son had meanwhile set up. Both parents and children now work together in this family enterprise, a clothing import firm.

Ms M. arrived in the Netherlands in 1978 as a 19-year-old woman. She came on her own, but was received by an aunt and a stepbrother. Her father was a civil servant in Surinam, occasionally earning additional income as a salesman. Her mother, having been forced out of school on becoming pregnant, worked mostly as a housewife caring for her 13 children. In her own view, Ms M. had not been an outstanding pupil. She completed the so-called advanced primary school in Surinam and obtained a typing certificate. In the Netherlands, she found an unskilled job in an envelope factory, but she left it two months later to embark on a career as a hospital orderly, combining work and study. Once she finished this junior secondary vocational training, she gradually rose in her career via senior secondary vocational education to higher professional education. Meanwhile, she worked in several jobs, consistent with her educational qualifications at the time and all in welfare work. She currently works in a project for school dropouts, while engaged in a one-year training course in management: she aspires to a managerial position.

These two examples may be said to typify the upward mobility patterns of Hindustanis and Creoles. It is not unusual for Hindustanis to have several sources of income at once, for instance a steady job with other activities on the side like cleaning jobs, commercial dealings, work in a family business, or letting a flat. For the Creoles, it is not so much the accumulation of incomes or economic activities that has priority, but the accumulation of educational qualifications. The second pattern illustrated is especially typical of the many Creole women who work in either the health care or the welfare sector. They gradually rise through the ranks by combining work and study.

This is not to say, however, that Creoles assign higher priority to education than the Hindustanis. Education is also highly valued among Hindustanis. Their children even appear to advance through school at a faster rate than the Creole youth. If we compare age categories, generations and educational levels of students and ex-students, all results indicate steady progress by the Hindustanis, while that of the Creoles is less straightforward. Obviously this also reflects a process of catching up – the Hindustanis started lower in education, so their progress seems swifter. But there is more to it than that. In the 18- to 22-year age category, Hindustani educational participation is higher than that of Creoles, while the reverse is true at higher ages.[20] That is to say, Hindustanis finish their educational careers sooner or at a younger age than Creoles. This appears to be linked to marriage and family patterns. Hindustanis traditionally marry young. Creoles may go on studying until a later age, even if they do have families, but that is rare among Hindustanis. Marriage or cohabitation, pregnancy and childcare do not form breaking points in the careers of Creoles as much as they do for Hindustanis. This is especially true of women: at age 25 to 30, the educational participation of Creole women is nearly three times that of Hindustani women.[21] Of course the traditional Hindustani family patterns are subject to change, but they are still discernible and represent a distinguishing feature between the two groups. At present, the average educational attainment of Creole women is higher than that of Hindustani women or men, and it is even somewhat higher than that of Creole men (Martens and Verweij 1997: 77). Traditional family patterns are also reflected in labour market participation data. Creole women are far more active in the labour market than Hindustani women. In 1994, labour market participation amounted to 63 per cent for Creole women, compared to 43 per cent for Hindustani women (ibid.: 80) and 53 per cent for Dutch women (ibid.: 32).[22] Thus, the traditional Creole woman's role does not seem to have lost any of its significance. This may be a sign of greater cultural continuity among Creoles than among the Hindustanis, where the gender gap seems to be gradually narrowing as a result of women's growing educational and labour participation.

Contrary to what one might expect, the successful, enterprising image of the Hindustanis is not substantiated by statistical data. In each of these two Surinamese populations, the number of self-employed persons is small: no more than 3 per cent of the working population (5 per cent if freelancers are included). The key question to be asked, then, is whether the Hindustanis' traditional route of mobility will still be as important for the generation to come as it has been in the past. In Surinam, self-employment had traditionally been the main road to upward mobility for the

Hindustanis, as immigrants in a Creole-dominated society. In more recent times, however, entrepreneurship had become more of a jumping-off point for a younger generation in pursuit of an educational career. Thus, on their way to integration in Surinamese society, the Hindustanis had already become committed to urban forms of employment and waged labour. According to some observers, the self-employment route will therefore diminish in importance for the younger generation as a route to integration in Dutch society (Choenni 1997). They argue that Hindustanis have already departed from their old path of entrepreneurship to continue their transition to an urban–educational route to integration. Although it may be too early yet for such a conclusion, such may well happen in the future.[23]

At the present time, however, it is questionable whether Hindustani entrepreneurship is as insignificant as the statistical data indicate. In two Amsterdam studies, the Hindustanis have been found to be overrepresented among Surinamese businesspeople (Boissevain and Grotenbreg 1988, Choenni 1997). Moreover, the low proportion of self-employed Hindustanis may reflect their position in the formal economy, but such figures do not cover the entire range of informal business-like activities. For that matter, it is well to remember that economic activities that were formal in Surinam may qualify as informal in the Netherlands.[24] The complex Dutch regulations transform, as it were, the income-generating activities that immigrants were accustomed to performing in their home countries from formal into informal. The institutional context of legislation, rules and regulations thereby determines whether entrepreneurship is called formal or informal (cf. Kloosterman *et al.* 1997: 19).

Creoles, of course, also have informal incomes. Both Creoles and Hindustanis who have low earnings or live on social benefits may develop various types of informal economic activities as ways of supplementing their meagre incomes. In fact, it would be difficult to distinguish between the business-like activities in the informal sphere, as described above, and the more 'hustling' type of activities. These should be regarded instead as the outer extremes of a whole range of informal income-generating activities. Yet apart from that, the more entrepreneurial, business-like mentality of Hindustanis, which leads to what I have called an accumulation of incomes, may still prove an advantage for their upward mobility in Dutch society. This lies perhaps not so much in the economic value it produces, but in the cultural messages it transmits to the younger generation.

Economic behaviour, social organization and cultural values

Historically, a crucial element in the Hindustanis' economic behaviour has been their collective performance as a family. This is arguably one of the keys to their economic success and upward mobility in Surinam (see van

Niekerk 1995; cf. Benedict 1979; Despres 1970). Such concerted efforts can still be witnessed in the way Hindustanis work in family enterprises, pool incomes and share housing blocks. Although poorer Hindustani families cannot always live up to this ideal of economic solidarity, this sense of responsibility for relatives is generally strong and highly valued. An example from the recent past is the way all family members combined forces to save for and invest in the education of one person from their midst to become a teacher, doctor or some other type of professional. Their migration to a welfare state, however, has meant that financial resources are now less important to the educational careers of a younger generation than they had been in Surinam (cf. Dronkers and de Graaf 1995). Yet the values that derive from the cultural ideal of collectiveness are still very much alive, and they instil into the younger generation a sense of family responsibility which could inspire them to high achievement.

At the other extreme, we find the more individualized, loosely knit family networks of the Creoles. Rather than acting together in an obligatory fashion, Creole families allow room for more individual freedom and responsibility. Patterns of mutual aid are not absent among the Creoles, however. Lower-class Creoles show strong moral obligations to relatives. Despite the transition to a welfare state through migration, lower-class Creole family networks may still function as a final safety net in times of trouble (van Wetering 1987; cf. Venema 1992). However, this seems more a reaction to a precarious state of affairs than a well-planned concerted action to attain a common goal.

Whereas Hindustanis regard themselves as people who 'push each other up', Creoles describe themselves as people who 'pull each other down'. Obviously that is a gross generalization, but the trust inherent to the Hindustani family networks seems in stark contrast to the so-called *kraboe* mentality of the Creoles (Wilson 1973; cf. Pierce 1973). Hindustanis readily lend sizeable sums of money to relatives. This sharing of resources as a means of realizing collective goals is still evident in practices such as their enormous outlays for weddings, which, in the Netherlands, seem to have increasingly become a means for status competition and display of material wealth. Creoles also incur huge expenditures for events such as a *bigi jari* or *winti pre*,[25] but such obligations seem less coercive. Creoles seem less caught up in heavy status competition between families within the ethnic community. Status competition certainly takes place, but more on an individual basis. As regards the sharing of resources, lower-class Creoles traditionally have their own rotating credit associations (*kas moni*), organized by women who are not necessarily relatives, but may also be neighbours or friends. In my field work I even came across one case in which young Creole women formed a *kas moni* system together with Dutch women, who had originally been totally unfamiliar with such a savings system. This may reflect the low social cohesion of the Creole community and, at the same time, their relative openness to outsiders. Depending on the circumstances, this can be either a benefit or a drawback to their upward mobility in Dutch society.

Related to the question of economic behaviour is the value the two ethnic populations attach to education. As we have seen, education is valued highly by both Creoles and Hindustanis. The motivations for this appreciation, however, may greatly differ. The Hindustanis' drive to achievement is informed in large part by materialistic incentives. This emphasis on material gain generates a more or less instrumental attitude towards education: it is first and foremost a route to a job and hence an income. Naturally this is also a motive for the Creoles, but for them the idea that one should derive pleasure from a job seems to carry more weight. This might also help explain the penchant of lower-class Creole youngsters for careers in the glamorous worlds of sports, pop music and fashion (Sansone 1992: 50). Parental authority and pressure from the older generation on the younger one are generally less forceful than among Hindustanis. Creole children have more room for choice and parents' advice is not as prescriptive as it seems to be for young Hindustanis. This may result in Creole children choosing the most agreeable (and perhaps more facile) educational routes. Creoles in general, however, seem to value education not only instrumentally but also for its intrinsic merits.

The Hindustani economic behaviour and mentality endow younger generations with a strong motivation for education. The traditionally high-status professions of doctor and lawyer are still pursued as means of independent, well-paid employment. Similar ambitions are also reflected in educational career choices for paramedical occupations, laboratory work, chemistry or biology. Such choices are reinforced by the strong status competition within the Hindustani community, where academic achievement is highly valued and academic titles are important status symbols. In part, the Creoles' educational ambitions are oriented towards different occupational careers. My young Creole informants showed greater preferences for fields such as social science, welfare work and health care than the Hindustanis, and they were less interested in some of the typical career choices of Hindustani young people as described above. Creole and Hindustani youth do exhibit a common interest in areas such as accountancy, clerical, technological or computer training. However, their divergent occupational preferences still have a differentiating influence on the patterning of their educational careers. Moreover, the educational aspirations of the younger Creole generation lack reinforcement from strong status competition within their ethnic community and Creole social networks are much more open to outside influences. If a form of downward assimilation does emerge (cf. Portes 1995), it will be Creoles sooner than Hindustanis who take on Dutch lower-class behavioural patterns. The stronger Hindustani social and family networks deter the younger generation from going astray. In this case, ethnic retention seems to further the upward educational mobility of the next generation.

Conclusion

Despite their successful image, the socioeconomic position of the Hindustanis cannot be said to be any better than that of the Creoles. On average, the educational, occupational and income levels of Creoles are higher. I have shown that such differences can be traced back to their pre-migration histories. In spite of the differences, however, the case of the Creoles and Hindustanis reveals some clearly convergent tendencies in their socioeconomic conditions since they migrated from Surinam to the Netherlands. The convergence can be attributed both to elements in the immigrants' premigration class positions (such as educational and occupational levels) and to the structure of opportunities they encountered in the Netherlands (which included high unemployment, unintended effects of the social security system and discrimination). This levelling effect of migration appears to be due to 'structural' rather than cultural factors (cf. Steinberg 1989). Yet in more detailed analysis ethnic differences do emerge. Despite the disadvantage they suffered as immigrants in Surinamese society, the Hindustanis never experienced a long-term period of urban poverty, as a section of the lower-class Creoles did in Paramaribo. Those Creoles brought with them to the Netherlands a set of behavioural norms and values forged in a context of urban poverty and irregular employment. In this sense, the sociocultural context that accompanies a position at the bottom of the Dutch labour market is different for young Creoles than for young Hindustanis growing up in the Netherlands. While the Hindustanis do not yet show any strong signs of 'ghetto-related behaviour' (Wilson 1996), subgroups of lower-class Creoles do. It could well be the case that these behavioural patterns will persist among the Creole population and be more open to change among the Hindustanis.

Structural factors, then, cannot entirely account for differences in mobility patterns. This can also be seen in educational mobility, which is more rapid among Hindustanis than among Creoles. Although Hindustanis still lag behind the Creoles as a whole, they seem to be making stronger progress. This is not what would be expected on the basis of parental levels of schooling. It seems, rather, that this differential pace of educational mobility can be traced to a difference in the *values* attached to education and to the ways these are reinforced in the ethnic social context. Seen in this light, the strength of the Hindustani community lies not so much in its economic potential, but in the strong drive towards upward mobility that parents are transmitting to their children. Such cultural messages seem to outweigh economic capital and entrepreneurial experience. Especially in a welfare state like the Netherlands, parents' economic resources are of less importance for the educational attainment of their children than social and cultural resources (Dronkers and de Graaf 1995).

So even though culture is only one element in a complex explanation, it obviously does make a difference in the way immigrants and their children are incorporated into the host society. Among the interesting questions yet to be asked are how much influence culture will have in the future, and how the relationship between the convergent and divergent tendencies will unfold. This complex issue cannot yet be unravelled, for at least two reasons. The period of immigration is, historically speaking, fairly recent. Little is known as yet about the second generation now coming of age. Secondly, any long-term effects of strong or weak social cohesion remain to be seen. Whereas the Hindustani community seemingly benefits at present from its close-knit family structures and social networks, the greater openness of the Creole community and the high degree of intermarriage might prove advantageous to it in the future. This question is still far from being answered (cf. Vermeulen and Penninx 1994: 225 ff). Whether or not a strategy of ethnic retention will eventually lead to assimilation into the dominant middle class is still debatable (see, for example, de Windt and Kasinitz 1997: 1101). The same can be said for the possibility of assimilation into the lower social strata of declining urban areas. It is uncertain whether the present conditions of long-term unemployment and welfare dependency will prove just a temporary phase in the adaptation process or a more permanent condition that will persist into the second or third generation. It should be noted that most of the Surinamese came to the Netherlands in a period of severe unemployment, whereas the economic climate in the 1990s is a good deal more favourable. Moreover, although processes in the Netherlands may be compared in some ways to those in the United States, the Dutch welfare state has strongly mitigated the negative effects of deindustrialization, particularly in the housing market (van Amersfoort and Cortie 1996). Such contextual differences may be the very reason why the results of this type of assimilation are likely to be different from those in the United States.

By way of conclusion, two final remarks. First, an examination of cultural differences as performed here might suggest that we are dealing with two distinctly separable and internally integrated ethnic groups. Obviously this is not the case, if only because intermarriage erodes ethnic boundaries. More important, perhaps, from a theoretical point of view is that culture cannot be equated with ethnic culture, because it is also linked to other social divisions such as class, gender and generation. These types of social divisions may generate differentiation within and across ethnic groups. If ethnic origin and gender are considered together, for instance, Creole women stand out, both in their active economic roles and their educational attainment.

Second, the focus on culture as one of the explanatory elements in differential success might lead to a 'judgment' of ethnic groups. Werbner, in this volume, questions the narrow economic yardstick against which 'success' or 'failure' is measured, and points instead to the production of cultural value as an alternative mode of measuring social success. This attempt at evaluating cultures in their own terms may be sympathetic, but the question is whether such relativism is justified. The goals that immigrants pursue on leaving their home countries are broadly the same: they are in search of a better future for themselves and their children, concretely expressed in better incomes, housing, education and other such amenities. As Roosens (1989) argued, a kind of transcultural consensus is reached about the value of certain products of the modern world. Immigrant groups or ethnic minorities want 'social security, comfort, all kinds of products, prestige, luxury, intellectual insights and technological mastery in many domains, in spite of all the ideologies that contend otherwise' (ibid.: 153). Although the primacy of economic models of value may be one-sided and their measure of 'success' narrowly defined, this global tendency as observed by Roosens still seems an undeniable and irreversible reality. Thus, the only legitimite way of assessing the 'success' and 'failure' of immigrant groups would seem to be their economic and educational progress – even when we use their own standards to measure it.

Notes

1. *Elsevier*, 22 February 1992, 'Een nijvere minderheid' [An industrious minority] by Gerlof Leistra.
2. The Creoles or Afro-Surinamese are of African or African-European descent.
3. Until independence in 1975, Surinamese people held Dutch nationality, enabling them to migrate freely to the Netherlands. A 1975 agreement for a five-year transitional period regulated migration until 1980. Since then, Surinamese nationals have needed visas to immigrate.
4. See also van Niekerk 1994, 1995, 1996 and 1997. The findings will be presented in full in the form of a PhD dissertation. The research project is financed by the Netherlands Organization for Scientific Research (NWO).
5. Since the main focus of the field work was on intragenerational and intergenerational social mobility, I collected individual and family histories, by way of single or repeated interviews and participant observation. By interviewing 102 family members, I collected information on 288 persons belonging to 64 families, 25 of which I regard as 'key cases'. All were roughly distributed between the two groups. I gathered additional information by interviewing key informants and doing participant observation in the ethnic communities.
6. This 1994 survey bore the name Social Position and Use of Provisions by Ethnic Minorities (*Sociale Positie en Voorzieningengebruik Allochtonen*, SPVA), and was carried out by the Institute of Sociological and Economic Research (ISEO) of Erasmus University Rotterdam. Prompted by the lack of data on immigrant groups, the Dutch government charged the ISEO in 1986 with developing a monitoring system to periodically assess the living conditions of the largest immigrant groups in the Netherlands. Up to now the survey has been held in 1988, 1991, 1994 and 1998 (data from this last survey were not yet available at the time of writing). The

SPVA survey can be considered representative on a nationwide basis for the groups studied. Unless otherwise indicated, all statistical data in the present article on the socioeconomic position of Surinamese people (including Creoles and Hindustanis) are derived from my interpretation of unpublished data from the 1994 SPVA. Wherever possible I refer to published data from this survey, contained in Martens and Verweij (1997). The ethnic origins of the Creoles and Hindustanis have been established by combining two criteria: self-identification and language spoken with relatives and friends besides Dutch.

7. Migration from Surinam to the Netherlands rose sharply in the 1970s, especially in two particular periods. The first peak occurred in 1974 and 1975, shortly before Surinam's independence in November 1975. In addition to the economic reasons, the exodus was also prompted by feelings of political insecurity among the Hindustani population. They feared Creole domination and ethnic conflict, as had occurred in neighbouring British Guiana. A second migration flow arose in the late 1970s, shortly before the Dutch government introduced a visa require-ment in 1980. Immigration has fallen sharply since then, but it has not ceased altogether. It has even shown a slight increase in the early 1990s as a consequence of the enduring economic and political crisis in Surinam.

8. In policy terms, Surinamese are defined as persons who were either born in Surinam themselves or have at least one parent born there. Under the terms of Dutch minority policy, the second-generation Surinamese, about half of whom are of mixed parentage (mostly Surinamese-Creole and Dutch), therefore belong to the Surinamese minority.

9. Similar findings emerged in our research in a neighbourhood with postwar hous-ing in the town of Haarlem. The Surinamese were attributed a higher position by the ethnic Dutch residents than were the Turks and Moroccans (van Niekerk *et al.* 1989: 104).

10. Many ethnic Dutch people fail to recognize Hindustanis as Surinamese, while they do recognize Creoles as such (van Niekerk *et al.* 1989: 56).

11. In his study on the integration of young Surinamese men in the Dutch army, Choenni (1995) noted that Creole men were more likely to report discrimination than Hindustani men and that they were more often convinced that discrimina-tion occurred in the army. These conclusions were based on the perceptions of informants. That problem was avoided in a so-called 'lifelike' experiment, in which discrimination was tested out (Gras *et al.* 1995). It showed that better-edu-cated Surinamese people (on further consideration these were probably Creoles) experience less discrimination in the labour market than lesser-educated ones, and that women experience less discrimination than men (Bovenkerk (1978) made comparable findings). The problem here, though, is that no comparison was made between Creoles and Hindustanis.

12. Between 1873 and 1917, more than 30 000 Indians were transported to Surinam. Although they had the right to return, most stayed.

13. In 1921 Hindustanis were working in three main sectors: commerce, transport and agriculture. Most were self-employed. Of the nonagriculturally self-employed Hindustanis, 45 per cent worked in commerce, 27 per cent in trans-portation and 13 per cent as artisan shopkeepers (de Bruijne 1976: 51).

14. The situation in Surinam may have changed just recently. The Hindustanis seem to have shown themselves better equipped than the Creoles to cope with the economic crisis that arose in the 1980s and took on serious proportions in the 1990s. The former are involved mainly in private sectors of the economy, whereas the latter work mostly in the public sector and are thus dependent on

an employer (the government) that has been forced to economize (cf. Buddingh' 1995: 373; Hassankhan *et al.* 1995).

15. This matrifocal family pattern has a long history. Ever since slavery (when slaves were not allowed to marry), cohabiting couples have been rather common, as have one-parent families consisting of a mother and child(ren). This so-called matrifocal family structure in the present day is not a mere historical residue, however. Its continued existence among lower-class Creoles is tied to social conditions of unemployment and poverty (Buschkens 1974). This family pattern is not conceived by the people involved as an ideal model, but since its emergence it has been a widely accepted sociocultural pattern among lower-class Creoles.

16. Female labour market participation now equals that of most European countries, although Dutch women are more likely to work part-time (van der Lippe and van Doorne-Huiskes 1995).

17. These percentages include those on national assistance (*bijstand*), unemployment benefit and disability benefit (*WAO*). Hindustani women, moreover, are more likely than Creole women to report having no income at all. The other notable difference between the two populations is in student grants, received by a higher proportion of Hindustanis (source SPVA'94, ISEO/EUR).

18. Source SPVA'94, ISEO/EUR. See also Martens and Verweij 1997: 74.

19. Such was also suggested in a radio programme (26 May 1997) from the Hindu broadcasting corporation in the Netherlands, entitled *Scheiden om extra bijstand* [Divorce for extra social assistance]. Furthermore, Mungra (1990), in his research on Hindustani families in the Netherlands, noted a discrepancy between the official number of one-parent families in a sample taken from the population register and the actual number.

20. At age 19, the educational participation of Hindustanis is nearly twice that of Creoles, but the differential vanishes by age 22 (Martens and Verweij 1997: 29).

21. Fourteen per cent of Creole women versus 5 per cent of Hindustani women (Martens and Verweij 1997: 78).

22. Labour market participation is the proportion of the working age population that actually takes part in the labour market, either employed or unemployed.

23. This may change yet again, however, if well-educated young people decide to set up their own businesses in response to racism or lack of employment opportunities, as has happened, for instance, among the Sikhs in Britain (Gibson and Bhachu 1988).

24. Moreover, the distinction between formal and informal economic activities is not as strictly defined in Surinam as it is in the Netherlands.

25. A *bigi jari* is a quinquennial birthday celebration. *Winti* is the Afro-Surinamese religion; a *winti pre* is a ritual *winti* celebration.

References

Amersfoort, H. van, and C. Cortie, 1996, 'Social polarisation in a welfare state? Immigrants in the Amsterdam region', *New Community* 22(4): 671–87

Barth, F., 1994, 'Enduring and emerging issues in the analysis of ethnicity', in: H. Vermeulen and C. Govers (eds), *The Anthropology of Ethnicity. Beyond 'Ethnic Groups and Boundaries'* (Amsterdam: Het Spinhuis)

Benedict, B., 1979, 'Family firms and firm families. A comparison of Indian, Chinese, and Creole firms in Seychelles', in: S.M. Greenfield, A. Strickon, and R.T. Aubrey (eds), *Entrepreneurs in Cultural Context* (Albuquerque: University of New Mexico Press)

Biervliet, W.E., 1975, 'The hustler culture of young unemployed Surinamers', in: H.E. Lamur and J.D. Speckmann (eds), *Adaption of Migrants from the Caribbean in the European and American Metropolis* (Amsterdam/Leiden: KITLV/ASC)

Boissevain, J., and H. Grotenbreg, 1988, 'Culture, structure, and ethnic enterprise: the Surinamese of Amsterdam', in: M. Cross and H. Entzinger (eds), *Lost Illusions. Caribbean Minorities in Britain and the Netherlands* (London: Routledge)

Bovenkerk, F., 1983, 'De vlucht. Migratie in de jaren zeventig', in: G. Willemsen (ed.), *Suriname. De Schele Onafhankelijkheid* (Amsterdam: De Arbeiderspers)

Bovenkerk, F. (ed.), 1978, *Omdat Zij Anders Zijn. Patronen van Rasdiscriminatie in Nederland* (Amsterdam/Meppel: Boom)

Brana Shute, G., 1979, *On the Corner. Male Social Life in a Paramaribo Creole Neighborhood* (Assen: Van Gorcum)

Bruijne, G.A. de, 1976, *Paramaribo. Stadsgeografische Studies van een Ontwikkelingsland* (Bussum: Romen)

Buddingh', H., 1995, *Geschiedenis van Suriname* (Utrecht: Het Spectrum)

Buiks, P., 1983, *Surinaamse Jongeren op de Kruiskade. Overleven in een Etnische Randgroep* (Deventer: Van Loghum Slaterus)

Buschkens, W.F.L., 1974, *The Family System of the Paramaribo Creoles* (The Hague: Martinus Nijhoff)

Centraal Bureau voor de Statistiek (CBS), 1998, *Allochtonen in Nederland 1998* (Voorburg/Heerlen: CBS)

Choenni, A., 1997, *Veelsoortig Assortiment. Allochtoon Ondernemerschap in Amsterdam als Incorporatietraject 1965–1995* (Amsterdam: Het Spinhuis)

Choenni, C., 1995, *Kleur in de Krijgsmacht. De Integratie van Surinaamse Jongemannen in Nederland* (Utrecht: Faculteit Sociale Wetenschappen, Rijksuniversiteit Utrecht)

Despres, L.A., 1970, 'Differential adaptations and micro-cultural evolution in Guyana', in: N.E. Whitten and J.F. Szwed (eds), *Afro-American Anthropology. Contemporary Perspectives* (New York: The Free Press)

Dronkers, J., and P.M. de Graaf, 1995, 'Ouders en het onderwijs van hun kinderen', in: J. Dronkers and W.C. Ultee (eds), *Verschuivende Ongelijkheid in Nederland. Sociale Gelaagdheid en Mobiliteit* (Assen: Van Gorcum)

Gelder, P.J. van, 1985, *Werken onder de Boom. Dynamiek en Informele Sector in Groot-Paramaribo, Suriname* (Dordrecht: Floris Publications)

Gibson, M., and P. Bhachu, 1988, 'Ethnicity and school performance. A comparative study of South Asian pupils in Britain and America', *Ethnic and Racial Studies* 11(3): 239–62

Gooskens, I., J. Hoolt, and M. Freeman, 1979, *Surinamers in Amsterdam. Deel 1: Analyses* (Amsterdam: Gemeente Amsterdam)

Gras, M., F. Bovenkerk, K. Gorter, P. Kruiswijk and D. Ramsoedh 1995, *Een Schijn van Kans. Twee Empirische Onderzoeken naar Discriminatie op Grond van Handicap en Etnische Afkomst* (Arnhem: Gouda Quint)

Hagendoorn, L., and J. Hraba, 1989, 'Foreign, different, deviant, seclusive and working class. Anchors to an ethnic hierarchy in the Netherlands', *Ethnic and Racial Studies* 12(4): 441–68

Hassankhan, M., M. Liegon, and P. Scheepers, 1995, 'Sociaal-economische verschillen tussen Creolen, Hindoestanen en Javanen. 130 jaar na afschaffing van de slavernij', in: L. Gobardhan-Rambocus, M. Hassankhan, and J. Egger (eds), *De Erfenis van de Slavernij* (Paramaribo: Anton de Kom Universiteit)

Klerk, C.J.M. de, 1953, *De Immigratie der Hindostanen in Suriname* (Amsterdam: Urbi et Orbi)

Kloosterman, R., J. van der Leun, and J. Rath, 1997, *Over Grenzen. Immigranten en de Informele Economie* (Amsterdam: Instituut voor Migratie- en Etnische Studies, Universteit van Amsterdam)

Lenders, M., and M. van Vlijmen-van de Rhoer, 1983, *Mijn God, Hoe Ga Ik Doen? De Positie van Creoolse Alleenstaande Moeders in Amsterdam* (Amsterdam: Antropologisch-Sociologisch Centrum, Universiteit van Amsterdam)

Lier, R.A.J. van, 1971, *Frontier Society. A Social Analysis of the History of Surinam* (The Hague: Martinus Nijhoff)

Lippe, T. van der, and J. van Doorne-Huiskes, (1995) 'Veranderingen in stratificatie tussen mannen en vrouwen?', in: J. Dronkers and W.C. Ultee (eds), *Verschuivende Ongelijkheid in Nederland. Sociale Gelaagdheid en Mobiliteit* (Assen: Van Gorcum)

Martens, E., and A. Verweij, 1997, *Surinamers in Nederland. Kerncijfers 1996* (Rotterdam: Instituut voor Sociologisch Economisch Onderzoek)

Modood, T., 1991, 'The Indian economic success. A challenge to some race relations assumptions', *Policy and Politics* 19(3): 177–89

Modood, T., and R. Berthoud 1997, *Ethnic Minorities in Britain. Diversity and Disadvantage* (London: Policy Studies Institute)

Mungra, G., 1990, *Hindoestaanse Gezinnen in Nederland* (Leiden: COMT, Rijksuniversiteit Leiden)

Niekerk, M. van, 1992, 'Armoede en cultuur. Caraïbische vrouwen en meisjes in Nederland', *Migrantenstudies* 8(3): 18–33

Niekerk, M. van, 1993, 'Ethnic Studies in the Netherlands. An outline of research issues', *Research Notes from the Netherlands* (SISWO) 1: 2–14

Niekerk, M. van, 1994, 'Zorg en Hoop. Surinamers in Nederland nu', in: H. Vermeulen and R. Penninx (eds), *Het Democratisch Ongeduld. De Emancipatie en Integratie van Zes Doelgroepen van het Minderhedenbeleid* (Amsterdam: Het Spinhuis)

Niekerk, M. van 1995, 'A historical approach to ethnic differences in social mobility. Creoles and Hindustanis in Surinam', in: G. Baumann and T. Sunier (eds), *Post-Migration Ethnicity. Cohesion, Commitments, Comparison* (Amsterdam: IMES/SISWO)

Niekerk, M. van., 1996, *Culture and Gender. Male and Female Careers of Surinamese Creoles and Hindustanis in the Netherlands*, paper for the conference 'Does culture make a difference?', Amsterdam, 14–16 November

Niekerk, M. van, 1997, 'Surinaamse Nederlanders. Dilemma's van integratie', *Justitiële Verkenningen* 23(6): 36–48

Niekerk, M. van, T. Sunier, and H. Vermeulen, 1989, *Bekende Vreemden. Surinamers, Turken en Nederlanders in een Naoorlogse Wijk* (Amsterdam: Het Spinhuis)

Ogbu, J., 1987, 'Variability in minority school performance. A problem in search of an explanation', *Anthropology and Education Quarterly* 18: 312–34

Perlmann, J., 1988, *Ethnic Differences. Schooling and Social Structure among the Irish, Italians, Jews and Blacks in an American City, 1880–1935* (Cambridge: Cambridge University Press)

Pierce, B.E., 1973, 'Status competition and personal networks. Informal social organization among the nengre of Paramaribo', *Man* 8(4): 580–91

Portes, A., 1995, 'Children of immigrants. Segmented assimilation and its determinants', in: A. Portes (ed.), *The Economic Sociology of Immigration. Essays on Networks, Ethnicity and Entrepreneurship* (New York: Russell Sage Foundation)

Reubsaet, T.J.M., J.A. Kropman, and L.M. Mulier, 1982, *Surinaamse Migranten in Nederland. De Positie van Surinamers in de Nederlandse Samenleving* (Nijmegen: Instituut voor Toegepaste Sociologie)

Roosens, E., 1989, *Creating Ethnicity. The Process of Ethnogenesis* (Newbury Park: Sage Publications)

Sansone, L., 1992, *Schitteren in de Schaduw. Overlevingsstrategieën, Subcultuur en Etniciteit van Creoolse Jongeren uit de Lagere Klasse in Amsterdam 1981–1990* (Amsterdam: Het Spinhuis)

Speckmann, J.D., 1965, *Marriage and Kinship among the Indians in Surinam* (Assen: Van Gorcum)

Steinberg, S., 1989, *The Ethnic Myth. Race, Ethnicity and Class in America* (Boston: Beacon Press) [1981]

Venema, T., 1992, *Famiri Nanga Kulturu. Creoolse Sociale Verhoudingen en Winti in Amsterdam* (Amsterdam: Het Spinhuis)

Vermeulen, H., and R. Penninx (eds), 1994, *Het Democratisch Ongeduld. De Emancipatie en Integratie van Zes Doelgroepen van het Minderhedenbeleid* (Amsterdam: Het Spinhuis)

Wetering, W. van, 1987, 'Informal supportive networks. Quasi-kin groups, religion and social order among Surinamese Creoles in the Netherlands', *Netherlands Journal of Sociology* 23(2): 92–101

Wilson, P.J., 1973, *Crab Antics. The Social Anthropology of English Speaking Negro Societies of the Caribbean* (New Haven: Yale University Press)

Wilson, W.J., 1996, *When Work Disappears. The World of the New Urban Poor* (New York: Vintage Books)

Windt, J. de, and Ph. Kasinitz, 1997, 'Everything old is new again? Processes and theories of immigrant incorporation', *International Migration Review* 31(4): 1096–111

10

Does Culture Explain? Understanding Differences in School Attainment between Iberian and Turkish Youth in the Netherlands

Flip Lindo

Any assessment of the socioeconomic position of a migrant group will inevitably be based on a comparison, either implicit or explicit. Usually the social performance of immigrants is measured against the standards of mainstream society. Inherent in such a comparison is an expectation that generations born and reared in the host society should 'ideally' conform to mainstream standards. If they do not, something is wrong.

Society, however, is many-layered, and one might ask whether it is realistic to expect all migrant groups, coming as they do from different strata in their societies of origin, to all adapt at an equal pace (see Steinberg 1989). In real life there is considerable variation in the speed at which migrant groups become incorporated into the host society, in the routes they choose in their efforts to achieve social mobility and in the positions they occupy, at least initially, in the stratified system. Theories that try to account for these divergent paths and outcomes have highlighted contextual factors, as well as individual- and group-level factors, as possible determinants. Such theoretical arguments are often tied to central pairs of concepts – 'culture and society', for instance, or 'agency and structure'. The mutually exclusive use of such concepts lies at the root of the normative discussions that are likely to accompany any observation made about the differential success of migrant groups in daily life. Many of the claims made in such discussions can be traced to two opposing normative positions. These might be described, by way of caricature, as *blaming the victim* and *blaming the system*.

In many analyses of the success of some migrant groups compared to others, a distinction between *culture* and *structure* still plays a major role (for an extended discussion, see Lindo 1996). The culture of a given group is frequently presented as an explanation for success, with emphasis on certain properties deemed typical for the group in question: a family orientation, a sober life style, perseverance, a self-denying attitude, ability to formulate and live up to long-term goals and high ambitions for the children's educational careers.[1] Such qualities – often emphasized selectively because they resemble the ideals of the mainstream (Zhou 1997: 994) – symbolize an immigrant group's capacity to surmount problems and obstacles on its own, thus underlining its moral worth. Often without explicitly saying so, such a moral narrative passes judgement on less successful groups. In the process of incorporation into the receiving society, *their* culture has evidently failed to support them.

A recent theoretical framework, developed especially to make sense of the differing paths and outcomes in the incorporation processes of second-generation migrants, is the *segmented assimilation theory* (Portes 1995, Portes and Zhou 1993). This approach calls attention both to societal factors such as discrimination and the hourglass economy and to more group-specific factors such as a proliferation of transnational activities and the mechanisms of social control within migrant communities. The way in which societal and group-specific factors interact may influence, among other things, the potential for the emergence of an *adversial frame of mind* among migrant children raised in the host society (Portes 1997). Some proponents of the segmented assimilation theory claim that their approach diverges from other models by assuming that the specific determinants by themselves are of minimal importance. They emphasize instead the *interrelation* between contextual determinants and the determinants 'intrinsic' to the migrant group (Zhou 1997). If we try to analyse this interrelation more concretely within specific cases, however, we run into problems on how to conceptualize such determinants. The question arises, for instance, as to whether contextual determinants should always be understood as 'structure' and group determinants as 'culture' (that is, as frames of mind, orientations and other ideational constructs).

This study focuses on the interaction between individual-level, group-level and societal factors, and on some of the conceptual problems that come with this type of analysis. It contains an explicit comparison, an analysis of the differences in school success between (and to a lesser degree within) two specific groups of 'Mediterranean' migrants in the Netherlands. The analysis is based on largely qualitative research involving the children of Turkish migrants and the children of Iberian (Portuguese and Spanish) migrants. The research, conducted from 1989 to 1993, uncovered marked differences between these two groups in terms of the overall school performance of their offspring (Lindo and Pennings 1992). Portuguese and Spanish youth turned out to be quite successful in education, while most of their Turkish peers performed rather poorly.[2] In this type of comparative analyses, any divergence in school performance is usually brought into connection with one or more conspicuous differences in the social and cultural resources the children's families have at their disposal, their migration histories, or the social positions they occupy in the receiving country.

Let us now have a look at some of these factors, which can be sought at individual, group and societal levels. We can identify both differences and similarities between the two groups.

Migration and incorporation

Both Turkish and Iberian immigrants belonged to the category of 'guest workers' (*gastarbeiders*) from Mediterranean countries who, in the booming economy of the 1960s and 1970s, found employment in unskilled jobs in heavy industry (metals and textiles) which the Dutch labour force was no longer willing to perform. Both the Iberian and Turkish labour migrants began arriving in the Netherlands in the second half of the 1960s. Only males, mainly aged 20 to 30, migrated in that period. Until the 1970s, most Iberian and Turkish migrants used similar channels to get to the Netherlands: they came on employment contracts, or otherwise as 'tourists', sometimes on the invitation of a relative or friend already in the host country.

Another similarity was that neither group came to the Netherlands with the intention of staying and building a future there. The idea of staying only temporarily, to earn the wherewithal for a better future back home within a relatively short time, was not relinquished when the migrants later decided to send for their families. The fact that their children would grow up and take root in Dutch society was a consequence of this family reunification that had scarcely been thought through initially. Contrary to the facts, the image of the Mediterranean immigrant as an 'international commuter' persisted for a long time in Dutch society – partly because the migrants themselves saw no cause to dispute it. Until the late 1970s, government policy was founded on that assumption too. Only later did it become clear that, whatever the intentions of the first generation, Mediterranean migrants and their families were there to stay. Any policy changes by the authorities continued to approach the different Mediterranean groups in more or less the same fashion.

On arrival, the Iberian and Turkish migrants – that is, the males who came first – exhibited only minor differences in education and vocational skills, as shown in Table 10.1. In the *female* first generations, by contrast, the differences in educational profile between the Iberians and the Turks were far more pronounced. Spanish and Portuguese women of the first generation had enjoyed significantly more education in their home country than Turkish women. While the differential between men and women in the Iberian group was marginal, a wide gap existed between the Turkish men and women. As I will emphasize later, this contrast is crucial to understanding the differences in educational behaviour between the two groups of children.

The survey data also reveals other dissimilarities between the two groups. I will note the most important ones here. First of all, there is a difference in

Table 10.1 Educational levels of Turkish and Iberian first-generation migrants upon arrival in the Netherlands, and of the Dutch native population in the comparable age category, in percentages

	Turkish		Iberian		Dutch	
	Male	Female	Male	Female	Male	Female
no or unfinished primary school	17	60	28	29	0	0
primary school	74	40	57	60	26	37
junior vocational or general secondary school	6	0	13	9	30	36
senior vocational or general secondary school	3	0	1	2	23	19
higher professional/ university education	0	0	1	0	22	7
total (=100%)	391	244	231	216	305	309

*The figures on the Iberian first generation were collected in the 1989 study (Lindo and Pennings 1992), and they apply to the parents of the questioned youth. Since the qualitative research among the Turkish youth was not accompanied by a survey as in the Iberian group, quantitative data on the Turkish first generation have been drawn from the 1988 survey Social Position and Use of Provisions by ISEO, Erasmus University, which distinguished a similar age category of Turkish first-generation migrants. The data on the native Dutch population have been taken from the same survey (Ankersmit *et al.* 1989: 141; Lindo and Pennings 1992: 11–15).

the scale and duration of the migration process. The comparatively meagre school results of Turkish youth in the Netherlands can partly be accounted for by the ongoing immigration from Turkey. The Turkish population in the Netherlands is much larger than the Portuguese and Spanish ones. Whereas Iberian immigration came to a halt in the 1970s, and the communities that remained grew little after that point, the Turkish group continued to grow exponentially well into the 1990s as a result of family reunification and (partly illegal) chain migration. Most Portuguese and Spanish immigrants had long been reunited with their families by that time.

In line with this demographic trend, a larger proportion of Turkish young people than Iberian ones were having to break off their education in their homeland to start a school career in the Netherlands at a relatively late age and without any command of the Dutch language. Obviously this was detrimental to their educational performance. Even if we leave them aside, though, the evidence shows that the Turkish children who begin their school careers in the Netherlands reach only a marginally better position than the 'in-between generation'. Their attainment is hence significantly lower than that of their Portuguese and Spanish peers as shown in

Table 10.2 (Lindo 1996: 145). In the 1970s and 1980s, major shifts in the Dutch economy rendered many labour migrants jobless. Although the first-generation Turks, Spaniards and Portuguese had occupied similar types of jobs in the beginning, the Turkish were harder hit by the closures of traditional industries and they had more difficulties in recovering from unemployment. The reason is not entirely clear. One difference may be that Iberian first-generation migrants had more success in obtaining Dutch training certificates than their Turkish coworkers. Although those who secured such qualifications saw their job levels increase only marginally, this may have just shielded them from unemployment (Lindo and Pennings 1992: 29–31).

Even so, the educational underachievement of Turkish young people cannot be explained by the unemployment of their fathers. The survey data indicate that children in Turkish families dependent on benefit have an educational profile practically identical to that of their Turkish peers whose fathers have jobs (Lindo 1996: 132). By the same token, the children of Iberian fathers with Dutch training certificates do no better at school

Table 10.2   Educational level attained by Turkish and Iberian migrants' children who finished their education in the Netherlands, in percentages, 1989 and 1991

	Turkish						Iberian		
	Older than 6			6 or Younger					
	Male	Female	Total	Male	Female	Total	Male	Female	Total
no education or primary school junior vocational or general	54	70	62	43	55	49	18	19	19
secondary school senior vocational or general	34	22	28	39	36	38	48	35	42
secondary school higer professional/	10	9	9	18	9	13	39	35	33
university education	1	0	1	0	0	0	3	10	7
total (=100%)	174	199	373	61	56	117	60	62	122

Notes: Turkish children are distinguished into two categories based on their age of arrival in the Netherlands: those who presumably began their education in the Netherlands ('6 or younger') and those who had presumably started school in Turkey ('older than 6'). The Iberian figures are not broken down by age of arrival; only 18 per cent of the Iberian sample arrived after age 6, compared to 76 per cent of the Turkish sample.
Source: Roelandt *et al.* 1992.

than those whose fathers had no Dutch qualifications (Lindo and Pennings 1992: 29–31).

Any variable impact of (intended or unintended) racism and discrimination on the social position of Iberian or Turkish migrant families is difficult to assess. At the bottom of the labour market, where competition among poorly educated youths for the few decent jobs is especially fierce, it is possible that Turkish young people, more than their Iberian peers, suffer from negative stereotyping in Dutch society. But we are dealing here with education. Research into how the expectations and behaviour of teaching staff may affect the educational careers of migrant children (the large majority of whom are Moroccan or Turkish) has produced contradictory findings (Tesser and van Praag 1995; Tesser and Veenman 1997). There is little conclusive evidence that racism in the school context accounts for differences in achievement between minority groups, either in the Netherlands or in any other Western European country (Fase 1994).

Not all schools are of the same quality, of course, and the presumed negative effects of high concentrations of minority pupils in schools often receive particular notice. Although no conclusions can be drawn from survey material, my qualitative research suggests that a higher proportion of Turkish children than Iberian ones are enrolled in so-called 'black schools', schools with large percentages or even a majority of migrant children. However, research on whether such schools affect educational attainment is not conclusive (Tesser and van Praag 1995: 223–301). The question remains as to why Portuguese and Spanish children avoid 'black schools' more than Turkish children do. Parents and children in the Netherlands are basically free to choose between schools. There are few financial impediments, nor do formal restrictions exist as to the location of the school. Iberian children, however, do seem better able to overcome social and structural obstacles to attending 'whiter' schools, such as distance from home or inadequate family knowledge about the Dutch education system. I shall address this and other questions in my analysis below, when I take a closer look at the behavioural patterns in the families and communities in question.

In my introduction I have noted that various factors at the level of the individual, the group and the host society can affect the social mobility of immigrant groups. Such factors may prove to have some bearing on the educational opportunities of Iberian and Turkish youth in the Netherlands. They may also account for some of the differences in their educational profiles. Yet if we make an overall comparison of the Iberian and Turkish first generations on the basis of their socioeconomic backgrounds and the extent of their incorporation into the Dutch economy, we find more similarities than differences. From a distance there are many resemblances in terms of the education and skills that the family heads brought from their country of origin, in their initial migration histories, and in the positions they were allocated in the Dutch economy. It also seems unlikely that the current enormous gap in educational attainment between Iberian and Turkish children can be explained by other allocation processes in the host society, such as racism or school environment.[3]

Of course there are differences between the two groups as well, and small differences may add up to a greater divergence in the next generation (Zhou 1997). One question I address in this chapter is how to interpret such relatively small differences (such as the differential education levels of the first-generation women) in ways that can help us understand the wide educational divergence of the second generation.

The qualitative research

The analysis below is based on a qualitative study of children from 94 Portuguese, Spanish and Turkish migrant families in the Netherlands, conducted between 1990 and 1993.[4] During the children's school careers, the family heads had all been employed in the same sector and at the same level (most had cleaning jobs in the transport sector). Because I wanted my informants to be able to look back on a major part of their educational career, I chose adolescents and young adults aged 16 to 27. One should bear in mind that some of the school careers had been completed several years earlier (with varying degrees of success).

Viewed from a microlevel perspective, the similarities between the groups predominate at first glance. Both Iberian and Turkish parents were reported to have stressed the importance of education for their children, and their manifesto was clearly heartfelt: 'My children have to go to school. Otherwise they will end up doing the same kind of job I do.' Or, 'I say to them, "Look at me. Do you want to clean toilets later too?" But they have to decide for themselves!' The children confirmed the sincerity of these good intentions, but also pointed to the parents' ignorance in matters of education. This was another similarity between Iberian and Turkish parents: they were constantly aware of their ignorance, a condition that made it difficult for them to formulate more specific aspirations for their children's careers. Notwithstanding their generally positive attitude, their ignorance fostered a certain ambivalence towards Dutch education. Because of the parents' lack of knowledge of Dutch education (and of Dutch society in general), in some respects the children were delegated responsibility for their own future at a relatively early age.

The diverging educational careers of Iberian and Turkish migrants' children did not correspond to positive versus negative educational attitudes. Apart from the general pronouncements on the importance of education heard in both groups, I could detect no particular group-level 'folk theory of success' among the families of the relatively successful Portuguese and Spanish children, analogous to that recorded by Gibson (1987) in the folk sayings of Californian Sikhs that stress the value of formal education. Nor could I identify any overt parental educational strategies (Bhachu 1985; Ogbu 1987). No overt or covert pressure was exercised on children to achieve in school, as has been reported in studies on social mobility patterns in Asian families (see, for example, Pieke 1989). As mentioned above, both the Turkish and the Iberian immigrants to the Netherlands were reluctant settlers and they certainly did not go there with their children's educational opportunities in mind.

Behavioural patterns in families

Any causal analysis of the differential educational profiles of migrant children should also look at patterns of behaviour in areas not directly related to education. These may have unintended effects on the children's school performance. Such interaction patterns can be sought both in the relations *within* families and in the relations *between* those families and their ethnic communities. Is it meaningful, for a deeper understanding of the observed divergence in school careers, to designate such behavioural patterns as 'culture'? I will address this question in the final section of this chapter. At this point I will briefly introduce the behavioural patterns I have in mind.[5]

In Turkish, more than in Iberian families, implicit and explicit rules of behaviour seem to operate which act as impediments to a successful school career. Families in both groups may be classified under the general category of 'command households' (du Bois-Reymond 1992). In this household type, the mother mediates between her children and her husband, an authoritarian father. Portuguese and Spanish mothers, however, appear more successful in conveying their children's aspirations to their husbands and more adept at supporting their children at key junctures in their school careers. In other words, they occupy a more strategic position in this respect than the Turkish mothers do. More often than not, the Iberian mothers' interest is first aroused *after* one of their children turns out to do well in school. They then begin following their child's educational accomplishments more keenly. Mothers show pride in their children's school success in a general and emotional way, while fathers observe it more from a distance, evaluating the children's achievements in terms of objectives. While they often react positively to good results, they may question the benefits of schooling when their child is doing poorly, accentuating the negative aspects of long school careers. Such behaviour betrays the absence of any 'traditional' orientation to an educational career. The crux simply appears to be that the role of the mother in the Iberian families, and her function as a link to the world outside the ethnic group, give her more latitude for action than is generally granted to Turkish mothers. I found Iberian mothers to be more likely to carry on contacts with people like Dutch neighbours and coworkers. Such acquaintances furnish them at an early stage with basic information about the Dutch educational system. This better equippes the Iberian mothers to defend their children's interests vis-à-vis their husbands, and to support their children when they ask for things to facilitate their integration into the school environment (acceptable clothing, permission to take part in social events, money for school outings, books, even computers). Through their contacts in the outside world, Iberian mothers are also in a position to get basic advice about the quality of different schools. They can then act as a sounding board for their children in decisions affecting their educational careers. This may partly explain why Iberian pupils more often go to predominantly ethnic Dutch schools.[6]

Turkish mothers have a less influential position, especially in matters outside the home. This is reflected in quantitative data, that show that they are significantly less likely than Iberian mothers to have finished primary school, and that their participation in employment is very low indeed. That of the Iberian mothers is above the national average (Lindo and Pennings 1992: 11–23). A matter in which Turkish mothers do have an important say is the age of marriage and the choice of their children's marriage partners. Women and girls are thought to be safer if they stay at home and do not mingle too much in the outside world. The younger Turkish girls get married, the greater the chance they will still be virgins. Boys that get married are at less risk of going off the rails than unmarried schoolgoers. Many of my respondents were hence subjected to strong social pressure to marry before they turned 18. In the eyes of the Turkish parents, marriage was the best way to safeguard their children from the dangers of adolescence in Dutch society. But adolescence is also the period in which young people are in school, and as I have argued elsewhere (Lindo 1996: 50–8), the preoccupation with early marriage seriously interferes with the school careers of Turkish adolescents.

For boys, marriage does not mean deliverance from parental authority. They continue to be dependent on the head of the family, even after they have children of their own, and they are expected to contribute to the income of the enlarged family household. In many cases they transfer their income to the household head (their father) and are dependent on him for regular allowances and gifts. This can keep them from realizing their aspirations (Lindo 1996). With few exceptions, parents do not look positively on any plans their sons might have to proceed with daytime education after marriage.

A daughter is expected to wait until a candidate presents himself (or is presented by his family) to her parents. The parents then decide whether the suitor is acceptable; if so, the daughter has little leeway to withstand their pressure to accept. Girls sometimes have their own reasons for marrying early. In theory, they are then subordinated to their spouse's family, but in practice many men who marry migrants' daughters come over from

Turkey to start a household in the Netherlands, and thus have no immediate kin in the vicinity. Several Turkish girls told me that the prospect of having a relatively independent household without much meddling from in-laws was a comparatively attractive one. The new family would likely settle near the girl's parents and may count on help from them. At the same time, as a married woman she anticipates having a more independent position in her family of origin than she did as an unwed daughter. Some girls are so eager to escape from a situation of dependence and confinement that they are prepared to accept a complete stranger, even if his views on women's freedom of action are unknown. In any ambition to gain more independence from their parents, a decision to go for more schooling is ultimately seen by many Turkish young people as a high-risk investment whose yields are too uncertain and too distant. In the vast majority of cases in my research, marriage means the end of a school career, for girls and boys alike.

As in Turkish families, marriage in Portuguese and Spanish families is seen by both parents and children as the most important event in the life cycle. But the children themselves choose when to get married and marriage signifies full independence from their parents. In their behaviour towards their children, Iberian parents show a continual awareness of that future independence. In Turkish families, by contrast, the parents' goals are taken for granted even after the children are married. In Iberian families, parents are likely to climb down after a conflict with one of their children, fearing lasting estrangement. Turkish adolescents are the ones who conform to their parents' agenda, not because they agree with the content of the underlying norms, but out of fear that pressure from the migrant community will compel their parents to impose severe sanctions. The situation might lead to a total break with their parents, and for most of them that is an unbearable, even unimaginable prospect.

Community and migrant networks

These patterned differences in expectations and behaviour within families broadly coincide with group boundaries. On closer inspection, though, interesting differences emerge between different families within the ethnic groups, while some patterns also overlap group boundaries. Among the Turkish families I studied, some parents manifested a more lenient attitude towards the dangers their children might encounter in Dutch society, and in this respect they showed more resemblance to the Iberian families. Without exception, these Turkish families were 'atypical' for their ethnic group in one other way: they lived largely *outside* networks of family and covillagers. This provides a clue to a variable that could be crucial to understanding the *overall* differences in patterned behaviour (and hence in school attainment) between the Turkish and Iberian populations. The networks that Turkish and Iberian migrant families participate in are different in character. Turkish networks exercise effective social control to uphold the norms from their villages of origin. Although networks of Iberian migrants also apply social control, it is far less rigid. Such differences can be traced to differences in the migration histories of the two groups.

As I have observed, Turkish immigration to the Netherlands, far more than that from the Iberian peninsula, has been characterized by a steady influx of migrants. The fact that Turkey's economic development has lagged behind that of other European emigration countries is in large part responsible for this ongoing migration. This chain migration, however, is not entirely due to macrostructural forces. Behaviours inherent in the kinship system and the household cycle in the communities of origin have also played a key structuring role in the Turkish migration pattern. Migration is often made possible by the migrant's family of orientation. Those who stay behind in Turkey have, both in their own view and in that of their migrant relatives, a legitimate stake in the undertaking (Engelbrekston 1978; Schiffauer 1991).

One consequence of this migration pattern is that Turkish families have not built their communities in the Netherlands from scratch, but often had ready-established connections upon arrival (Böcker 1994; Engelbrekston 1978). A large number of tightly knit communities of former covillagers (or migrants from clusters of neighbouring villages) have come into being. Many such communities also have strong ties to communities elsewhere in the Netherlands and Western Europe. Most importantly, they still maintain ties with their villages and regions of origin in Turkey. Membership in these communities is ascribed and it is very difficult to withdraw oneself or one's family from them. The nature of the relationship between family and community makes social control very effective indeed. Social control is the prime mechanism through which the behavioural patterns described above are consolidated. Because the communities of origin are so tightly linked to the local migrant communities, transgressions of norms by members of migrant families are immediately transmitted 'back home'. Sanctions for noncompliance with group norms can be harsh: a family's reputation can be destroyed, and this can have devastating social and economic consequences. Children normally go along with their parents' wishes not so much because they agree, but for fear of repercussions, and because they are educated to understand their parents' situation.

This constant surveillance by group members, and the virtual impossibility of evading the watchful eyes of the community, is accompanied by almost inescapable claims of reciprocity. Turkish immigrants often feel obliged to take up related newcomers and to allow their kindred in Turkey to share in the profits of migration. Many heads of family are absorbed by the question of how to fulfil all sorts of obligations towards kin. Parents expect their children to help in meeting such obligations, and in such situations the children's own behaviour and ambitions can readily be interpreted as running counter to family interests. Community scrutiny also extends to the children's marriage: partners, age of marriage, and especially the abundance of the wedding and the gifts are all subject to evaluation, which in turn may enhance a family's prestige or damage its reputation. Many fathers perceive all such obligations as problematic, and that is recognized by their children. Everything is subordinated to the maintenance of norms and to the avoidance of loss of face.

In contrast to the Turkish population, Portuguese and Spanish families in the Netherlands are not grouped into relatively exclusive communities linked to regions and villages of origin. In part this derives from the scale and the genesis of the Iberian communities. The Spanish and Portuguese populations as a whole are far smaller than the Turkish population. Although the Portuguese, concentrated in tightly knit local communities in cities in the west of the country, display greater social cohesion than the Spanish, such communities are still too small and too diverse in origin to contain viable region- or village-based subsections. The members come from many parts of their home country. Chain migration has played no major role. Families formerly unknown to one another began organizing for various purposes, not in the least because there was a strongly felt need for a structural context for teaching the children Portuguese. This emergent community first experienced processes of fission and fusion as a result of political developments in Portugal. Region- and village-based ties never developed to the point where they dominated the community. This is why mechanisms of social control are less well developed among the Portuguese than among the Turks in the Netherlands. Sanctions such as loss of reputation in the local migrant community are unlikely to have repercussions in the communities of origin. The same applies to Spanish families. Iberian parents can thus deal more leniently with the aspirations of their children and the problems they encounter in Dutch society. Although young people in the Portuguese community especially are encouraged to mix with compatriots, friendships with Dutch peers (or age mates from other ethnic groups) are not discouraged. The personal networks of the Turkish youth are much more restricted. For girls, the limited opportunities to develop contacts outside their parents' social circle have been well documented (Rişvanoğlu *et al.* 1986; de Vries 1987). Although boys enjoy more freedom than their sisters, what struck me in my research was that only a few of them had developed stable friendships, even in their own surroundings, or were participating in peer groups that they valued for themselves. Parents welcome such relations for their children only if they are with people from their own region-based network. They are distrustful of friendships their children develop with Turkish peers from outside their moral community. As these local networks are often very limited in size, many young people have trouble finding peers to be friends within the areas where they live.[7] The exclusiveness of Turkish region- and village-based networks, and the approach taken there to ethnic difference, also limit the members' possibilities of developing affective relationships with Dutch people. The scarcity of durable contacts with Dutch society, and the lack of diversity in children's contacts with their Turkish school-age peers, results in a relative paucity of examples and role models for school behaviour.

The lack of positive, enduring relationships with people outside the Turkish community also makes it harder to put experiences with discrimination into perspective. Revealingly, both the Iberian and the Turkish young people I encountered who had cherished contacts, even one or two, with Dutch persons, were all able to take extremely insulting confrontations with racism and discrimination in their stride. Unlike the migrant young people who lacked such meaningful external relationships, they did not let such incidents affect their attitude towards Dutch society at large, nor their motivation to continue their schooling or their search for a good job (for an extended discussion, see Lindo 1996: 79–84).

Conclusion: does the concept of culture matter?

In a search for the influences that underlie behavioural patterns, the question of how to conceptualize such influences inevitably arises. It is obviously no solution just to call them 'culture' and leave it at that. Culture can be a hazardous tool in sociological analysis. In using culture as a guiding concept, one risks glossing over the ambiguities and variations that exist inside the group, as well as behavioural patterns that transcend the (not-so-neatly demarcated) boundaries. A second, more serious danger is reification. Cultural specificity is not an explanation; it *demands* explanation. The cultural factor is not autonomous. To ascribe something to the domain of culture – for instance, to label certain identified behavioural patterns as traditions, attitudes or orientations carried across from the country of origin – can never be an explanation in itself. If processes and characteristics have been identified in the direct social environments of migrant young people which are seen as interfering with their educational careers, an observation such as 'culture plays a role' marks the beginning of the analysis rather than the conclusion. As I have used the culture concept here, it is in the first place an indicator to help us recognize behavioural patterns that seem specific to one group or another. The real work of interpreting and explaining their specificity starts from there. The approach should be both situational and diachronic.

The differences in behavioural patterns observed between the migrant communities studied here can definitely be linked to differences in kinship in the communities of origin. Let me take the differences in the position of the wife and mother as an example. In Spain and Portugal, relations with kin outside the nuclear family are bilateral and are relatively insignificant in terms of obligations. The wife is closely involved in virtually all important decisions, also concerning matters outside the home. Submission to the husband's will is in many ways ritualistic (Collier 1997; Cutileiro 1971), and in the community of origin it is more highly emphasized in the public sphere, in the presence of non-kindred significant others, than inside the home. The position of Iberian mothers tends to gain strength in the immigration country, because almost all of them contribute to the family income. At the same time, the more ritualistic aspects of the subordination of wife to husband, as emphasized in the communities of origin, tend to lose their function, given the more relaxed social control in the immigration country.

The position of women in the patrilineal kinship system that functions in Turkish villages is far weaker. Within the home, they are not only dominated by their husband, but they are often subordinated to other in-laws too (see, for example, Delaney 1991). Their position tends to weaken further after migration as a consequence of the strong social control within the region-based migrant networks. Such control is bolstered by the dominant view in these networks that the temptations of Dutch society form a threat to a family's reputation. The same may be said of the pressure put on Turkish migrants' children to marry during adolescence. This custom from the communities of origin is maintained, and even reinforced, by the parents' fear of 'Dutchification' of the children.

The explanatory emphasis in this contribution has lain on fairly recent historical forces of migration and community formation. If we refer to the described group-specific behavioural patterns as culture, then this culture is transmitted by these historical forces in differential ways. In other words, in situations where the social cohesion of the migrant community is stronger and the ties back to the community of origin are better maintained, behavioural patterns originating in the latter communities tend to establish themselves in migrant families more firmly than in situations where the cohesion and home-country ties are less strong. Whether we call it culture or not, such a behavioural pattern should be viewed as a set of relations with a specifiable history, and not as an indigenous characteristic of the people involved. The behaviour of the Turkish migrants, in particular, is shaped and directed by processes of migration and community formation. Obviously these processes are themselves a partial product of group-specific behaviours in the communities of origin. They are not generated with the approval of all the actors; in fact, individuals have little influence on them. Most Turks did not make a conscious decision to participate in the local migrant community. They left Turkey under the auspices of kinship, and in the Netherlands they have remained part of the same network of kinspeople and covillagers. In the case of the Iberian migrants, the support of kin in the migration process was of less consequence than it was for most Turks. Yet there are also Turkish families with more individualistic migration histories, and their direct social environments appear to be more integrated into Dutch society. They are far less extensively, if at all, incorporated into networks of family and covillagers. If we consider behavioural patterns such as these in the wider perspective of the historical relationship between the migrant group and the community of origin, that can help us explain behavioural differences both between and within groups.

Notwithstanding the importance of this wider historical viewpoint, processes like these should at the same time be analysed at the level of the actors and their direct environment. Considered this way, the question of whether group-specific interaction processes should be understood in terms of ideational constructs or of structural impediments and possibilities is inappropriate. From the standpoint of the actors studied here, these two dimensions cannot be considered in isolation from one another. The 'structural' relations of Turkish region-based networks are indescribable without their 'cultural' content in terms of reciprocity, ethnicity and social control (to give but a few examples). And the converse is equally true. As Goody (1992: 10) has argued, people

> act and interact in ways that may allow one to discern beliefs, symbols and values, but these are intrinsic to their interaction; social action must include such a dimension and would be meaningless without it (...). Any more separable notion of a 'framework' emerges from the analytic perception of the observer rather than from the action perspective of the actor.[8]

The behavioural patterns which have been shown in this study to exert influence on educational attainment do not combine to produce a single unified attitude, either positive or negative, with respect to Dutch education or the benefits of learning in general. This may seem to be stating the obvious. After all, attitudes or orientations are never absolute, but always contain relative values and priorities. In the orientation of parents, education has its place in a ranking order of priorities, which is revealed in the choices they make at various moments, in various situations. My point here is that this orientation appears to be strongly bound up with and influenced by the context. For instance, if Turkish migrant families are not part of region-based networks, parents exert less pressure on their children to get married in adolescence. By implication, then, the negative orientation towards education – expressed in the priority other parents might give to marriage at the expense of school – is being imposed by the community.

A further point is that the social careers of Turkish young adults are almost never subject to just one of the described interaction patterns. It is the relative and combined impact of a number of these patterns that makes Turkish adolescents decide to abandon their educational career. From the children's perspective, it would not be reasonable to interpret the considerations they make in such situations as a positive or negative educational orientation or strategy. And the same applies to their parents. From the point of view of individual parents, phenomena such as reciprocal obligations and social control are, at least in part, contextual effects that can influence their decisions in spite of themselves.

In the cases examined here, then, any assumption that Iberians and Turks hold contrasting attitudes towards education would not do justice to the observed interaction within the families and communities under study. Concepts like 'orientation' and 'attitude' can be misleading, because they imply that 'culture' is imprinted in the individual. Nonetheless, one can say that ambivalence towards education, which can be observed in both groups, is greater in the case of the Turkish parents. But this is the consequence of real dilemmas that parents encounter through their participation in village- and region-based networks. They are more likely than Iberian migrants to find themselves in situations where they have to set priorities that interfere with their children's education.

Are we to conclude that culture plays little or no role in the educational divergence between the groups studied? That depends on what we understand by culture. If we reserve the concept for the ideational domain only, it does not have much explanatory value. But culture cannot be explained away by 'class' or 'social position' either. It is best to view culture as a concept that makes us aware of the historical singularity of the interaction patterns we observe within the direct social environments of individuals. Ethnic groups are products of distinct histories, as Perlmann (1988) has put it. We should not view ideational and structural domains as mutually exclusive explanatory categories. People are not just victims or passive receptors of social, economic or other 'contextual' mechanisms, nor are they bearers of cultural traits or traditions that programme them to behave in predetermined ways. They are themselves agents in society, giving form to the social context they are part of, and moulding 'inherited' behavioural patterns (usually called 'culture') in the process. Understood in this way, culture does make a difference in the educational careers of Turkish and Iberian migrants' children.

Notes

1. See, for instance, Caplan *et al.* 1989, Gibson 1989, Gibson and Bhachu 1988, Modood 1991.
2. The data that uncovered the success of the Iberian school leavers were collected in 1989 in a small quantitative study (Lindo and Pennings 1992) among children of southern European migrants (Portuguese, Spanish and Yugoslav). A total of 131 Portuguese and 132 Spanish young people were questioned on topics that included the social position and migration history of their parents. The findings of that study, taken together with those of other research in which southern

Europeans were represented as one category alongside other migrant groups (see, for example, van Langen and Jungbluth 1990), and with more 'circumstantial' statistical evidence relating to secondary school pupils, led the Dutch government in 1994 to conclude that southern European migrants have been successfully integrated into Dutch society. The data on the Turkish school leavers were collected in the 1991 migrant survey Social Position and Use of Provisions conducted by the ISEO of Erasmus University Rotterdam (see Table 10.2).

3. The allocating power of intended and unintended discrimination in the educational environment can be strongly influenced by the attitude the victim takes towards such occurrences. I will come back to this later on.

4. With the children semi-structured interviews were held, most of them were interviewed more than once. The interviews were tape-recordered. Also, with most of the fathers and about half of the mothers conversations were held.

5. These behavioural patterns are analysed more extensively in Lindo 1994, 1995, 1996 and 1997.

6. Another reason is that southern European families are more likely than Turkish families to have moved outside areas with large migrant populations (Tesser and van Praag 1995).

7. As a rule, networks of Turkish parents are multilocal, and they often extend not only back to the communities of origin but also to various cities in the Netherlands and other European countries that host covillagers and kinspeople. Children do develop warm friendships with cousins in other places, but those friendships can only be pursued at distant intervals.

8. See also Foner 1997.

References

Ankersmit, T., T. Roelandt, and J. Veenman, 1989, *Statistisch Vademecum* (Voorburg: CBS)

Bhachu, P., 1985, *Parental Educational Strategies. The Case of Punjabi Sikhs in Britain.* Research Paper in Ethnic Relations no. 3 (Warwick: University of Warwick)

Böcker, A., 1994, *Turkse Migranten en Sociale Zekerheid. Van Onderlinge Zorg naar Overheidszorg?* (Amsterdam: Amsterdam University Press)

Bois-Reymond, M. du, 1992, *Pluraliseringstendenzen en Onderhandelingsculturen in het Gezin*, paper presented at the Sociaal-wetenschappelijke Studiedagen, Vrije Universiteit Amsterdam, 28–29 April

Caplan, N., J.K. Whitmore, and M.H. Choy, 1989, *The Boat People and Achievement in America. A Study of Family Life, Hard Work, and Cultural Values* (Ann Arbor: University of Michigan Press)

Collier, J.F., 1997, *From Duty to Desire. Remaking Families in a Spanish Village* (Princeton: Princeton University Press)

Cutileiro, J., 1971, *A Portuguese Rural Society* (Oxford: Clarendon Press)

Delaney, C., 1991, *The Seed and the Soil* (Berkeley: University of California Press)

Engelbrektson, U.-B., 1978, *The Force of Tradition* (Gothenburg: Gothenburg Studies in Anthropology)

Fase, W., 1994, *Ethnic Divisions in Western European Education* (New York: Waxmann)

Foner, N., 1997, 'The immigrant family. Cultural legacies and cultural changes', *International Migration Review* 31(4): 961–75

Gibson, M.A., 1987, 'The school performance of immigrant minorities. A comparative view', *Anthropology and Education Quarterly* 18(4): 262–75

Gibson, M.A., 1989, *Accommodation Without Assimilation. Sikh Immigrants in an American High School* (Ithaca: Cornell University Press)

Gibson, M.A., and P.K. Bhachu, 1988, 'Ethnicity and school performance. A comparative study of South Asian pupils in Britain and America', *Ethnic and Racial Studies* 11(3): 239–62

Goody, J., 1992, 'Culture and its boundaries. A European view', *Social Anthropology* 1(1A): 9–32

Langen, A. van, and P. Jungbluth, 1990, *Onderwijskansen van Migranten. De Rol van Sociaal-Economische en Culturele Factoren* (Amsterdam: Swets en Zeitlinger)

Lindo, F., 1994, 'Het stille succes. De sociale stijging van Zuideuropese arbeidsmigranten in Nederland', in: H. Vermeulen and R. Penninx (eds), *Het Democratisch Ongeduld. De Emanciptatie en Integratie van Zes Doelgroepen van het Minderhedenbeleid* (Amsterdam: Het Spinhuis)

Lindo, F., 1995, 'Ethnic myth or ethnic might? On the divergence in educational attainment between Portuguese and Turkish Youth in the Netherlands', in: G. Baumann and T. Sunier (eds), *Post-Migration Ethnicity. Cohesion, Commitments, Comparison* (Amsterdam: IMES/SISWO)

Lindo, F., 1996, *Maakt Cultuur Verschil? De Invloed van Groepsspecifieke Gedragspatronen op de Onderwijsloopbaan van Turkse en Iberische Migrantenjongeren* (Amsterdam: Het Spinhuis)

Lindo, F., 1997, 'Integratie op kousevoeten. Het snelle succes van de Zuid-Europeanen in Nederland', *Justitiële Verkenningen* 23(6): 21–36

Lindo, F., and T. Pennings, 1992, *Jeugd met Toekomst. De Leefsituatie en Sociale Positie van Portugese, Spaanse en Joegoslavische Jongeren in Nederland* (Amsterdam: Het Spinhuis)

Modood, T., 1991, 'The Indian economic success. A chalenge to some race relations assumptions', *Policy and Politics* 19(3): 177–89

Ogbu, J., 1987 , 'Variability in minority school performance. A problem in search of an explanation', *Anthropology and Education Quarterly* 18: 312–34

Perlmann, J., 1988, *Ethnic Differences* (Cambridge: Cambridge University Press)

Pieke, F.N., 1989, 'Chinezen in het Nederlandse onderwijs', *Migrantenstudies* 5(2): 2–17

Portes, A., 1995, 'Children of immigrants. Segmented assimilation', in: A. Portes (ed.), *The Economic Sociology of Immigration* (New York: Russell Sage Foundation)

Portes, A., 1997, 'Immigration theory for a New Century. Some problems and opportunities', *International Migration Review* 31(4): 799–826

Portes, A., and M. Zhou, 1993, 'The new second generation. Segmented assimilation and its variants among post-1965 immigrant youth', *Annals of the American Academy of Political and Social Science* 530: 74–98

Rişvanoğlu, S., L. Brouwer and M. Priester, 1986, *Verschillend als de Vingers van een Hand. Een Onderzoek naar het Integratieproces van Turkse Gezinnen in Nederland* (Leiden: COMT)

Roelandt, Th., J.H.M. Roÿen and J. Veenman, 1992, Minderheden in Nederland: Statistisch Vademecum 1992 (The Hague: SDU)

Schiffauer, W., 1991, *Die Migranten aus Subay. Türken in Deutschland: Eine Ethnographie* (Stuttgart: Klett-Cotta)

Steinberg, S., 1989, *The Ethnic Myth. Race, Ethnicity and Class in America* (Boston: Beacon Press)

Tesser, P.T.M., and C.S. van Praag 1995, *Rapportage Minderheden 1995. Concentratie en Segregatie* (Rijswijk: SCP)

Tesser, P., and J. Veenman, 1997, *Rapportage Minderheden 1997. Van School naar Werk* (Rijswijk: SCP)

Vries, M. de, 1987, *Ogen in Je Rug. Turkse Meisjes en Jonge Vrouwen in Nederland* (Alphen a/d Rijn: Samsom)

Zhou, M., 1997, 'Segmented assimilation. Issues, controversies, and recent research on the new second generation', *International Migration Review* 31(4): 975–1009

11
Breaking the Circle of Disadvantage. Social Mobility of Second-Generation Moroccans and Turks in the Netherlands

Maurice Crul

Moroccan and Turkish migrants of the first generation are low on the socioeconomic ladder in Dutch society. They hold the worst paid jobs, suffer the highest unemployment rates and live in the poorest neighbourhoods of the cities (see Eldering 1997). To a considerable extent, the children replicate the socioeconomic position of their parents. Many Turkish and Moroccan immigrant youngsters have left school without diplomas, winding up in the same types of menial jobs as their parents. Researchers have offered a range of cultural and structural explanations for this school failure. Recent research, however, has been focusing more specifically on the so-called second generation – the children born and bred in the Netherlands – rather than on immigrant youth in general. Such studies have found that a growing number of second-generation Turkish and Moroccan children are doing very well indeed.[1] In view of the well-documented internal and external factors that lead to school failure, it would be interesting to know why this latter group is so successful. Most such children have parents who either are illiterate or who enjoyed only a few years of primary education. The children that have achieved success have thus made a spectacular leap upwards.

In a chapter like this one which deals with the social mobility of second-generation Turks and Moroccans, the reader might expect the focus to be on differences between the two groups. Indeed, when I began my research I was looking for such differences. As we shall see, however, the educational profiles of Turkish and Moroccan young people hardly diverge. I will therefore attempt here to explain the differences *within* the two groups, rather than those between them. In analysing the various second-generation outcomes, I stress the historically dynamic nature of the immigrant cultures of the two ethnic groups. Two different temporal considerations are crucial. One of these concerns the arrival of the groups in the Netherlands – how many people migrated, how long they have been in the country, and whether migration has continued within the family in question into the present day. The other consideration involves what is called birth order effects. The specific factors with the strongest influence on individual members of the second generation will be seen to vary in the interplay of these two temporal mechanisms. Such time-related factors affect the nature of both the migration process and the process of cultural change.

I begin by briefly introducing the second-generation Turks and Moroccans and their parents in the Netherlands.

The Turkish and Moroccan communities in the Netherlands

The first Turkish and Moroccan labour migrants came to the Netherlands in the 1960s on the basis of treaties with the governments of their countries. Their numbers grew steadily in the course of that decade, with the bulk of the immigrants arriving in the first half of the 1970s. In 1976 the Dutch government put an official end to migration, as a result of the economic recession then prevailing. Although that considerably slowed the migration, smaller numbers still managed to arrive through chain migration. At first, only men were involved, but in the early 1970s they began reuniting with their families, a process that resulted in the substantial Moroccan and Turkish communities of the present day. By 1996, 272 000 Turks and 225 000 Moroccans were officially residing in the Netherlands (Tesser and Veenman 1997). The majority of them originated from rural areas. Most of the men had no more than a rudimentary education and most women had never been to school at all (Crul 1994). As a consequence, first-generation parents today generally have scant knowledge of educational systems – a state of affairs which was repeatedly emphasized by both the parents and the children I interviewed. This has severely constrained the parents' ability to help their children with their schoolwork. The majority of parents nonetheless encouraged their children to study hard.

The children of the first Turkish and Moroccan migrants are now mostly adolescents. Some came to the Netherlands due to family reunification, others were born there. This article deals only with the latter group, the second generation. The initial wave of the second generation is now moving on to the labour market and concluding its educational careers, but the majority of the young people are still at school or college. I have analysed the educational position of the second generation using the survey Ethnic Minorities, Their Position in Society and Their Use of Facilities (ISEO/EUR, SPVA'94).[2] The success rates of children currently attending school are difficult to determine precisely, since only time will tell whether and how they will complete their education. Notwithstanding this reservation, we may still conclude that a fairly large group has achieved success. I have defined as 'successful' those survey respondents who were in an educational stream

(Havo/Vwo) that affords direct access to higher (university or professional) education, as well as those who were already in higher education. One quarter of the Turkish and Moroccan pupils and students between 15 and 24 years of age were successful by this criterion. The SPVA survey revealed that Turkish and Moroccan pupils have educational profiles that are roughly similar, as do males and females. The latter finding indicates a significant improvement, as much of the previous literature has dwelt on school neglect and school dropout rates among Turkish and Moroccan girls (Vlug 1985: 85, 95) – a trend that seems to have been effectively reversed by the second generation.[3] Turkish and Moroccan girls are now just as likely as boys are to enter general secondary school.

The empirical research

In the period 1994 to 1997 I interviewed 86 second-generation Moroccan and Turkish pupils and students, both male and female. The interviews took place in seven schools and colleges located in different parts of Amsterdam, the city with the largest Moroccan and Turkish communities in the Netherlands. Respondents were chosen at random from the students of Moroccan and Turkish descent in the official school registries and were between 16 and 24 years of age. In addition, I interviewed one or both parents in 30 families. The numbers of 'successful' and 'nonsuccessful' students in the sample were virtually equal. We spoke about their experiences so far with education, starting with primary school. The questions were designed to reconstruct the educational routes of the pupils and students in the greatest possible detail, with special attention to selection processes in the educational system. A range of topics were covered, which included problems with subjects in the school curriculum, disputes with teachers, and parental support.

From the data thus obtained, I reconstructed the educational careers of all of the respondents. My information included the recommendations made by primary schools on the choice of a secondary school type, the secondary school streams pursued towards higher education, and in some cases the longer routes followed through secondary vocational education up to higher education. The resulting patterns provided important information about the selection processes undergone by Turkish and Moroccan pupils in the Dutch educational system. The system provides pupils with various possibilities for reaching higher education,[4] and these are utilized by the Turkish and Moroccan pupils to varying degrees. This enables us to assess the significance of the different routes pupils can follow to attain success in school.

A minority of the successful respondents (13) received high primary school recommendations and directly gained access to the highest streams of secondary education (Figure 11.1, route 1). The largest group, 20 respondents,

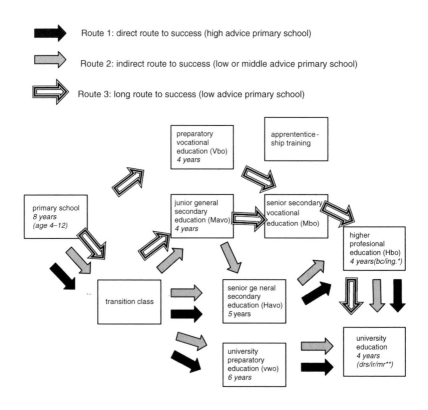

Route 1: direct route to success (high advice primary school)

Route 2: indirect route to success (low or middle advice primary school)

Route 3: long route to success (low advice primary school)

*Hbo titles granted:
(in engineering and agriculture): 'ingenieur' (ing.)
(in all other fields): 'baccalaureaat' (bc)

** university titles granted:
• (in engineering): 'ingenieur' (ir)
• (in law): 'meester' (mr)
• (in all other fields): 'doctorandus' (drs)

Figure 11.1   School routes of successful students

achieved their success in the course of secondary school (Figure 11.1, route 2). A third group of 8, the smallest group in the sample, reached higher education via the long route through preparatory and senior vocational education (Figure 11.1, route 3). Thus, for some pupils the crucial period was at the beginning of their school career, for others it was in the middle or more towards the end. The success of each group was associated with a different educational phase and a different age. In other words, success appears to be governed by various factors; it cannot be explained by one factor alone or reduced to one decisive period.

In the sections to follow I will identify the factors associated with the success of each of the three successful groups. Taken together, the groups reflect a certain evolution over time. The oldest of the successful students generally took the long route. Most successful students in the intermediate age category took the direct route. The youngest students were most likely to have achieved their success in the course of secondary school. This development over time may be explained by the changes in the circumstances of the various second-generation age categories. I shall highlight the most significant characteristics of each successful group. Although these characteristics obviously applied more to some members of each group than to others, the descriptions the students gave of their situations were strikingly similar. Given the limited number of cases studied, my argument derives its validity not from statistics but from a detailed microlevel analysis of the school careers. It identifies specific processes that seem to be at work within the community, among family members and between the family and the school.

Mutual help and support of peers

The pupils who took the long, indirect route to higher education are the oldest second-generation children in my research. Most were also the oldest children in their families and their parents had no experience with the Dutch educational system. They attended school with children who had arrived in a later phase of their schooling as a result of family reunification, the so-called 'in-between generation'. Just as the in-between children in their class, most of my older respondents received low primary school recommendations and were channelled into the lowest educational options. Their parents did not feel confident enough to disregard the recommendation. Most youngsters thus entered preparatory vocational education, the lowest available educational stream. Those successful pupils who followed the long route through the educational system shared a good deal of their educational careers with their nonsuccessful counterparts. During the first 12 years of school, they distinguished themselves little from the non-successful pupils. However, they subsequently went on studying, while the others left school after getting their pre-vocational or senior vocational school diplomas. The successful ones had to overcome numerous obstacles on their long route towards higher education, and many now harbour anger and frustration about the ways they have been treated by schools and teachers in the past. Characteristic of this group, however, is that such treatment did not cause them to give up.

It might seem logical to assume that these children's parents did more than others to encourage and stimulate them to continue their studies, but that was by no means the case. Instead, the children themselves used their success to stimulate their parents' involvement.

> I just dragged my dad along to my school, whether he wanted to go or not, and then he heard all these really positive things about me like, 'Yes, your daughter is bright, we don't see that very often, she's really going to get somewhere.' Well, of course he really enjoyed hearing that (young Moroccan woman [1], university).

Most young people who decided to move on to higher education could reckon on at least some passive support from within their families. Many parents contributed to the educational expenses and reserved a room especially for their son or daughter. In this way the study became a project for the whole family. Some other young people received more ambivalent support.

> My parents didn't give me constant encouragement. If I ever complained they would say, 'See, why are you studying, then? Go get a job!' Then I didn't dare to complain any more. I was also scared to admit it if I had problems, like if I failed a test or a course. It's all up to you. It's something inside you that pushes you to go on, to prove yourself, especially to society and to everyone (young Moroccan woman [2], university).

One may conclude that although many children were not really encouraged by their parents, at least they were not obstructed either. An early marriage, desired by the parents, is the most salient factor identified so far that thwarts children's school careers (Lindo 1995: 158). For the second-generation youth, this no longer seems to carry much weight. Fewer than 5 per cent of the Turkish and Moroccan youth now get married before age 21 (ISEO/EUR, SPVA'94). Even most children who leave school between 16 and 21 do not marry early. The overwhelming majority of the young people who are over 21 and still studying are in higher education. I found this category of students in particular to be deeply convinced of the importance of education and they would not let themselves be denied an education they had struggled so hard to achieve.

Parents, then, do not seem to have been a determinant factor, in either a positive or a negative sense. The young people themselves emphasized the role played by their peers. Notably, all the children who took the long, indirect route to higher education reported how important their Turkish and Moroccan peers were to them, some even stating explicitly that these peers were the main reason they had come so far. They often formed closely knit study groups with one or two other Turkish or Moroccan students in their class, who then supported each other psychologically as well as practically.

> Most of the time we did our homework together. I went to his place and he came to mine. We usually started by chatting and drinking tea, learning some French words in between and testing each other quickly. That went very well. He couldn't understand mathematics very well, he was better at languages. I was better at technical things (young Turkish man [1], higher professional school).

Peer groups of Turkish or Moroccan descent have hitherto often been perceived as detrimental to the school performance of Turkish and Moroccan children. The successful students, however, benefited immensely from their close contacts with friends from their own group. The help they gave one another was a key factor in their success (see also Rumbaut 1997: 38).

Shared background was a binding element between peers. As one Turkish student succinctly put it, 'You can't expect that sort of help from Dutch people, you only get that from real friends.' Other shared experiences in the Dutch educational system, such as with racism or discrimination from teachers or with the feeling of being excluded by Dutch pupils, also played an important part. Ostensibly, such peer group support might be interpreted as a manifestation of the mutual help that is typical of the Turkish and Moroccan communities at large, where such commitments are of vital importance within family and regional networks. Although the friends that formed the peer groups at school did not usually come from the same family or regional networks, they acquired a similar status. Because of the clearly positive influence the peers had on one another, they were welcomed in each other's families and, with the passage of time, family-like relationships between the peers and their friends' parents started to emerge. The young people often spoke of their friendships in family terms, such as 'we are like brothers to each other'. We might describe such peers as 'fictive kin'.

As students advanced through their educational careers, the peer group became an increasingly central point of reference in their lives. This was true both for the students who took the long route through education as well as for those who reached higher education through quicker routes. Turkish and Moroccan students still form tiny minorities in the Dutch institutions of higher education. Without exception, the students I interviewed were part of smaller or larger peer groups of Turkish and Moroccan students. Within such groups, problems with course content were discussed, jobs were arranged and arrangements were made to attend social activities together. Almost everyone belonged to a Turkish or Moroccan students' association or at least took part in the activities organized by one. Such organizations were very important, for they provided a discussion forum on opinions and behaviour in the community. The existence of such small or larger networks which provided support and protection more or less independently of the family made it easier for the students to *confront* their parents and negotiate with them about their plans for the future (see also Sung 1987: 126). The students could point to the opportunities enjoyed by other Turkish and Moroccan young people, so that they no longer stood alone in their discussions with their parents.

White schools, black schools

The school careers of the second group of successful students I have identified can be described as real success stories from start to finish. They received a good recommendation right after primary school and they reached the highest streams of education without delay. Other children repeated one or more classes in primary or secondary school. Only a minority of all the successful respondents received high primary school recommendations.

Primary school is the most critical period in the explanation of their success and for that reason I focus mainly on that period in this section. Every primary school pupil in the Netherlands receives an official recommendation at the end of their final year. It is crucial for admission to certain schools and streams of secondary education. Most children's recommendations are based on the nationwide CITO examination which assesses their knowledge of mathematics and Dutch, as well as their overall intellectual development by means of general questions. I have defined a high recommendation as one that affords admission to the secondary school levels that give direct access to higher education.[5]

High primary school recommendations proved to be strongly associated with the school context in which pupils had been educated. Almost all the children with a high recommendation had attended so-called 'white schools', ones with few children of foreign descent.[6] Children who went to a 'white school' either lived in neighbourhoods with few migrant families, or their parents had deliberately sent them to 'white schools' even though they lived in neighbourhoods with many migrants. Most often the 'white school' was a Protestant or Roman Catholic school, which were avoided by other Muslim parents for religious reasons.[7]

Pupils attending 'white schools' distinguished themselves from other children primarily in their far superior Dutch language skills (see also Klatter-Folmer 1996: 237). Children who scored high on the CITO exam had no major problems with Dutch by the end of primary school. As the interviews revealed, Turkish and Moroccan pupils in 'white schools' had received plenty of individual attention from the teachers as they learned Dutch. Such was hardly feasible in schools with high shares of migrant children – the so-called 'black schools' – because 10 or 15 children in each class needed help with their Dutch. Among them were children who had just arrived in the Netherlands and had little knowledge of the language. In the early 1980s, schools in many working-class neighbourhoods were transformed within a few years' time from predominantly ethnic Dutch in composition into schools with a majority of migrant pupils, and this plunged the schools into a long-term crisis. Teachers complained in this period that it was almost impossible to teach well, because of the wide differentials between the children within each class in terms of age, language abilities and years educated in Dutch schools (de Jong 1986).[8] My respondents who had attended 'white schools' also reported having read more than other respondents and having begun to read earlier. In addition, they had far more intensive language contacts with their ethnic Dutch schoolmates, since they did not belong to separate Turkish of Moroccan peer groups like many of those attending schools with large migrant populations. Many children who went to 'white schools' related in the interviews how teachers had stimulated them to go for higher education and how they were pushed to deliver good results. I rarely heard such comments from the children who attended 'black schools'.

The overwhelming majority of children who visited 'white schools' lived in neighbourhoods with few migrant inhabitants, suburbs built in the 1950s. The Turkish and Moroccan families were the first migrant families to settle there and their children were the first migrant pupils in the schools. At the time, these had been predominantly lower-middle-class, ethnic Dutch neighbourhoods (see also van Amersfoort and Cortie 1996). That situation did not last long, though, since more and more Turkish and Moroccan families were moving into the areas. The families that first moved there had also been pioneers in coming to the Netherlands.[9] The fathers had been among the first migrants to arrive from Turkey and Morocco, five to ten years earlier than the fathers of other respondents in the sample. Their process of incorporation into Dutch society had been quite different from that of the later migrants. They had first lived in boarding houses or had rented a room from Dutch people. The interviews suggest that, in those early days, the immigrants had friendly relations with the Dutch.

> My father arrived in 1966. Compared to other families that was very early; most of them came five or even ten years later. They're not like us, you know. The people who came in the 1970s are more disadvantaged and cut off from Dutch people. My parents made an effort to get to know Dutch people; they also lived with Dutch families and got to know their way round. It was normal, as normal as daylight (young Turkish man [2], higher professional school).

Soon after their families joined them, a considerable proportion of the early migrants began moving from the older working-class districts surrounding the city centre into postwar, lower-middle-class housing developments on the outskirts of Amsterdam. Their move was always motivated by a combination of practical and social reasons. The flats were larger and the neighbourhoods were more attractive for children to grow up in. Many people also wanted to move because of the increasing concentrations of Turks and Moroccans in their old neighbourhoods. Although their motives for moving are not yet well documented, there is some evidence that people who move to predominantly ethnic Dutch neighbourhoods have a greater desire not to live near their compatriots than people who stay in areas of ethnic minority concentration (Bolt and van Kempen 1997).[10] Other value and behavioural patterns of parents that moved out of the older districts also suggest they were more oriented to Dutch society. Earlier than other parents, for instance, they were convinced that the future of their children was in the Netherlands, rather than in Turkey or Morocco. A key indication is that none of them sent their children to study in Turkey or Morocco. Many other second-generation children were sent to Morocco or Turkey to learn the language, in case the family should ever move back there. When they returned to the Netherlands one or two years later, many such children encountered serious problems at school, especially with the Dutch language.

Use of Dutch at home is another indicator of significant differences between families in the sample. In many of the families in the newer districts, the use of Dutch at home was encouraged by the parents. Children in these families spoke Dutch among themselves and some even spoke it with their parents. This formed a major contrast with other families, where the emphasis was put on learning the original immigrant language. Parents who settled in the newer districts were also more likely to encourage their children to play with Dutch friends. They were allowed to bring their Dutch friends home with them and they would go to play in the Dutch homes. Other parents were more reluctant about contacts with Dutch children. This may also partly explain the differences in Dutch language proficiency that already existed between children in the sample in their preschool period. Some did not speak a word of Dutch when they started school, others spoke it almost fluently. Parents in the newer districts also allowed their children more freedom to join activities with Dutch children organized by schools or community centres. Some parents reported that they consciously encouraged their children to take part because they did not want them to be isolated from Dutch children. This does not mean that such parents failed to demand respect for Turkish or Moroccan values and norms – they also put considerable effort into conveying their cultural heritage to their children. But they did not want that to impede their children's integration into Dutch society.

The differential conditions in primary education continued to give these children advantages over other children when they moved on to secondary school. The children I have just described had more opportunities to play-fully develop social skills that are essential if one is to function within the Dutch educational system. At first glance, the system appears strict and for-mal, but in practice there is considerable latitude for manoeuvre and nego-tiation between teachers and pupils. Pupils who possess the social skills to discuss things with the teachers in a relaxed manner have more manoeu-vring space when problems arise or decisions have to be made. The inter-views demonstrated that such pupils had close, regular contacts both with their teachers and with their ethnic Dutch classmates. Because they had moved directly into the highest streams of secondary education, they were once again in classes with predominantly Dutch pupils. The lower sec-ondary school types have much higher percentages of Turkish and Moroccan pupils.

Fathers who migrated in later years arrived in a far more closed society than their predecessors, one which could be blatantly hostile to for-eigners. A clear connection is evident between the migrants' reception into Dutch society and their subsequent attitude towards it. In the initial years after migration, the latecomers had far less contact with ethnic Dutch people. By that time they also had available their own emergent ethnic infrastructures consisting of organizations, mosques and shops (Bovenkerk *et al.* 1985, Vermeulen 1984). There was less need to socialize with Dutch people. They became integrated not so much into Dutch society as into the already existing Turkish or Moroccan communities in the older working-class districts. A similar process has been described by Portes and Zhou (1993) in their model of segmented assimilation. Migrants who came later were focused far more on their own ethnic community, and when their wives and children arrived, they too automatically became part of that community. To a significant degree this determined the latecomers' hori-zons. A small proportion even became openly hostile to Dutch society. They tried to keep their children away from it, believing it undermined true values. Although the majority of the late arrivers in my research did not have outspokenly negative attitudes towards Dutch society, neither did they encourage their children to speak Dutch or associate with Dutch people (see van der Hoek and Kret 1992; Klatter-Folmer 1996; van der Leij *et al.* 1991). Their children therefore grew up in mainly Turkish or Moroccan surroundings.

The outlook and the behaviour of the early migrants directly and indirectly fostered the swift integration and acculturation of their chil-dren into Dutch society during the primary school period. Such young people would seem to fit perfectly into the classical assimilation thesis, but one critical remark should be made. Assimilation is often depicted as a one-way process, involving only the migrants (van der Hoek and Kret 1992; Pels 1991). The dedication to integration among the parents, however, can also be explained in part by the way they were received in the host society in the first place. The exceptional position of the early migrants was due not only to the needs or intentions of the migrants themselves; it was also rooted in the way the receiving Dutch society interacted with the newcomers. For the later migrants, assimilation was a far less attainable, and attractive, option than it was for their early counterparts.

Help and support from siblings

The largest group of successful students in my research had climbed to the highest rungs of the Dutch educational system during the course of general secondary education. These children were clearly distinguishable from those in the previous section. They grew up in the older districts and attended 'black schools'. Most were among the youngest respondents in the sample. Their situation more closely resembled that of young Turkish and Moroccan children in general. In many ethnic minority concentration areas, primary schools are now attended almost solely by Moroccan and Turkish migrant children. A considerable number of respondents that grew up in those circumstances nevertheless achieved success, gaining 'promotion' to the highest curriculum levels in the course of their secondary school careers. They did not do this without difficulty. Many had to repeat a year because they could not cope with the pace of study or with the new demands of a more difficult curriculum. But eventually they got there. The overcoming of such hurdles in their educational career was a prominent topic in the interviews with these students. Their parents usually played no role of importance in their education. As one young woman reported, 'They just know you're going and they know you come back again.' The most significant success-related factor that emerged was the help and support provided by older brothers and sisters.

Respondents that rose to success in the course of secondary school were a good deal more likely than those in the other two groups to say they had been helped by older siblings. For many of them, that support tipped the balance between going to higher streams of education and having to opt for a lower stream. Time and again, older siblings were mentioned in connection with important decisions, advice and practical help with homework. As I became more aware of their importance, I began asking more specifically about the part elder brothers and sisters played and this helped to reveal the socioemotional aspects of educational support. The elder brothers and sisters were often the ones who 'dragged' the successful students-to-be through difficult times; they were the ones the younger children could rely on. Sibling care in Turkish and Moroccan families has been documented in a number of studies (van der Hoek and Kret 1992; Pels 1991).

Van der Hoek (1995: 653) later linked the role played by older siblings to two factors: the culture-specific ideas about mutual dependency and responsibility within Turkish and Moroccan families and certain structural factors such as family size (see also Greenfield and Cocking 1994; Zukow 1989).[11] It is more the rule than the exception that older children in the families have a task in rearing younger children. The fact that both Turks and Moroccans have a special name for their oldest brother or sister under-lines this special status within the household. In Moroccan Arabic, the eldest sister is called *eaziza* and the eldest brother *eaziz;* in Turkish they are called *abla* and *abi.*

When researchers write of such tasks, they commonly mention the duties of the oldest daughter in the household. She is to take responsibility for the younger children in the family. The relation between the eldest daughter and the younger children in the family resembles a parent–child relationship. From a young age, many elder sisters in my respondents' families were responsible for the well-being of their younger brothers and sisters and cared for them like a mother. Many of the mothers had jobs, so older children had to collect the younger ones from school and look after them. Although older brothers were not usually given those responsibilities, they still had other tasks to fulfil in the household. The eldest son was often designated to deal with the family's Dutch contacts if the parents could not understand and speak Dutch well enough. They would go to the housing corporation to arrange to rent a flat, or to the registry office to handle official business. If a Dutch person rang the doorbell, one male respondent remembered, he was always called to see what they wanted. The oldest children of the family had to be mature at a young age. The role of older brothers and sisters takes on a deeper dimension when it comes to education. The oldest children in the family, whether born in their countries of origin or in the Netherlands, had been through at least a part of the Dutch educational system, so they had considerable knowledge of it from their own experience. Unlike their parents, they had no problem speaking and understanding Dutch.

In the interviews with respondents who achieved success in the course of secondary school, the involvement of older brothers and sisters in the school careers of younger siblings came up in one way or another. Most referred to a combination of concrete help and emotional support.

[Does your brother help you?] Sure, he gives me tests! [ha, ha] Is that what you mean? Well, for example I had to decide whether or not to do Latin after the third form. My brother had done it and when I was trying to decide he said, 'No, don't do it, it's too hard.' If I don't understand something, then I go to him. Last year, too. He's good at physics and he explains it to me. It's a real advantage (Moroccan boy [1], higher stream of secondary school).

During the period of primary school, most parents had enough knowledge of school matters to guide their children, but by secondary school they had more trouble understanding exactly what their children were doing. Many were no longer able to check their children's homework or to make sure they were spending enough time on it. An additional factor was that the beginning of secondary school coincides with the onset of adolescence. If parents attempted to involve themselves at this point, they might unwittingly betray their ignorance of the school environment, and that could be a source of irritation and resentment. At the same time, brothers and sisters were growing closer, and older brothers and sisters were far closer to the younger children's school experiences. They exchanged stories and anecdotes about the teachers and passed on school news to one another. Obviously this created opportunities for help and support.

If there was a major age difference, older brothers and sisters often supported their younger siblings quite intensively. Sometimes they shared or discussed this role with their parents, but more often it was entirely up to them. Unlike the parents, they understood the school system well enough to intervene constructively. Many older children exacted high standards from their younger siblings, often because they were so painfully aware of their own missed opportunities. They were determined to not let that happen to their brothers and sisters. A Turkish pupil attending senior general secondary school (Havo) recalled how he ended up doing Havo because his older brother wanted him to. The brother, who (much to his own regret) had only finished pre-vocational school (Vbo) and was now working as a car mechanic, had persuaded him to continue school after his junior (Mavo) diploma. It took a lot of convincing, and the brother even promised a financial reward. Since the brother had pressured him into this decision, he also accepted the resulting responsibility. Although he himself had a family with two children, he never failed to attend the contact evenings at his younger brother's school, speaking to the teachers of the subjects his brother was having difficulty with. He was also in regular touch with the brother's mentor to hear how things were going at school.

Now and then, older brothers or sisters would intervene when a younger sibling was in danger of not being promoted to the next form. Contrary to the parents, they knew whom to talk to at school and what opportunities there were to arrange extra tutoring. The parents were mostly in the dark about where the problems lay. Often they would just keep telling their children to work harder if they came home with insufficient marks. Such well-meant encouragement was not particularly motivating in cases where children were having trouble with the subject matter.

In addition to giving practical help and support, older brothers and sisters may act as 'cultural brokers' (van der Hoek 1995: 651), intermediating between the worlds of parents and children. For example, to some Turkish and Moroccan parents it is not assumed that a young woman will continue studying after secondary school. Second-generation girls tend to be very self-assured, but even for them it can be difficult to choose a prolonged course of study against the will of their parents. In such cases, an elder brother or sister might act as their advocate. Since the parents had delegated part of the supervision over the children's schooling to the older children, they were more or less obliged to listen to their opinion. That opinion could be decisive in whether a daughter would be allowed to continue school. Such changes in outlook came gradually. Slowly but surely the parents' viewpoints shifted towards those of their children (see also Gibson and Bhachu 1988: 246). Such processes occur in many families simultaneously, and at some point a young woman at university is no longer an exception in the community. This makes it easier for parents to consent to their daughters' prolonging their education. Such intergenerational dynamics are important in explaining processes of cultural change. Within families, different generations have different interests, as do men and women. In this respect, the family is also an arena of negotiation and conflict (see also Foner 1997: 961).

Using the SPVA data, I was able to gauge the association between the academic success of second-generation young people and their position in the family. A very strong connection emerged between the two. The second-, third- or fourth-born children in families did significantly better at school than the first-born children. The oldest children of the family were the real pioneers when it came to education and subsequent children could take advantage of their experience and knowledge. Among Moroccan school children, the second, third or fourth child in a family was twice as likely as the first child to enter educational streams that give access to higher education and comparable Turkish children were one-and-a-half times as likely. Almost three quarters of the first-born children who had already left school had no qualifications at all. A greater proportion of the younger children in the family had gained diplomas, especially in the higher educational streams. Even though the children had similar starting points in the sense of all being born in the Netherlands, they got much further in education if they were the second, third or fourth child in the family to start school. This birth order effect became stronger as children came later down the row, because each could theoretically make use of the expertise of all the preceding children. The effect was also associated with family size and with the quality of the education the older brothers and sisters had enjoyed. The more older brothers and sisters one had, the more chance they had of being helped by one of them. The receipt of help and support was more likely in cases where there were large age differences between siblings. This applies especially, of course, to any so-called afterthoughts in the family.

The success of the children described in this section seems surprising in some ways. They grew up in neighbourhoods with high concentrations of migrants, they attended 'black schools', and their parents did not involve themselves much in Dutch society or strongly encourage their children to do so. As I have noted, some parents were also not very involved in their children's education, and some were even averse to the idea of their children's continued schooling. At the close of primary school, the children tested as average or even below average pupils, but they caught up during secondary school. In contrast to other groups with strong community ties who do well at school (Gibson 1988; Ogbu 1987), I could not identify here any distinct educational strategy on the part of the parents. The help of older siblings, though, could be just as effective as that of the parents in other groups. They could be crucial intermediaries between the younger children and their school, and they possessed a great deal of practical knowledge that was useful for educational success. The part played by older siblings may have derived from values and behavioural patterns both in Turkish and in Moroccan families, according to which older siblings are traditionally assigned key childrearing tasks. Such tasks take on added meaning in the Netherlands because of the parents' lack of experience with Dutch education.

Discussion and conclusion

I have described here three groups of successful students. How can their success be linked to existing theories of social mobility in migrant groups? It cannot be pinned down to any one explanatory factor. Portes and Zhou (1993), in their model of segmented assimilation, have shown that there is more than one path leading to social mobility for migrant groups. To paraphrase later work by Zhou, three possible multidirectional patterns exist: the time-honoured upward mobility pattern that entails acculturation and economic integration into the normative structures of the middle class; the downward mobility pattern, in the opposite direction, that involves acculturation and integration into an underclass; and economic integration into the middle class, with lagging acculturation and deliberate preservation of the immigrant community's values and solidarity (Zhou 1997: 984). The classical assimilation pattern seems to apply to the group of students who went to primary school in the ethnic Dutch neighbourhoods. The adaptive assimilation pattern (the third pattern described by Zhou) puts more emphasis on the social capital available within the community. Help and support from siblings and mutual support from peers – both of which have proved so important to groups of Moroccan and Turkish students – may be regarded as forms of social capital. Though differently constituted than in the groups examined by Zhou, they are still major resources for academic success. The second path, that of downward social mobility, is not encountered in the groups studied here. Family dynamics and the community building process, as well as the interaction between migrants and the host society, are constantly altering the ways subgroups become incorporated into the Dutch society. Immigrant culture, as I have described it, is very dynamic when observed in a time framework. Even for this limited age category in the second generation, the effects of immigrant culture on the processes of incorporation are widely varied.

The success of this part of the second generation may be viewed against the failure of other second-generation children. The question for the future is which tendency will prove stronger. The group of people within the second generation that drop out of school without a diploma is just as big as the group that go on to higher education (Crul 2000). School dropouts tend to attract the most attention in research. Some boys in that group are marginalized and have got involved in petty crime (van Gemert 1998). An anti-school attitude is manifest among them. This applies only to a small group, however. There is little evidence of an anti-school attitude among the majority of children in migrant groups (Crul 2000). The fact that help and support within the community is of such crucial importance to academic success demonstrates that the communities in question are not dominated by a 'culture of poverty'. Tendencies towards marginalization within some segments of these groups, which might potentially affect the groups as a whole, are now developing simultaneously with tendencies in other segments to move up swiftly to a more comfortable social position. Often the dividing line runs right between family members. Compared to the capabilities the oldest parents of the first generation had to help their children, the migrant communities' experience with the Dutch educational system is now growing fast. It will be of great benefit to the younger children of the second generation, as well as to the children of the third generation yet to come.

Since the time that the first-generation men were recruited for manual labour over a quarter of a century ago, virtually no middle class has emerged within the Moroccan and Turkish communities. The successful second-generation students are the emerging elites within these communities. They are already taking over leading positions there (Crul 1998; Strijp 1996; Sunier 1996). This will greatly enhance the resources available to the community. Cautious optimism thus seems warranted, and this has been substantiated by recent findings that the educational position of Turkish and Moroccan children is improving in every new cohort that emerges in the statistics (Crul forthcoming.).

Notes

1. Crul 1994, 1996 and 1998, Veenman 1996, Veenman and Martens 1995.
2. At first I had defined as belonging to the second generation all those children from the SPVA survey who were born in the Netherlands. When the resulting group proved too small, I extended the definition to include children who,

though born in the country of origin, had spent their entire school careers in the Netherlands. Although strictly speaking they do not belong to the second generation, statistical analysis showed that there was little difference between this group and the children born in the Netherlands in terms of my research theme – the school success of the second generation. The socializing effect of attending Dutch schools thus appears to be the key differentiating criterion. I compared the data on the second-generation children to data on the parents and the paternal grandfather. The SPVA survey was representative for the ethnic minority population in the Netherlands (Roelandt *et al.* 1991: 202), and it included 398 Turkish and 363 Moroccan pupils and students aged 12 or older who had spent their entire school career in the Netherlands. In view of these sizeable numbers and the random nature of the survey, I believe the results of my analysis are representative for the nationwide population of Turkish and Moroccan youth of this category.

3. ISEO/EUR, SPVA'94, see also Binnenlandse Zaken 1996: 28–30, Veenman and Martens 1995: 26–8.

4. Research by Timmerman (1995) and by Hermans (1995) on successful Turkish and Moroccan pupils and students in Belgium (the country most similar to the Netherlands with regard to the migration histories and settlement processes of Turkish and Moroccan migrants) has shown that in Belgium the most crucial selection takes place in the final year of primary school. Pupils who do not succeed in primary school get few subsequent chances to move on to higher streams of education.

5. I also included in this group the 'borderline children', those pupils with an above average recommendation. Without them, the group achieving success through this route would have been smaller.

6. Timmerman (1995), in her comparison between successful and less successful Turkish girls in Belgium, draws a distinction between 'immigrant schools' and 'elite schools'. The immigrant schools are best compared to the so-called 'black schools' in the Netherlands. Timmerman argues that the school makes the difference. Elite schools enable swift acculturation of children into Belgian society. Hermans (1995), who compares successful and less successful Moroccan boys in Belgium, distinguishes between 'concentration schools' and schools with few pupils of foreign descent. He, too, sees the school context as the major source of success or failure in primary school.

7. The former parents deviated from customary practice in their communities. Most Turkish and Moroccan children attended state schools, because the parents did not want their children going to a 'school with the Bible'.

8. Much has changed since then in the 'black schools'. Special programmes have now been developed for children recently arriving from abroad and schools with high percentages of migrants receive supplementary funding.

9. The parents of the Turkish children described in this section were no different socioeconomically from other Turkish parents. They were equally likely to have originated from rural areas of Turkey and they had equally low levels of education. As for the Moroccan parents, fathers with slightly more education (unfinished secondary school) and those originating from cities were overrepresented. For a more detailed account, see Crul 1996.

10. In a study on a newly built district in the town of Haarlem, van Niekerk and her coauthors (1989) reported that many Turkish residents had consciously opted to live in a predominantly ethnic Dutch neighbourhood in order to escape from the social control in the Turkish community in their former neighbourhoods.

11. When relations between brothers and sisters in Turkish and Moroccan families were mentioned in the interviews, that was almost always in the plural. Turkish and Moroccan families are much bigger than Dutch ones: four or five children are no exception. In many families there is a considerable age difference between the oldest and the youngest child. In very large families this can be more than 10 years.

References

Amersfoort, H. van, and C. Cortie, 1996, 'Social polarisation in a welfare state? Immigrants in the Amsterdam region', *New Community*, 22(4): 671–87

Binnenlandse Zaken, 1996, *Minderhedenbeleid 1996. Jaaroverzicht Integratiebeleid Etnische Groepen 1996* (The Hague: Ministerie van Binnenlandse Zaken)

Bolt, G., and R. van Kempen, 1997, 'Segregation and Turks' housing conditions in middle-sized Dutch cities', *New Community*, 23(3): 363–83

Bovenkerk, F., K. Bruin, L. Bruin, L. Brunt, and H. Wouters, 1985, *Vreemd Volk, Gemengde Gevoelens. Etnische Verhoudingen in een Grote Stad* (Amsterdam: Boom)

Crul, M., 1994, 'Springen over je eigen schaduw. De onderwijsprestaties van Marokkanen en Turken van de tweede generatie', *Migrantenstudies* 10(3): 168–86

Crul, M., 1996, 'Marokkaanse en Turkse jongeren van de tweede generatie. Schoolsucces, hulpbronnen en netwerken', in: H. Heeren, P. Vogel and H. Werdmölder (eds), *Etnische Minderheden en Wetenschappelijk Onderzoek* (The Hague: NWO)

Crul, M.R.J., 1998, 'Onderlinge hulp en schoolsucces van Marokkaanse en Turkse jongeren. Een optimistische visie', in: I. van Eerd and B. Hermes (eds), *Pluriform Amsterdam* (Amsterdam: Vossiuspers AUP)

Crul, M., 2000, *De Sleutel tot Succes: Over hulp, Keuzes en Kansen in de Schoolloopbanen van Turlise en Marokkaanse Jongeren van de Tweede Generatie* (Amsterdam: Het Spinhuis).

Eldering, L., 1997, 'Ethnic minority students in the Netherlands from a cultural-ecological perspective', *Anthropology and Education Quarterly*, 28: 330–50

Foner, N., 1997, 'The immigrant family. Cultural legacies and cultural changes', *International Migration Review* 31(4): 961–73

Gemert, F. van, 1998, *Ieder voor Zich. Kansen, Cultuur en Criminaliteit van Marokkaanse Jongeren* (Amsterdam: Het Spinhuis)

Gibson, M., 1988, *Accommodation Without Assimilation. Sikh Immigrants in an American High School* (Ithaca, NY: Cornell University Press)

Gibson, M., and P. Bhachu, 1988, 'Ethnicity and school performance. A comparative study of South Asian pupils in Britain and America', *Ethnic and Racial Studies* 11(3): 239–62

Greenfield, P.M., and R. Cocking, 1994, *Cross-Cultural Roots of Minority Child Development* (London: Laurence Erlbaum Associates)

Hermans, P., 1995, 'Moroccan immigrants and school success', *International Journal of Education* 23(1): 33–44

Hoek, J. van der, 1995, 'Broers en zussen als opvoeders in migrantengezinnen', *Jeugd en Samenleving* 25(11/12): 644–56

Hoek, J. van der, and M. Kret, 1992, *Marokkaanse Tienermeisjes. Gezinsinvloeden op Keuzen en Kansen* (Utrecht: Jan van Arkel)

Jong, W. de, 1986, *Interetnische Verhoudingen in een Oude Stadswijk* (Delft: Eburon)

Klatter-Folmer, J., 1996, *Turkse Kinderen en hun Schoolsucces* (Tilburg: Tilburg University Press)

Leij, A. van der, R. Rögels, H. Koomen, J. Bekkers, 1991, *Turkse Kinderen in Onderwijs en Opvoeding* (Amsterdam: VU Uitgeverij)

Lindo, F., 1995, 'Ethnic myth or ethnic might? On divergence in educational attainment between Portuguese and Turkish youth in the Netherlands', in: G. Baumann and T. Sunier (eds), *Post-Migration Ethnicity. Cohesion, Commitments, Comparison* (Amsterdam: Het Spinhuis)

Niekerk, M. van, T. Sunier, and H. Vermeulen, 1989, *Bekende Vreemden. Surinamers, Turken en Nederlanders in een Naoorlogse Wijk* (Amsterdam: Het Spinhuis)

Ogbu, J., 1987, 'Variability in minority school performance. A problem in search of an explanation', *Anthropology and Education Quarterly* 18: 312–34

Pels, T., 1991, *Marokkaanse Kleuters en hun Culturele Kapitaal. Opvoeden en Leren in het Gezin en op School* (Amsterdam: Swets & Zeitlinger)

Portes, A., and M. Zhou, 1993, 'The new second generation. Segmented assimilation and its variants among post-1965 immigrant youth', *Annals of the American Academy of Political and Social Science* 530: 74–98

Roelandt, T., J.H.M. van Roijen, and J. Veenman, 1991, *Minderheden in Nederland. Statistisch Vademecum 1991* (The Hague: SDU/CBS)

Rumbaut, G., 1997, 'Ties that bind. Immigration and immigrant families in the United States', in: A. Booth, A. Crouter, and N. Landale (eds), *Immigration and the Family* (Mahwah, NJ: Lawrence Erlbaum)

Strijp, R., 1996, *Moroccan Associations in a Dutch Town. The Politics of Identity, Lanquage and Religion*, paper for the conference 'Does Culture Make a Difference?', Amsterdam, 14–16 November

Sung, B.L., 1987, *The Adjustment Experience of Chinese Immigrant Children in New York City* (New York: Center for Migration Studies)

Sunier, T., 1996, *Islam in Beweging. Turkse Jongeren en Islamitische Organisaties* (Amsterdam: Het Spinhuis)

Tesser, P., and J. Veenman, 1997, *Rapportage Minderheden 1997* (Rijswijk: SCP)

Timmerman, C., 1995, 'Cultural practices and ethnicity. Diversifications among Turkish women', *International Journal of Education* 23(1): 23–32

Veenman, J, 1996, *Keren de Kansen? De Tweede Generatie Allochtonen in Nederland* (Assen: Van Gorcum)

Veenman, J., and E.P. Martens, 1995, *Op de Toekomst Gericht. Tweede Generatie Allochtonen in Nederland* (The Hague: VUGA)

Vermeulen, H., 1984, *Etnische Groepen en Grenzen. Surinamers, Chinezen en Turken* (Weesp: Het Wereldvenster)

Vlug, I., 1985, *Schoolverzuim van Turkse en Marokkaanse Meisjes* (Rotterdam: Erasmus Universiteit)

Zhou, M., 1997, 'Segmented assimilation. Issues, controversies, and recent research in the new second generation', *International Migration Review* 31(4): 975–1008

Zukow, P.G., 1989, *Sibling Interaction across Cultures. Theoretical and Methodological Issues* (New York: Springer)

Subject Index

absorption, 76
accommodation, 34
acculturation, 29–30, 84, 238, 240, 242
achievement motivation, *see* cultural
    factors and social mobility
African Americans, 35, 55, 57, 167–9
Africans, 61
Afro-Brazilians, 152–5, 159, 167–70,
    173, 177
Afro-Caribbeans, *see* West Indians
Afro-Surinamese, *see* Surinamese Creoles
agency, *see* culture as agency
Americanization, 75, 87, 139, 168–9
amoral familism, 5–6, 135, 142, 146
    see also cultural factors and social
        mobility
Amsterdam, 150–1, 154–6, 161–5, 167,
    169, 173–4, 176, 178–9, 185
anti-school culture, *see* oppositional
    culture
Antilleans (Dutch -), 154–5, 172
Armenians, 130–2, 143
artisans, 104–5, 114–15, 119, 130,
    145–6, 187–9, 201
    see also workers, skilled
Asians, 2, 4–5, 17, 30, 35, 41, 43–4, 46,
    51–4, 57, 184, 187, 213
assimilation, 34, 36, 97, 179, 199,
    235–6, 240
    see also segmented assimilation

Bangladeshis, 51–3
behavioral patterns, 12–13, 66, 69, 211,
    213–16, 218–21, 234, 240
    see also culture
birth order effects, 226, 229, 236–40
Black Atlantic, 165, 168, 174
black culture, 6, 49, 150–2, 154, 167–8,
    174–7
'black schools', 211, 232–6, 240, 242
blacks, 35, 47, 49, 53–5, 62–4, 66–9,
    75, 77, 80, 98, 127, 140, 144,
    150–80
Buddhism, 30
Bulgarians, 128, 132, 134

California (Central Valley, 'Valleyside')
    72, 82–9, 92–4, 96–7, 99
Candomblé, 159
capital, *see* cultural capital, social
    capital, symbolic capital *and*
    human capital
Caribbeans, *see* West Indians
chain migration, 43, 83, 89, 94, 135,
    137, 209, 216–17, 226
childrearing practices, *see* socialization
Chinese, 36, 143, 147, 185
Christianity, 62, 171, 242
class, 8, 17, 28, 39, 127, 153–4, 174,
    176, 178
class position/structural location, 8–10,
    23–7, 32, 36, 51, 61, 74–80, 83–4,
    86, 89, 92–5, 98, 116–18, 127–8,
    136–7, 141–3, 151–3, 171, 176,
    184–7, 192, 198, 201, 206–7, 225
    see also lower class, middle class, elite
        and premigration class position
class structure and relations, 61–3,
    67–70, 73, 76, 78–80, 95–6, 126,
    134–6, 142–3, 145, 156, 159, 165,
    174, 178
    see also social structure
class culture, 9, 14, 18, 26, 39, 55–6, 64,
    67, 78–81, 95–6, 98, 107, 125, 130,
    141, 151, 154, 171, 174–8, 199, 202
cohesion, 11–12, 44, 84, 88, 94, 97, 127,
    134–5, 138, 140–3, 152, 171, 196,
    199, 216–17, 219, 230, 234, 240
colonial minority, *see* ethnic minority
colonialism, 61–2, 75, 80, 100, 126, 135,
    142, 146, 157, 164, 170–1, 173–4,
    177, 179, 187
Confucianism, 4–5, 30, 35
consumption and consumerism, 5, 17,
    35, 38, 40, 42, 47–51, 56, 152–4,
    156–7, 160–1, 163, 165–9, 171,
    174–6, 179, 197
context of receiving society, *see*
    opportunity structures
contextual effects, *see* ethnic
    community context

Author Index